THE HITTITES AND THEIR WORLD

Society of Biblical Literature

Archaeology and Biblical Studies

Andrew G. Vaughn, Editor

Number 7

THE HITTITES AND THEIR WORLD

THE HITTITES AND THEIR WORLD

by

Billie Jean Collins

Society of Biblical Literature
Atlanta

THE HITTITES AND THEIR WORLD

Library of Congress Cataloging-in-Publication Data

Collins, Billie Jean.
  The Hittites and their world / by Billie Jean Collins.
    p. cm. — (Society of Biblical literature archaeology and Biblical studies ; no. 7)
  Includes bibliographical references and index.
  ISBN 978-1-58983-296-1 (paper binding : alk. paper)
  1. Hittites. I. Title.

DS66.C65 2007b
939'.3—dc22

                                                2007038041

13 12 11 10 9 8   5 4 3 2
Printed in the United States of America on acid-free, recycled paper
conforming to ANSI/NISO Z39.48-1992 (R1997) and ISO 9706:1994
standards for paper permanence.

For Gary Beckman

CONTENTS

PREFACE

THE HITTITES RULED A MAJOR EMPIRE during one of the most exceptional periods of human history, the Late Bronze Age. Yet, when they disappeared from history's radar, they did so completely. No direct memory of them survived outside of a handful of references in the Hebrew Bible; classical sources are entirely silent about them. Although rediscovered in dramatic fashion over the past century, as described in chapter 1, the Hittites are still known to few people. This is understandable given that their contribution to world culture has been difficult to pin down, let alone to package and market to a waiting public, particularly in the face of competition from other great civilizations of the ancient Mediterranean world like Egypt, Mesopotamia, Greece, and Rome. Happily, a new interest in the Hittites has arisen in recent years. This is due, first, to the recent availability of excellent popular books, museum exhibits, and documentaries about the Hittites. Also key to their resurgence is the long-overdue recognition within the academy of the value of Hittite studies for understanding the background of classical and biblical—and hence, of Western—traditions.

Only a decade ago, a book such as this would scarcely have been possible. Major new finds have allowed Hittitologists to fill in major gaps in the historical events of the Late Bronze Age in Anatolia. Although much remains to be learned, so much progress has been made in recent years in reconstructing Hittite history that Bryce's *Kingdom of the Hittites* published in 1998 was reissued in significantly updated form only a few years later. Without his extraordinary efforts and those of Horst Klengel in his *Geschichte des hethitischen Reiches*, my task here would have been considerably more difficult.

The Hittite kingdom lasted for approximately four hundred years (*ca.* 1650 to 1180 B.C.E.) but the story hardly begins or ends with these dates. Any history of the Hittites that does not include the formative centuries of the Middle Bronze Age (1800–1650 B.C.E.) and the subsequent Iron Age (1180–717 B.C.E.) is incomplete at best. Hence, chapter 2 covers all one thousand years of "Hittite" history. This history is presented in brief and is designed for those wanting an overview of political events unencumbered by minutia. Readers requiring a more detailed history are directed to the list of "Further

Reading" for excellent detailed histories of the Hittites of the Late Bronze Age, including those just cited.

For decades, biblical scholars and Hittitologists alike have eagerly mined the Hittite documents for nuggets of information that could illuminate biblical passages. These excursions have proved overhwelmingly fruitful, and the literature documenting the resulting parallels between the Hittite and biblical worlds is considerable. Nowhere, however, have these findings been collected together in one place. This volume is an attempt to fill the need for a comprehensive and up-to-date survey of the contributions of Hittite studies to biblical interpretation. It is directed at anyone interested in viewing the cumulative work on this subject as well as those seeking a succinct introduction to the history, society, and religion of the Hittites.

All quotes of biblical passages are taken from the New Revised Standard Version (NRSV). Translations of Hittite and Akkadian passages are acknowledged in the footnotes unless they are my own. For the sake of consistency and simplicity, in this volume I follow the so-called Middle Chronology and the sequence and lengths of reigns of the Hittite kings established by Bryce in *Kingdom of the Hittites*.

It remains only to thank those who kindly read drafts of chapters and offered helpful comments, namely Trevor Bryce, Gary Beckman, and Brian Schmidt. I am indebted to Itamar Singer for graciously making his paper "The Hittites and the Bible Revisited" available to me in advance of its publication, to Susanne Wilhelm for her excellent maps, and to Katie Chaple for her editorial advice. Thanks also to Andrew Vaughn for inviting me to contribute a volume to the SBLABS series and to my colleagues at SBL, and most especially Bob Buller, for their support and encouragement. Finally, I am beholden to Chris Madell for supporting, cajoling, tolerating, and encouraging me at all the right times.

LIST OF FIGURES

ABBREVIATIONS AND KEYS

AA	*Archäologischer Anzeiger*
AASOR	Annual of the American Schools of Oriental Research
AB	Anchor Bible
ABD	*Anchor Bible Dictionary*
ÄHK	Elmar Edel, *Die ägyptisch-hethitische Korrespondenz aus Boghazköi in babylonischer und hethitischer Sprache* II. 2 vols. Opladen: Westdeutscher Verlag, 1994.
AJA	*American Journal of Archaeology*
ANES	Ancient Near Eastern Studies
AOAT	Alter Orient und Altes Testament
AoF	*Altorientalische Forschungen*
ArOr	*Archiv Orientální*
AT	Alalakh Text
BA	*Biblical Archaeologist*
BagMitt	*Bagdader Mitteilungen*
BAR	*Biblical Archaeology Review*
BASOR	*Bulletin of the American Schools of Oriental Research*
B.C.E.	before the common era
BCSMS	*Bulletin of the Canadian Society for Mesopotamian Studies*
BiOr	*Bibliotheca Orientalis*
BN	*Biblische Notizen*
ca.	circa
CANE	*Civilizations of the Ancient Near East*. Edited by Jack M. Sasson. 4 vols. New York: Scribner's Sons, 1995.
CBQ	*Catholic Biblical Quarterly*
CHD	*The Hittite Dictionary of the Oriental Institute of the University of Chicago*. Chicago: The Oriental Institute of the University of Chicago, 1980–.
CHLI I	*Corpus of Hieroglyphic Luwian Inscriptions,* Vol. I: *Inscriptions of the Iron Age*. 3 vols. Berlin: de Gruyter, 2000.
CHLI II	Halet Çambel, *Corpus of Hieroglyphic Luwian Inscriptions*, Vol. II: *Karatepe-Aslantaş*. Berlin: de Gruyter, 1999.

CHM	Cahiers d'histoire mondiale
ChS	Corpus der hurritischen Sprachdenkmäler
CM	Cuneiform Monographs
CoS	Context of Scripture. Edited by William W. Hallo. 3 vols. Leiden: Brill, 1997–.
CTH	Emmanuel Laroche, Catalogue des textes hittites. Paris: Klincksieck, 1971.
d	a determinative preceding the name of a Hittite divinity
DBH	Dresdner Beiträge zur Hethitologie
DMOA	Documenta et monumenta Orientis Antiqui
EA	El Amarna
ELO	Elementa Linguarum Orientis
HdO	Handbuch der Orientalistik
HED	Jaan Puhvel, Hittite Etymological Dictionary. 6 vols. Berlin: de Gruyter, 1984–.
HKM	Sedat Alp, Hethitische Keilschrifttafeln aus Maşat. TTKY VI/34. Ankara: Turk Tarih Kurumu Basımevi, 1991.
IBoT	İstanbul Arkeoloji Müzelerinde bulunan Boğazköy Tabletleri. 4 vols. İstanbul: Maarif, 1944, 1947, 1954; Ankara: Türk Tarih Kurumu Basımevi, 1988.
IBS	Innsbrucker Beiträge zur Sprachwissenschaft
IEJ	Israel Exploration Journal
IOS	Israel Oriental Studies
IstMitt	Istanbuler Mitteilungen
JANER	Journal of Ancient Near Eastern Religion
JAOS	Journal of the American Oriental Society
JBL	Journal of Biblical Literature
JCS	Journal of Cuneiform Studies
JIES	Journal of Indo-European Studies
JNES	Journal of Near Eastern Studies
JSOT	Journal for the Study of the Old Testament
KBo	Keilschrifttexte aus Boghazköi. Berlin, Gebr. Mann, 1916–.
KUB	Keilschrifturkunden aus Boghazköi. 60 vols. Berlin, Akademie Verlag, 1921–1990.
MAOG	Mitteilungen der Altorientalischen Gesellschaft
MARI	Mari Annales de Recherches Interdisciplinaires
MDOG	Mitteilungen der Deutschen Orient Gesellschaft
MVAeG	Mitteilungen der Vorderasiatisch-ägyptischen Gesellschaft
NEA	Near Eastern Archaeology
NINO	Nederlands Instituut voor het Nabije Oosten
NRSV	New Revised Standard Version
obv.	obverse

OLZ	*Orientalistische Literaturzeitung*
Or	*Orientalia*
PEQ	*Palestine Exploration Quarterly*
PIHANS	Publication de l'Institut Historique et Archéologique Néerlandais de Stamboul
r.	ruled
RA	*Revue Assyriologique*
rev.	reverse
RGTC VI	Giuseppe F. del Monte and Johann Tischler, *Repertoire Geographique des Textes Cuneiformes*, Band 6: *Die Orts- und Gewassernamen der hethitischen Texte*. Wiesbaden: Reichert, 1978.
RHA	*Revue hittite et asianique*
RlA	*Reallexikon der Assyriologie*
RS	Ras Shamra
RSO	Ras Shamra-Ougarit
SAOC	Studies in Ancient Oriental Civilization
SMEA	*Studi Micenei ed Egeo-Anatolici*
StBoT	Studien zu den Boğazköy-Texten
StMed	*Studia Mediterranea*
s.v.	sub voce
THeth	Texte der Hethiter
TUAT	Texte aus der Umwelt des Alten Testaments
UF	*Ugarit-Forschungen*
VT	*Vetus Testamentum*
WO	*Die Welt des Orients*
ZA	*Zeitschrift für Assyriologie*
ZAW	*Zeitschrift für alttestamentliche Wissenschaft*
ZDPV	*Zeitschrift des Deutschen Palästina-vereins*

KEY TO TRANSLITERATED WORDS

handandatar	Hittite words are indicated by italics.
HAZANNU	Akkadian words in a Hittite context are indicated by italicized capitals Otherwise, Akkadian words are indicated by lowercase italics
SANGA	Sumerian word signs are indicated by capital letters

KEY TO PRONUNCIATION OF TURKISH LETTERS

c = j
ç = ch
ı = uh
ö = oe
ü = ue
ş = sh

EXPLANATION OF SYMBOLS

Single brackets [ ] enclose restorations.
Angle brackets < > enclose words omitted by the original scribe.
Parentheses ( ) enclose additions in the English translation.
A row of dots . . . indicates gaps in the text or untranslatable words.

1
A Brief History of Hittite Studies

When architect and explorer Charles Texier first rode on donkey-back up the rutted road to the ancient ruins near the village of Boghazköy on the high plateau of central Anatolia, Queen Victoria was four years away from ascending the throne of England, Charles Darwin was sailing home on the Beagle, Architect Leo Klenze was beginning restoration of the temples of the Acropolis in Athens, and Sultan Mehmet II was ruling the great Ottoman Empire from his palace in Constantinople. The year was 1834, and at the time no one had heard of a people called the Hittites except through a handful of references in the Hebrew Bible. Texier's discovery was the first in a series of events that would change all that. On that July day, however, the Frenchman was not thinking about the biblical Hittites. He was looking for ancient Pteria, a Roman city thought to be located in the vicinity.

Discovery

What he found instead were the ruins of a great city that was not at all Roman. Texier could not know it at the time, but the great blocks of stone laid out in long, straight rows were the ruins of a monumental temple complex; the miles-long fortification wall interrupted by great carved gates once protected the captial of an empire, and the mysterious and utterly inexplicable reliefs carved into the walls of a broad, rocky outcropping (called Yazılıkaya "inscribed rock" in Turkish) northeast of the ruins held the key to the religious beliefs of an entire civilization.[1] No Roman ruins these, but what and who could account for them? Their like had never been seen before.

---

1. Texier thought that the scene portrayed a meeting between Amazons and Paphla-gonians. William J. Hamilton, who visited the site a year after Texier, suggested that they portrayed a peace treaty between the Lydians and Persians. See Johan de Roos, "Early Travellers to Boğazköy," in *Studio Historiae Ardens* (ed. Theo P. J. van den Hout and

Fig. 1.1. Charles Texier made extensive, if not entirely true-to-life, drawings of the ruins at Boghazköy. This drawing is of the central vignette carved onto the face of the rock sanctuary called Yazılıkaya today. From Charles Texier, *Description de l'Asie Mineure* (3 vols.; Paris: Didot, 1839–49). Photo courtesy Pitts Theology Library, Emory University, Atlanta, Georgia.

Other travelers followed after Texier, adding to and improving on his observations and rather idealized sketches of the ruins (fig. 1.1).[2] One of these was Karl Humann, a trained civil engineer, who in 1882 took casts of some of the Yazılıkaya reliefs, which he sent to the Royal Museum in Berlin, and who produced the first plans of the architectural remains at the site. At the time, Humann was in the middle of his excavations at Roman Pergamon on the west coast of Anatolia, and he would soon travel east to excavate a place called Zincirli (ancient Samal).

But the next major event in this story of rediscovery had already come twelve years earlier, in 1870, when two Americans, Consul J. A. Johnson and Rev. S. Jessup spotted four stones inscribed "with a number of small figures and signs" while strolling through the bazaar at Hama in northern Syria. In fact, one of these stones had already been sighted in 1812 by the legendary

---

Johan de Roos; Leiden: Nederlands Historisch-Archaeologisch Instituut te Istanbul, 1995), 264.

2. For the story of some of the less-celebrated participants in the rediscovery of the Hittites, see ibid., 261–69. Henry J. van Lennep's drawings following a visit in 1864 were considerably more accurate.

Johann Ludwig (John Lewis) Burckhardt, who spent his short life studying and traveling throughout the Near East as Sheik Ibrahim. His posthumously published *Travels in Syria and the Holy Land* made mention of a stone embedded in the corner of a building in the Hama bazaar, and he was able to identify the "figures and signs" on the stone as a kind of hieroglyphic writing.[3] A year after the two Americans discovered the stones in Hama, another inscribed stone was found in the wall of a mosque in Aleppo. In neither case could the Westerners make a cast or drawing of them, for the locals appeared to revere the stones, attributing to them the power to cure illnesses such as eye disease and rheumatism, and would not let any Westerners approach them. In 1872, an Irish missionary, William Wright, with the support of a more liberal local pasha (governor), had somewhat more success. Wright was able to chisel the stones out of the walls of the buildings, although the effort was plagued by demonstrations on the part of the local population. The stones were shipped to a museum in Constantinople, where Wright took impressions of them and sent the casts to the British Museum.[4]

Suddenly the hieroglyphic symbols were turning up everywhere, not just in northern Syria, but throughout Anatolia, and it was becoming clear that the inscriptions that Texier and others had encountered at Yazılıkaya were a part of this same script tradition. Comparison of these reliefs with the Hama stones and those that had been found at Karkamis (also spelled Carchemish), where excavations had begun in 1878, made it clear that one continuous cultural tradition covered an area from western Anatolia to northern Syria.

In 1879, the English Assyriologist Archibald Henry Sayce visited two reliefs carved into the rock in the region around Smyrna (now Izmir) in western Anatolia (at Akpınar and Karabel). Pausanias had referred to the former as "a petrified mourning Niobe" (*Descr. Greece* 1.21), in reference to the Greek daughter of Tantalus, who became a symbol of eternal mourning after Apollo and Artemis slew her fourteen children. Herodotus identified the latter as a representation of the Egyptian king Sesostris (*Hist.* 2.106). The following year Sayce delivered a lecture before the Society for Biblical Archaeology in London in which he made a connection that seemed at the time as unlikely as it was daring. He announced that the various monuments and inscriptions found scattered throughout Anatolia and northern Syria should be attributed to the "Hittites" mentioned in the Bible.

---

3. John Lewis [Johann Ludwig] Burckhardt, *Travels in Syria and the Holy Land* (London: Murray, 1822), 146–47.

4. As of 1953, one set of these casts was in the possession of the Palestine Exploration Fund and the other in the hands of the Royal Asiatic Society (R. D. Barnett, "Karatepe, the Key to the Hittite Hieroglyphs," *AnSt* 3 [1953]: 55).

In fact, William Wright had already made this claim two years earlier in a small article, but it was Sayce's public and provocative announcement that put the Hittites in the headlines throughout England. Wright's publication in 1884 of the book *The Empire of the Hittites*, however, was a watershed event because it asserted that the Hittites had ruled an empire and because it established the point at which the field of Hittitology may be said to have begun.

Fortunately, the Egyptian and Akkadian (Assyrian) languages had both by now been deciphered, and the texts written in them provided immediate corroboration for this new theory. The Assyrian texts made repeated mention of a land called "Hatti" (*ḫatti*), and the Egyptian texts referred to the *Ḫt* (arbitrarily vocalized *Ḫeta* by Egyptologists). The identification of the biblical term (*ḫittîm*, rendered "Hittites" in English) with either the Akkadian or Egyptian forms would not have been obvious to anyone prior to 1880. These Akkadian and Egyptian sources provided a historical context for the Hittites from the fifteenth century B.C.E. through the end of the eighth. Yet they also presented a bit of a problem, for in these accounts the Hittites seemed always to be on the losing side of one battle or another. This simply did not make sense for a kingdom that apparently had ruled such a large area for such a long period of time. Moreover, no one at this time thought to question the assumption that the Hittites' political center was at Karkamis in northern Syria.

The world did not have to wait long for the next twist in the plot. In 1887, a great diplomatic archive dating to the reign of the heretic king, Akhenaton, was discovered at El Amarna in Egypt. It contained hundreds of diplomatic letters, including one from Suppiluliuma, king of Hatti, which was written in the now-understandable Akkadian language. In addition, there were two letters, also in cuneiform script but in an unknown language, between Tarhundaradu king of Arzawa and Pharaoh Amenhotep III.[5] To this language scholars naturally applied the name "Arzawan." When in 1893 French archaeologist Ernest Chantre made test diggings at Boghazköy and turned up tablets that were also found to be written in this "Arzawan" language, the "Arzawa problem" became all the more acute.

In 1902, J. A. Knudtzon, a Norwegian scholar who had been working independently on the two "Arzawan" letters from El Amarna as part of his

---

5. The two letters were an exchange regarding a diplomatic marriage between the pharoah and the daughter of Tarhundaradu. The Egyptian scribe was required to compose the letter in Hittite, presumably because the scribes in Tarhuntaradu's court were not educated in Akkadian, the diplomatic language of the major powers of the time. Notably, the Egyptian scribe's knowledge of Hittite was not perfect either (see Frank Starke, "Zur Deutung der Arzaua-Briefstelle VBoT 1, 25–27," *ZA* 71 (1982): 221–31).

larger study of the Amarna archive, concluded that the language probably belonged to the Indo-European family of languages.[6] The Indo-European family includes most of the major languages spoken in the West today (including the Germanic and Romance languages), as well as the Slavic and Indo-Iranian languages. Knudtzon's was a remarkable accomplishment, given that his conclusions were based on so little material.[7] Owing to this and also to the fact that the syllabic cuneiform script distorted the Indo-European elements of the language almost beyond recognition, his announcement failed to find acceptance among his colleagues. Moreover, the idea that an Indo-European language should have been spoken in the ancient Near East, where Semitic languages clearly dominated, seemed too improbable, and Knudtzon's announcement was met with such skepticism that he subsequently retracted his claim.

Excavations finally began at Boghazköy in 1906 under the auspices of the German Oriental Society (Deutsche Orient-Gesellschaft [DOG]). It was the capriciousness of politics that gave the concession to dig the site to the Germans rather than the British, who were also set to go. The Deutsche Bank had financed the Berlin-to-Baghdad railroad in 1899, and the Boghazköy concession was a gesture of friendship to the Kaiser, with whose government the Turks were on better terms than they were with the British. This one decision would forever shape the field of Hittite studies, as we will see.

The expedition, conducted under the direction of Hugo Winckler, a German Assyriologist, in collaboration with the seasoned Turkish excavator and government official Theodor Makridi, was focused entirely on the retrieval of tablets. It is fortunate, therefore, that in 1907 the German Archaeological Institute (Deutsches Archäologisches Institut [DAI]) sent Otto Puchstein to map and partially excavate the monumental buildings, especially the fortifications and temples. The young British archaeologist John Garstang stopped at Boghazköy that same year during his travels through Turkey. Although little archaeological work had actually been carried out in Anatolia up to that time, he was able to publish an exhaustive survey of the landscape and visible material remains in *The Land of the Hittites: An Account of Recent Explorations and Discoveries in Asia Minor* (London:

---

6. EA 31 and 32. J. A. Knudtzon, *Die Zwei Arzawa Briefe: Die ältesten Urkunden in Indogermanischer Sprache* (Leipzig: Hinrichs, 1902). His conclusions were enthusiastically supported by two prominent linguists and colleagues, Alf Torp and Sophus Bugge, who contributed commentaries to the 1902 publication. Knudtzon also correctly concluded that Arzawa must have been located in Anatolia (p. 28).

7. Petr Vavroušek, "Zur Geschichte der Lösung des hethitischen Problems," *ArOr* 47 (1979): 69.

Constable, 1910). This volume represents the first attempt to synthesize the documents and monuments in a comprehensive picture of the Hittite Empire. By the same token, before the language of the tablets had been deciphered, prominent historian Eduard Meyer was able to write his *Reich und Kultur der Chetiter* (Berlin: Curtius, 1914), based purely on the evidence of the Akkadian documents from Boghazköy.

Winckler was by all accounts a disagreeable character whose approach to excavation would not redeem him in the eyes of posterity.[8] His interest in excavating Boghazköy was to find tablets, and this he did in the very first year, extracting from the ground some 10,400 clay fragments. It was an incredible discovery and achievement, but it came at great cost to subsequent scholarship. No notes were taken of the find spots of the tablets, information that might have been used to learn about the organization of the libraries and the relationship of the various documents with one another.[9] Worse, since little care was taken in the retrieval of the tablets from the ground, many were broken into pieces, and many more that were deemed too fragmentary to be of interest were dumped into a heap. Even by the standards of the day, these techniques were dubious.

This assault on scholarship was nevertheless overshadowed by the significance of the finds. Among the tablets recovered in that first year was an Akkadian-language clay copy of the very treaty between the Egyptians and the Hittites that was inscribed on the walls at Karnak in Egypt. The presence of so many texts in the diplomatic language of the period led Winckler to the correct conclusion that Boghazköy, not Karkamis, was the captial of the Hittite civilization.[10] Although Winckler could read these Akkadian texts, the majority of the tablets were inscribed in the still-unknown Hittite language. Although Winckler was making important strides toward its decipherment at the time of his death in April 1913, he did not live to see either the excavations at Boghazköy brought to an abrupt halt in 1914 or the announcement in 1915 of the definitive decipherment of the language of the Hittites.[11]

---

8. For Winckler's own account of these events, see the posthumously published *Nach Boghazköi!* (Leipzig: Hinrichs, 1914).

9. On the possibility that the find spots were recorded only to be lost later, see Theo van den Hout, "Another View of Hittite Literature," in *Anatolia Antica: Studi in Memoria di Fiorella Imparati* (ed. Stefano De Martino and Franca Pecchioli Daddi; 2 vols.; Eothen 11; Firenze: LoGisma, 2002), 2:859 n. 5.

10. In fact, credit for the identification of the capital of the Hittites rightfully belongs to Georges Perrot, who expressed his preference for Boghazköy over Karkamis in an article in 1886. See de Roos, "Early Travellers," 269.

11. Winckler's papers contained references to years of work on the deciphering

Decipherment

The important contributions of Wright, Sayce, and Winkler notwithstanding, the honor of the title "father of Hittitology" must go to the Czech Assyriologist Friedrich Hrozný, who finally deciphered the language of the Hittites.[12] For his research, Hrozný, a young professor at the University of Vienna, was able to utilize the wealth of tablets that Winckler had uncovered at Boghazköy, which the German Oriental Society had now made available for study. Although drafted into the Austro-Hungarian army, he had the good fortune to have an understanding superior officer who allowed him to continue his work, and he was even given the opportunity to travel to Constantinople to study the Hittite tablets there. In a 1915 article entitled "The Solution to the Hittite Problem," which he wrote and published while in the service, Hrozný vindicated Knudtzon by asserting that the language of the Hittite Empire was, after all, Indo-European.[13] The centerpiece of Hrozný's lecture before the German Oriental Society that year was the Hittite sentence ⸗⸗ 𒉿𒀀𒋫 𒃶𒀷𒋼𒉌𒌍 𒀊𒍝𒀜𒁄 𒉌𒌓𒐊𒌍 (*nu* NINDA-*an ēzzatteni wātar-ma ekutteni*). The sign NINDA was an ideogram for bread; this much Hrozný knew from Akkadian cuneiform. Hrozný guessed that the following word, *ezzatteni*, might be a form of the verb "eat," and so he looked, and found, cognates for it in other Indo-European languages (compare, for example, German *essen* and Latin *edō*). The next word, *watar*, bore an undeniable resemblance to English *water*, German *Wasser*, and so on. Recognizing that the suffix -*teni* at the end of both verbs suggested a second-person plural form, Hrozný was able to offer a translation: "Then you will eat bread and

---

of "cuneiform Hittite." In a postcard dated 26 December 1907, Winckler was already aware that the language of the Boghazköy tablets must be Indo-European (Horst Klengel, *Geschichte des hethitischen Reiches* [HdO 34; Leiden: Brill, 1999], 8 n. 20). According to Hrozný's main rival, Ernst Weidner, in his review of Hrozný's work (*OLZ* [1920]: 114–20), Winckler destroyed his notes before he died.

12. The story of the decipherment is recounted in various useful sources. See in particular Gary Beckman, "The Hittite Language and Its Decipherment," *BCSMS* 31 (1996): 23–30; C. W. Ceram, *The Secret of the Hittites: The Discovery of an Ancient Empire* (New York: Knopf, 1956; repr., London: Phoenix, 2001); Johannes Friedrich, "Die bisherigen Ergebnisse der hethitischen Sprachforschung," in *Stand und Aufgaben der Sprachwissenschaft* (Heidelberg: Winter, 1924), 304–18; Petr Vavroušek, "Zur Geschichte der Lösung des hethitischen Problems," 67–77.

13. Hrozný was motivated to publish the article because he was not the only one working on the problem. His main competitor, Ernst Weidner, however, was on the wrong track. In his *Studien zur hethitischen Sprachwissenschaft* (Leipzig: Hinrichs, 1917), he concluded that Hittite was a Caucasian language.

you will drink water."[14] C. W. Ceram summed up this momentous discovery with his characteristic expressiveness: "How staggering it is to realize that with three thousand years intervening, a Frisian living on the North Sea coast of Germany and a Pennsylvania Dutchman of eastern North America would understand a Hittite's cry of thirst!"[15]

Hrozný followed his preliminary article with a book in 1917 that served as the first systematic study of Hittite grammar and remained the standard work on the subject for years.[16] Despite the conclusiveness of his decipherment, the old preconceptions that did not allow for the possibility of an Indo-European presence in biblical lands stayed alive for another decade.[17] It simply did not fit the picture that historians had drawn up to that point. Moreover, the identification of the Hittites as Indo-Europeans forced upon the scientific community a revision of the racial assumptions that had settled in on the basis of the rock reliefs. Viewed through some eyes, the reliefs had provided visual evidence that the Hittites were an "ugly" people "with yellow skins and 'Mongoloid' features," with "receding foreheads, oblique eyes, and protruding upper jaws."[18] Still, the incontrovertable nature of the evidence soon silenced critics, and progress on the language from that point was swift.

Hittite studies in this period were carried by five scholars in Germany: Hans Ehelolf (Berlin), Emil Forrer (Berlin), Johannes Friedrich (Leipzig), Albrecht Goetze (Heidelberg and Marburg), and Ferdinand Sommer (Munich). The United States had Edgar Sturtevant (Yale University), and France had Louis Delaporte, editor of *Revue hittite et asianique*, who, tragically, would later die in a German concentration camp. By 1930, many historical texts had been translated in German editions that were accurate enough that they are still referenced today. These publications also set a

---

14. Hrozný wrote his own retrospective on the decipherment in 1931: "Le Hittite: Histoire et progrès du déchiffrement des textes," *ArOr* 3 (1931): 272–95.

15. Ceram, *Secret of the Hittites*, 86.

16. Friedrich Hrozný, "Die Lösung des hethitischen Problems," *MDOG* 56 (1915): 17–50; idem, *Die Sprache der Hethiter: Ihr Bau und ihre Zugehörigkeit zum indogermanischen Sprachstamm* (Leipzig: Hinrichs, 1917). Hrozný also concluded that Hittite belonged to the western (*centum*) branch of Indo-European and thus was more closely related to Greek and Latin, for example, than to Sanskrit and Old Persian.

17. E. O. Forrer, "The Hittites in Palestine I," *PEQ* (1936): 191–92. Hrozný's work would also come under fire from linguists, since he had made many errors in individual examples of word relations (Vavroušek, "Zur Geschichte der Lösung des hethitischen Problems," 72).

18. Archibald Henry Sayce, *The Hittites: The Story of a Forgotten Empire* (2nd ed.; London: Religious Tract Society, 1890), 15.

standard for scholarly rigor against which all subsequent philological studies have been measured.

Even while understanding of the Hittite cuneiform texts was advancing in leaps and bounds, the struggle to unravel the mystery of the hieroglyphs dragged on with painful slowness. Hrozný had been aided by his ability to apply phonological values to the cuneiform signs in which the Hittite texts were written. This allowed philologists to look for familiar word formations and grammatical usage. It also helped that the Hittite scribes divided words and paragraphs, something that we take for granted today but that was by no means typical in ancient scribal traditions. Although most assumed the language behind the hieroglyphs was Hittite or a language closely related to it, the values of the signs were at first completely unknown. As a result, the process of decipherment, which had begun with Sayce thirty years before the decipherment of cuneiform Hittite, continued for decades and required the input of many of the best minds in the field.

Before decipherment could even begin, it was necessary first to establish the direction of the writing, whether the script was logographic, syllabic, or alphabetic, and whether it used determinatives (word signs that classify the following word, e.g., man, woman, city, stone, god). Investigators correctly determined that the direction of the writing alternated from line to line, that is, it was meant to be read *bustrophedon* ("as the ox plows"), a conclusion that was arrived at on the assumption that the signs must face the direction from which the particular line was to be read (fig. 1.2). The identification of about one hundred distinct signs (at the time) pointed to a syllabary, as an alphabet would require many fewer signs and a purely logographic script would have many more. In addition to syllabic signs, the script also used logograms and determinatives.

Beyond these insights, decades would pass with little progress. Not even the so-called Tarkondemos seal, which was inscribed both with cuneiform and hieroglyphs and thus was a possible bilingual, had offered additional insights into the script (fig. 1.3).[19] At the beginning of the century, Leopold Messerschmidt had published a corpus of hieroglyphic inscriptions that comprised a total of sixty-one texts as well as a number of seals and epigraphs.[20] The British Museum excavations at Karkamis from 1911 to

---

19. J. David Hawkins and Anna Morpurgo-Davies, "Of Donkeys, Mules and Tarkondemos," in *Mír Curad: Studies in Honor of Calvert Watkins* (ed. Jay Jasanoff, H. Craig Melchert and Lisi Oliver; IBS 92; Innsbruck: Institut für Sprachwissenschaft der Universität Innsbruck, 1998), 243–60.

20. Leopold Messerschmidt, *Corpus Inscriptionum Hettiticarum* (4 parts; MVAeG 5/4–5, 7/3, 11/5; Berlin: Peiser, 1900–1906): see parts 1–2:113–60 and parts 3 and 4.

Fig. 1.2. A section of hieroglyphs from Karkamis containing a dedicatory inscription by Katuwa (tenth or early-ninth century). KARKAMIS A13d. From Sir Leonard Woolley, *Carchemish II: The Town Defences* (London: British Museum, 1921).

1914 under the direction of D. G. Hogarth, Sir Leonard Woolley, and T. E. Lawrence (Lawrence of Arabia) increased the number of known inscriptions considerably. Nevertheless, by the 1920s, the field could not boast of making significant inroads into the decipherment of the hieroglyphs, other than the identification of a few place names made possible with the help of Assyrian records.

Fig. 1.3. Archibald Sayce went to great pains to track down the so-called Tarkon-demos seal in the hopes that it would provide the key to the decipherment of the hieroglyphs. Unfortunately, the seal's short inscription had until recently proved resistant to interpretation. Sayce had managed at least to identify the signs for "god," "king," "city," and "country." He read the seal "Tar-rik-tim-me šar mat Er-me-e." We now read the inscription on the seal as follows: TARKASNA-wa LUGAL KUR URUMe-ra!-a! "Tarkasnawa, king of the land of Mira" (Hawkins and Morpurgo-Davies, "Of Donkeys, Mules and Tarkondemos," 243–60). Photo courtesy of the Walters Art Gallery, Baltimore.

Fortunately, the new generation of scholars was ready to tackle the problem of the hieroglyphs. In 1919, Swiss Assyriologist Emil Forrer had realized that there were more languages represented in the cuneiform texts from Boghazköy than just Hittite and Akkadian. Among the eight languages he identified was one that was introduced in the texts as *luwili* "in Luwian."[21] In 1932 the Italian scholar Piero Meriggi observed that the

21. Emil Forrer, "Die acht Sprachen der Boghazköi Inschriften," *Sitzungsberichte*

language of the Hittite hieroglyphs was more closely related to the Luwian of the cuneiform texts than to Hittite, and he applied the label "Luwian hieroglyphs" for the first time.[22] Forrer and Ignace J. Gelb, the latter at The Oriental Institute of the University of Chicago, devoted considerable energy to their decipherment, and both presented their results in 1931 at a congress in Leiden. Even Hrozný attempted to repeat his past success, although with less spectacular results. Also dedicating himself to these efforts was Helmuth Theodor Bossert, the man who would eventually provide the critical piece in the decipherment.[23] The combined efforts of these scholars resulted in basic agreement on the syllabic values of some fifty-five signs and on the meanings of many logograms and determinatives.[24]

The next break would come when excavations were resumed at the Hittite capital in 1931 under the auspices of the DAI and the DOG. Much had changed since World War I. Turkey was now a republic. The Oriental Institute of the University of Chicago had already begun excavations at Alişar Höyük in central Anatolia (1927–32), another site with Late Bronze Age remains, under the direction of the young German archaeologist Hans Henning von der Osten. The DAI chose Kurt Bittel to direct the renewed excavations at Boghazköy, his mission being to establish the stratigraphy of the site, something that had not been accomplished during Winckler's excavations. When it soon became clear that the flow of tablets from the ground was destined to continue, Hans G. Güterbock, a student of Friedrich in Leipzig, was invited to join the staff as epigrapher in 1933.[25] Güterbock, whose father was of Jewish heritage, had been denied a position at the Berlin Museum working under Hans Ehelolf but was allowed by the Istanbul branch of the DAI to participate in the German excavation. So in 1933, Güterbock began an exile that would eventually take him to The Oriental Institute of the University of Chicago.

---

der Preussischen Akademie der Wissenschaften, phil.-hist. Klasse 53 (1919): 1029–41. This brief summary cannot do justice to the contributions of Emil Forrer to the field of Hittitology. For an entertaining account of Forrer's insights, see Johannes Lehmann, *The Hittites: People of a Thousand Gods* (New York: Viking, 1975), 85–93.

22. Piero Meriggi, "Sur le déchiffrement et la langue des hiéroglyphes 'hittites,'" *RHA* 9 (1932): 1–57.

23. His early contributions to the decipherment are summed up in *Šantaš und Kupapa* (MAOG 6.3; Leipzig: Harrassowitz, 1932).

24. J. D. Hawkins, Anna Morpurgo-Davies, and Günter Neumann, *Hittite Hieroglyphs and Luwian: New Evidence for the Connection* (Göttingen: Vandenhoeck & Ruprecht, 1974), 148.

25. See Güterbock's retrospective, "Resurrecting the Hittites," in *CANE*, 2765–76.

In 1935, the excavations uncovered some two hundred bullae (lumps of clay stamped with a seal used to identify and secure consignments) from a storage room, many of them containing text in both hieroglyphs and cuneiform, others only in hieroglyphs. With the arrival of two new epigraphers on the scene, Hans Ehelolf and Heinrich Otten, Güterbock had to leave the excavation, and in 1936 he took a position at the new university in Ankara. As he no longer had access to the cuneiform tablets from the current excavation, he set to work cataloguing and analyzing the seals. These miniature bilinguals allowed him to identify the hieroglyphic names of kings, which could then be matched with the same names appearing on rock reliefs scattered about Anatolia.

Finally, in 1946, Bossert and Halet Çambel discovered the long-hoped-for bilingual at Karatepe in the mountainous Adana region of southeastern Anatolia. The text was written in Phoenician and Luwian hieroglyphic and was inscribed on the stone blocks that formed the monumental gateway of a late-eighth-century B.C.E. fortress.[26] It remains the longest inscription in either language yet found[27] and confirmed many of the readings and meanings of individual signs that had been proposed previously and allowed the assignment of values to many more. However, many signs to which incorrect values had been applied slipped through the corrective net, and, despite the best efforts of three generations of scholars, the decipherment remained incomplete. Nevertheless, the new information obtained from the bilingual was utilized by the French scholar Emmanuel Laroche in 1960 in a new systematic sign list.[28] This was quickly followed by Piero Meriggi's glossary and grammatical analysis,[29] and both works remain fundamental resources to this day.

The final step in the decipherment came only in 1974 with the publication of an article by J. D. Hawkins, Anna Morpurgo Davies, and Günter Neumann that corrected a number of readings for some common syllabic signs.[30] These new readings significantly revised the reconstruction of the language. It is now generally accepted that the language of the hieroglyphs, which were in use from the fifteenth century B.C.E. until the end of the eighth, is Luwian, but a form of Luwian distinct in certain respects from that which Forrer first

---

26. This is the same region (Cilicia) with which King Solomon had trade relations, according to 1 Kgs 10:29 and 2 Chr 1:17; see also R. D. Barnett, "Karatepe, the Key to the Hittite Hieroglyphs," 88.

27. The definitive edition of the Karatepe bilingual is Halet Çambel, *CHLI* II.

28. *Les hiéroglyphes hittites, Première partie, L'écriture* (Paris: CNRS, 1960).

29. *Hieroglyphisch-Hethitisches Glossar* (Wiesbaden: Harrassowitz, 1962).

30. *Hittite Hieroglyphs and Luwian*, 145–97.

identified in the cuneiform documents. Exactly how these two "dialects," as they are often referred to, relate to one another spatially and temporally is still far from clear.[31] Nor can we yet answer satisfactorily the question why the Hittite Empire felt it needed two distinct scripts, although a new theory suggests that the Hittite monarchy, increasingly in competition with Egypt and Mesopotamia for political domination, may have been motivated by a desire to have a writing system that was uniquely Anatolian.[32]

The Story Unfolds

The Boghazköy archives have produced more than thirty thousand cuneiform tablet fragments, and the enormous task of publishing copies of these documents is only now coming to a conclusion. The more than ten thousand tablets excavated by Theodor Makridi and Hugo Winckler were sent to Berlin for conservation and study by agreement between Otto Weber, the director of the Near Eastern Department of the Berlin Museum, and Halil Edhem, the director of the Istanbul Museum. These tablets provided the contents for the first six volumes of *Keilschrifttexte aus Boghazköi* (Cuneiform Texts from Boghazköy), published by the German Oriental Society, but this series was discontinued when Hans Ehelolf, as curator of the tablets in the Berlin Museum, initiated a new series, *Keilschrifturkunden aus Boghazköi* (Cuneiform Documents from Boghazköy), which began publication in 1921.[33] According to the agreement between Berlin and Istanbul, the tablets were to be returned to Turkey once published; however, by 1942, fewer than three thousand had been returned. More than seven hundred of those that were returned had not yet been published in *KUB*, and those make up the content of the *Istanbul Arkeoloji Müzelerinde Bulunan Boghazköy Tabletleri* (Boghazköy Tablets in the Archaeological Museums of Istanbul) published

---

31. H. Craig Melchert, "Language," in *The Luwians* (ed. H. Craig Melchert; HdO 1/68; Leiden: Brill, 2004), 171.

32. Annick Payne, "Writing Systems and Identity," in *Anatolian Interfaces: Hittites, Greeks and Their Neighbors. Proceedings of an International Conference on Cross-Cultural Interaction, September 17–19, 2004, Emory University, Atlanta, GA* (ed. Billie Jean Collins, Mary Bachvarova, and Ian C. Rutherford; Oxford: Oxbow, forthcoming).

33. Ehelolf himself published most of the early volumes in the series. For a personal account of his work, see Hans Gustav Güterbock, "Hans Ehelolf und das Berliner Boğazköy-Archiv," *Das Altertum* 33 (1987): 114–20. For a history of the Berlin archive, see Horst Klengel, "Das Berliner Boğazköy-Archiv: Geschichte und Textedition," in *Ägypten, Vorderasien, Turfan: Probleme der Edition und Bearbeitung altorientalischer Handschriften* (ed. Horst Klengel and Werner Sunderman; Berlin: Akademie, 1991), 73–81.

by Muazzez Çığ (1944, 1947, 1954) and Mustafa Eren (1988). The other approximately 7,400 Istanbul tablets remained in Berlin until 1989, when East Germany returned them, published or not, to Ankara. Some unpublished texts remain. The *KUB* series completed publication in 1990 with a total of sixty volumes.

The tablets found in the 1931–33 campaigns led by Bittel were also sent to Berlin and published in *KUB*. To accomodate the tablets found in the postwar excavations, the old series *KBo* was revived under the direction of Otten, epigrapher for the Boghazköy excavations. The first volume in this series had been published in 1916, while the most recent volume (57) appeared in 2007. Most of the published cuneiform texts have been translated and analyzed in one form or another, although few are published in a form or venue that is accessible to a nonspecialist audience. The entire Iron Age hieroglyphic corpus, on the other hand, is now available, thanks to the massive three-volume undertaking, *The Corpus of Hieroglyphic Luwian Inscriptions*, by J. David Hawkins of the School of Oriental and African Studies, University of London. Although Germany still leads the way in the study of cuneiform Hittite, the field today is truly international. Scholars not only in Germany, England, and the United States but also in the Netherlands, Italy, France, Israel, Japan, and, of course, Turkey are now engaged in this important work.

Much remains to be done, and the work of reconstructing the language, culture, and history of this fascinating people continues. The last few decades have seen significant new discoveries, and although they cannot match the excitement of those early revelations, they are nevertheless spectacular in their own right. While Hittitology continues to be a dynamic and evolving field of study, it is nevertheless still a relatively young and relatively small field, and it continues to struggle to gain a firm foothold in academe.

The story of the decipherment of the hieroglyphs provides a vivid testimonial to the importance of combining philology (the study of texts) and archaeology in reconstructing past languages, history, and culture. Archaeology has provided some of the most important inroads in recent years. Not least significant have been new discoveries at the Hittite capital. Political events had brought the excavations at Boghazköy to a halt in 1939, and they did not reopen until 1952. Archaeologists have been excavating continually ever since, initially under the direction of Kurt Bittel (1952–77), followed by Peter Neve (1978–93) and Jürgen Seeher (1994–present). To date, a total of thirty temples have been excavated in the Upper City (fig. 2.2), and it is becoming apparent that the Hittite capital was above all a religious and ceremonial center. The discovery of a sacred pool complex and the restoration of its two associated vaulted chambers, one with a well-preserved hieroglyphic inscription that records a military campaigns of the last Hittite king, Suppiluliuma II, from whose reign few records survive, provide valuable information about both the history and the religion of the Hittites. Further, the 1990 season turned up more than three thousand bullae in a "seal archive" located in the cellar of a building to the north of the rocky outcrop called Nişantaş, situated opposite the citadel. Typically stamped with the official seal of the Hittite kings or their officials, these bullae have provided valuable information about the genealogy of members of the Hittite ruling family.

Currently the excavations are focused on two goals. The discovery of a major food storage and redistribution center on the rock summit known as Büyükkaya in the lower town has encouraged investigators to focus on the economic basis of the city as one major goal. The second focus is the new excavations (since 2001) in the western part of the Upper City in the valley west of the rock of Sarıkale, which may provide evidence of the elusive residential quarter. One major challenge remaining for excavators is to find a royal tomb.

Outside of the Hittite capital, new excavations along the Aegean and Mediterranean coasts are yielding data relating to the Late Bronze Age; even the Black Sea area, historically an archaeological "no man's land," is now being surveyed. Information from these "peripheral" areas should shed light on the relationship of the Hittites with their Anatolian neighbors. Sites in the Hittite heartland that had been subjected to "premodern" excavations have recently undergone new study. These include Alişar, Atchana (ancient Alalakh), and Karatepe (ancient Azatiwadaya). For other key sites, such as Karkamis (modern Jerablus) and Alaca Höyük,[34] we must impatiently await future excavation. The rock monuments at Gavurkalesi,[35] Sirkeli,[36] and Eflatun Pinar have also recently been excavated, with surprising results.

Most dramatic has been the identification and excavation of several Hittite regional centers with cuneiform archives of their own: Maşat (ancient Tapikka), an administrative center northeast of Hattusa; Ortaköy

---

34. Excavated by the Turkish Historical Society in the 1930s under the direction of Hamit Z. Koşay, work is once again underway under the direction of Aykut Çınaroğlu.

35. See, e.g., Stephen Lumsden, "Gavurkalesi: Investigations at a Hittite Sacred Place," in *Recent Developments in Hittite Archaeology and History* (ed. K. Aslihan Yener and Harry A. Hoffner Jr; Winona Lake, Ind.: Eisenbrauns, 2002), 111–25.

36. Barthel Hrouda, "Vorläufiger Bericht über die Ausgrabungsergebnisse auf dem Sirkelihöyük Südtürkei von 1992–1995," *Kazı Sonuçları Toplantısı* 18 (1997): 291–312; H. Ehringhaus, "Hethitisches Felsrelief der Grossreichszeit Entdeckt," *Antike Welt* 26/1 (1995): 66; idem, "Ein neues hethitisches Felsrelief am Sirkeli Höyük in der Çukurova," *Antike Welt* 26/2 (1995) 118–19.

(ancient Sapinuwa), southeast of Hattusa; and Kuşaklı (ancient Sarissa), a religious center southeast of Hattusa. These archives stored letters, land grants, inventories of goods and personnel, and religious and cultic texts.[37] Ortaköy, which once served as a royal residence, is the most substantial of these, having produced a cache of more than three thousand tablets.[38] Their publication will provide valuable information about Hittite regional administration. Other sites with Hittite-period occupations that have recently undergone excavation are Çadır and Kaman-Kale in central Turkey, Kinet (Issos) in the Hatay, and Mersin and the mound at Sirkeli (adjacent to the rock reliefs mentioned above) in Cilicia. The excavators of Sirkeli propose an identification with Hittite Lawazantiya, the Kizzuwatnean city in which King Hattusili III took Puduhepa as his queen (see ch. 2).[39] Finally, the recent discovery of a hieroglyphic inscription adjacent to a massive fortified Late Bronze Age site at Hatip near Konya has raised hopes of finding the Hittites' second capital, Tarhuntassa, and the archives it no doubt possessed (see ch. 2).[40]

Although the quality of the style of art showcased on the Hittite rock reliefs is difficult to defend when set beside the magnificent works of art from Egypt and Mesopotamia, it has the advantage, at least, of being original. The style of the reliefs cannot be attributed to poorly trained artists, as the Hittites also produced undeniably exquisite works of art, including rhyta (animal-shaped vessels) and other ceremonial vessels, but appears rather to have been a matter of taste. Hittite art has also revealed some surprises of its own. A vase that has recently come to light in the vicinity of Hüseyindede bears a relief decoration that points to an Anatolian origin for the "sport" of bull-leaping well known from Minoan Crete.[41] In addition, the Boghazköy excavations recently revealed that the walls of at least one temple (Temple 9)

37. Trevor R. Bryce, "The Hittites—Discoveries and Ongoing Research," *History Compass* (2004). Online (by subscription): http://www.blackwell-compass.com/subject/history/article_view?highlight_query=Trevor+Bryce&type=std&slop=0&fuzzy=0.5&last_results=query%3DTrevor%2BBryce%26submit%3DGo%26content_types%3Dcja&parent=void&sortby=relevance&offset=0&article_id=hico_articles_bsl072.

38. Aygül Süel, "Ortaköy-Šapinuwa," in Yener and Hoffner, *Recent Developments in Hittite Archaeology and History*, 157–65.

39. See http://www.sirkeli-project.info/en/index.html.

40. Ali M. Dinçol, "Die Entdeckung des Felsmonuments in Hatip und ihre Auswirkungen über die historischen und geographischen Fragen des Hethiterreiches," *TÜBA-AR* 1 (1998): 27–34.

41. Piotr Taracha, "Bull-Leaping on a Hittite Vase: New Light on Anatolian and Minoan Religion," *Archeologia* 53 (2002): 7–20.

in the Upper City were covered with colorful paintings, which points either to unexpected versatility on the part of Hittite artists or to the presence of foreign (Mycenaean?) artists in the Hittite capital.[42]

In 1929, Garstang wrote, "no one can claim to the satisfaction of the others to have made much progress as regards the position, grouping, and organization of the central Hittite states."[43] Indeed, until recently, few historians held out hope that the complex geography of the Hittite Empire could be sorted out. Locating the geographical position of the Hittites' political dependencies in Anatolia with any precision was daunting enough, but the cuneiform documents refer to hundreds of towns and villages under Hittite control, and locating them precisely seemed an impossible task. Nevertheless, significant progress has been made, again thanks to a combination of philological and archaeological detective work. For example, the discovery of an inscription of Tudhaliya IV in Yalburt allowed scholars to pinpoint towns in the southwest of Anatolia. In addition, the decipherment of the inscription of a local king at Karabel has led to the identification of Ephesos (Hittite Apasa, modern Selçuk) as the captial of ancient Arzawa, an identification that is now confirmed by an analysis of the composition of the clay of one of the Arzawa letters from the El Amarna archive.[44]

No less productive are the advances that have been made in archaeological techniques and data-handling methods. Geophysical prospecting, the use of computer-aided research, paleo-zoological and environmental research, improved dating methods, and analysis of exchange networks are improving the quality of our information about Anatolia's past.

A NOTE ON CHRONOLOGY

The greatest challenge still facing historians is to establish an absolute chronology for second-millennium Anatolia. The surviving records of the Hittite administration make no use of a formal system for reckoning the passing of the years. Royal annals track the annual campaigns of individual kings, but these are not assigned to a specific regnal year and do not provide the total length of a given reign.[45] Nor do the Hittite "king lists" help, as these

---

42. The wall paintings are currently undergoing study, which hopefully will determine whether Mycenaean or Anatolian artists were responsible for them.

43. John Garstang, *The Hittite Empire: Being a Survey of the History, Geography and Monuments of Hittite Asia Minor and Syria* (London: Constable, 1929), viii.

44. See Sanna Aro, "Art and Architecture," in Melchert, *The Luwians*, 286.

45. For example, it has recently been proposed that the long forty-year reign of Suppiluliuma I should be reduced to about half; see G. Wilhelm and J. Boese, "Absolute

were compiled for the purpose of recording the sacrificial rations for the royal ancestor cult and are inaccurate and unreliable as tools for reconstructing a workable chronology. We can only assume that a civilization as complex as that of the Hittites had such a system. Perhaps the wooden tablets used for economic documents employed a system of year reckoning, but if so, it is permanently lost to us.[46]

For Hittite history, absolute dates are few and are dependent primarily on synchronisms with events in Mesopotamia and Egypt. Thus, for example, following the so-called Middle Chronology favored by most Hittitologists, we know that Mursili I brought an end to the dynasty of Hammurabi in 1595 B.C.E., that the battle of Qadesh was fought in the fifth year of Ramesses II (1274 B.C.E.), and that Tudhaliya IV fought the battle of Nihriya in the first few years of the reign of Tukulti-ninurta (r. 1233–1197 B.C.E.). In addition to such synchronisms, a prayer of Mursili II reports a solar omen that occurred while the king was on campaign in the land of Azzi in his ninth or tenth year. If this omen was a solar eclipse, then we are able to calculate that Mursili II celebrated his tenth year as king in 1311 B.C.E. It is important to remember that even these dates are provisional and will continue to shift as the absolute chronological framework for the entire ancient Near East continues to be refined. For example, an attempt has been made recently, based on pottery analysis, to lower the date of Mursili's attack on Babylon to 1499.[47] This would require compressing Hittite history by about one hundred years, a revision that the Hittite evidence does not easily support.[48]

Although the few absolute dates available to us provide some important anchors for Hittite history, the reconstruction of the sequence of Hittite kings and the length of their reigns is still mostly educated guesswork. As a result, for most of Hittite history we must be satisfied with a relative chronology, that is, the reconstruction of the sequence in which a particular set of events occurred. Analysis of the paleography of the cuneiform tablets—the changes over time in the style of expression, duktus (handwriting), grammar, and orthography—has allowed us to date particular compositions to within a

---

Chronologie und die hethitische Geschichte des 15. und 14. Jahrhunderts v. Chr." in *High, Middle or Low? Acts of an International Colloquium on Absolute Chronology Held at the University of Gothenburg, 20th–22nd August 1987* (ed. Paul Åström; Gothenberg: Åströms, 1987), 74–117.

46. Gary Beckman, "Hittite Chronology," *Akkakdica* 119–120 (2000): 20.

47. H. Gasche, J. A. Armstrong, S. W. Cole, and V. G. Gurzadyan, *Dating the Fall of Babylon: A Reappraisal of Second-Millennium Chronology* (Chicago: The Oriental Institute of the University of Chicago, 1998).

48. See Beckman, "Hittite Chronology," 25.

fifty-year period, providing a relative chronology for most of Hittite history. But only when absolute dates—the pinpointing of an event to a particular moment in time—are known are we able to anchor the tablets and the events they describe in a precise chronological and historical context.

New investigations at Boghazköy-Hattusa have provided an absolute chronological framework for the second half of the second millennium that will be important for applying absolute dates to future finds as well as allowing precise dating of the architecture of the Hittite capital.[49] In addition, Cornell University's dendrochronology project is on the verge of establishing an unbroken tree-ring sequence for central Anatolia. When the sequence is complete, the tables will turn and Anatolia will provide the master chronology according to which the historical chronologies of Mesopotamia and Egypt will be calibrated.[50]

---

49. Ulf-Dietrich Schoop and Jürgen Seeher, "Absolute Chronologie in Boğazköy-Ḫattuša: Das Potential der Radiokarbondaten," in *Strukturierung und Datierung in der hethitischen Archäologie* (ed. D. P. Mielke, U.-D. Schoop, and J. Seeher; BYZAS 4; Istanbul: Veröffentlichungen des Deutschen Archäologischen Instituts Istanbul, 2006), 53–75.

50. Colin Renfrew, "Kings, Tree Rings and the Old World," *Nature* 381 (1996): 733–34.

2
THE POLITICAL HISTORY OF THE HITTITES

TUCKED INTO THE NORTHEASTERN CORNER of the Mediterranean basin, the Anatolian peninsula is geographically diverse. The fertile river valleys of the west give way to a high, rugged, semiarid plateau in the east. Over two thousand feet high in most places, the plateau is flanked by two mountain systems, the Taurus and Pontus ranges. Beyond these, in both south and north, narrow coastal plains stretch in relative isolation, framing the Mediterranean and Black Seas, respectively. Hot in summer and sometimes bitterly cold in winter, much of the central highlands was once covered by forests, but centuries of human activity have turned forest to grassland. The system of steppeland and river basin, punctuated by high mountainous areas, has defined the cultural development of the land. Communication flowed with the east-to-west orientation of the valleys, and contacts with the rest of the world depended either on the narrow passes that cut through its mountains or on the ships that navigated its coastlines. The peoples who entrenched themselves in this land were as diverse as its geography, with the result that Anatolia's cultural development is not the story of one civilization but of many. Before the Hittites came on the scene, Anatolia had already played host to any number of cultures. Although often viewed as peripheral to the better-known civilizations of Greece in the West and Mesopotamia in the East, Anatolia was center court for some of the most important developments in human prehistory.

ORIGINS

Çatal Höyük in Anatolia's fertile Konya Plain is one of the earliest and most significant agricultural villages in the ancient Near East. Its sixteen or so levels of occupation date from 7400 to 6200 B.C.E. The 21-meter-high mound covers an area of 13 hectares, making it the largest Neolithic period (New Stone Age) site in the Near East. Lying outside the Fertile Crescent, the site is important for understanding humanity's early efforts to domesticate plants and animals. Yet it is the art that decorated the rooms in this settlement that has, understandably, received the most attention from scholars and the public alike. "The wall paintings and relief sculpture were unique, and even today … it remains the densest concentration of symbolism so far found in the eastern Mediterranean at this time."[1] The discovery of additional sites in southeastern Anatolia with elaborate art suggests that Çatal belongs to a larger regional development the nature of which has yet to be fully defined.

The Neolithic gradually gave way to the transitional Chalcolithic period (Copper and Stone Age) and then to the Bronze Age, a phase of human history that is marked by the intensified use of bronze, an alloy of copper and tin. The Early Bronze Age covers most of the third millennium in Anatolia and is characterized by a growing demand for luxury items, which required an increasingly complex trade network. This period is best represented in Anatolia by the sites of Troy in the northwest, Beycesultan in the southwest, and Tarsis and Mersin in Cilicia in the southeast.

Toward the end of the third millennium, central Anatolia was heavily settled, with power centers at Kültepe, Boghazköy, Alişar, and Alaca. A text recorded nearly a millennium later describes the rebellion of a coalition of seventeen Anatolian rulers against the Akkadian king Naram-Sin (2380–2325 B.C.E.), including Pamba king of Hatti, Zipani king of Kanes, Tisbinki king of Kursaura (Kussar), and probably also Nur-Dagan king of Purushanda (Burushattum).[2] The narrative describes a region under the control of a constellation of organized kingdoms, a picture that is fully consonant with the archaeological data, which indicate a conglomeration of small polities with kings or princes who ruled a city and its surrounding territory from a palace perched atop a citadel.

The advances in metallurgical techniques that are the hallmark of the Early Bronze Age are lavishly represented by the artifacts found in the thirteen tombs excavated at Alaca Höyük in the 1930s. Located only a few kilometers north of Boghazköy, the site of the later Hittite capital, Alaca in the Late Bronze Age was a royal retreat. But for the Early Bronze II period (2300–2100 B.C.E.), the tombs are the only material remains thus far uncovered at the site. The artifacts from the Alaca tombs are the product of a long-standing tradition in metalworking, one that is also evident in similar

---

1. Ian Hodder, "Ethics and Archaeology: The Attempt at Çatalhöyük," *NEA* 65 (2002): 174–81.

2. An alabaster stela from southern Iraq dating to the reign of Naram-Sin and depicting tribute bearers, one carrying a depas vase, a ceramic style characteristic of Cilicia, along with Anatolian-style weaponry, provides supporting evidence that the conquests of the Akkadian king may have taken him into Anatolia; see Machteld Mellink, "An Akkadian Illustration of a Campaign in Cilicia," *Anatolia* 7 (1963): 101–15.

finds at Horoztepe near the Black Sea. These "visually striking and intri-
cately crafted metal objects have been plausibly identified as standards and
sistra intended for cult processions and performances. Several are cast from
a copper alloy over which sheets of silver or electrum were wrapped around
antlers, horns, head, or feet, or used to form patterns on the body, yielding a
rich, polychrome effect."[3] No architecture was found that could be assigned
to the period of the tombs, leaving investigators to speculate as to who the
people buried in them were and where they came from, questions that are
key for understanding the origins of the Hittites.

INDO-EUROPEANS IN ANATOLIA

The question of Hittite origins is inevitably linked to the ongoing debate
over the original homeland of the Indo-Europeans. The earliest evidence of
Indo-European anywhere in the world is in the cuneiform texts of the Old
Assyrian trading colonies (see below). Here we find names that can already
be identified as one of the three dialects of Indo-European attested for the
second millennium in Anatolia: Hittite, Luwian, and Palaic.[4] How and when
these groups found a home on the Anatolian plateau is a question that has yet
to be answered to everyone's satisfaction.

Hittite, Luwian, and Palaic diverged very early from the other Indo-European dialects and thus display the most archaic linguistic features of all the
Indo-European languages.[5] For this reason, they constitute important evidence
for the reconstruction of the parent language. Although a speaker of one could
not have understood a speaker of the other, the similarities between Hittite and
Luwian are clear. Several hundred years of individual development must be
assumed for Hittite and Luwian in order to explain the linguistic differences
between them. Therefore, the ancestors of these languages must have penetrated into their respective territories within Anatolia sometime in the third
millennium, perhaps as early as 3000 B.C.E.,[6] a minimum of several hundred
years before we first see Indo-European names in the Old Assyrian texts.

---

3. Ann Gunter, "Animals in Anatolian Art," in *A History of the Animal World in the
Ancient Near East* (ed. Billie Jean Collins; HdO 1/64; Leiden: Brill, 2002), 83.

4. In addition, a handful of Hittite vocabulary words appear in the documents from
Kaneš; see Craig Melchert, "Indo-European Languages of Anatolia," in *CANE*, 2152.

5. See the papers collected in *Greater Anatolia and the Indo-Hittite Language
Family: Papers Presented at a Colloquium Hosted by the University of Richmond, March
18–19, 2000* (ed. Robert Drews; Journal of Indo-European Studies Monographs 38;
Washington, D.C.: Institute for the Study of Man, 2001).

6. Melchert, "Prehistory," in Melchert, *The Luwians*, 24.

One theory for the direction of immigration of the Indo-Europeans into Anatolia rests on the appearance in the Russian steppe north of the Black Sea and Caucasus at about 3100 B.C.E. of a new form of burial, the *kurgan*, Russian for "tumulus," referring to an underground shaft covered with a mound. The *kurgan* burials, which have been associated with warrior-like, horseback-riding pastoralists of Indo-European "ethnicity," begin to appear in Transcaucasia just before 3000 B.C.E. (e.g., at Uch Tepe in the Milska steppe). The presence of horse bones at a few sites in eastern Anatolia, such as Norşuntepe and Tepecik, where they had not previously been known, seems to support an intrusion of steppe pastoralists from the northeast. The Early Bronze tombs at Alaca Höyük are reminiscent of some of these *kurgans*, suggesting that the people buried in them were Indo-Europeans.[7]

Another theory argues that the homeland of the Indo-Europeans was in Anatolia itself, perhaps even centered at Çatal Höyük. In this scenario, the Indo-Europeans spread westward from central Anatolia, bringing agriculture with them, during the seventh millennium B.C.E. as part of the Early Neolithic expansion into Europe. This theory is especially contentious because of the very early date it requires for the divergence of Proto-Anatolian from Proto-Indo-European—several thousand years earlier than most linguists would put it. Recently, however, the theory has received support from a surprising source, evolutionary biology. Applying the methods that they use to reconstruct the process of human evolution, biologists from the University of Auckland have determined that the split must have occurred around 6700 B.C.E. ± 1200, thousands of years earlier than linguists have supposed.[8]

A final theory maps the arrival of the Indo-Europeans from the northwest late in the fourth or early in the third millennium. Archaeological evidence of Early Bronze Age links between southeastern Europe and western Anatolia, at sites such as Troy and Demirci Höyük, combined with the wide distribution of Luwian in the west and south of Anatolia in the second millennium, support the possibility of a westward migration of the Anatolian branch of Indo-European.[9]

---

7. Horst Klengel (*Geschichte des hethitischen Reiches*, 19 with references) supports the eastern theory based on a silver goblet from Karašamb in western Armenia, which he believes could date to the period of the Indo-Eurpean migration, that shows similarities to later Hittite artistic tradition.

8. Russell D. Gray and Quentin D. Atkinson, "Language-Tree Divergence Times Support the Anatolian Theory of Indo-European Origin," *Nature* 426 (November 2003): 435–39.

9. See, e.g., Gerd Steiner, "The Immigration of the First Indo-Europeans into Anatolia Reconsidered," *JIES* 18 (1990): 185–214; J. Makkay, "Pottery Links between Late Neo-

Each of these theories has support within the scholarly community, but none has managed to attract a critical majority of adherents. The material evidence remains inconclusive, as it is not possible to assign any of the Early Bronze Age polities unequivocally to a particular ethnolinguistic group. In the period when we know that Indo-Europeans are present in central Anatolia, at the beginning of the second millennium, there is nothing in the material remains to distinguish them from the native populations that preceded them. In other words, the polities were composed of populations that may have been linguistically diverse but shared the same material culture. Thus, until more information becomes available, perhaps through further excavation, the question of who was buried in the Alaca tombs, Hattians or Hittites, will remain a matter of faith.

THE ASSYRIAN COLONIES

Anatolian history begins at Kanes (modern Kültepe), for it is in this large metropolis that the Assyrians established a merchant colony in the beginning of the second millennium, bringing with them a knowledge of cuneiform writing. Shortly after Erishum, king of Assur (r. 1939–1900 B.C.E.), authorized the trade by establishing "freedom (of circulation) of silver, gold, copper, tin, barley and wool" for Assur,[10] the first donkey caravans began making the arduous six-week journey to bring tin (for making bronze) and high-quality wool textiles to trade with the Anatolians in exchange for silver and gold bullion.[11] Later epic tradition relates a much earlier expedition of Sargon of Akkad into Anatolia to protect the interests of Mesopotamian merchants dwelling in Purushanda (Burushattum), hinting at Mesopotamia's interest in the metals trade with Anatolia well before these merchant colonies.[12] How-

---

lithic Cultures of the NW Pontic and Anatolia, and the Origins of the Hittites," *Anatolica* 19 (1993): 117–28; Bill Darden, "On the Question of the Anatolian Origin of Indo-Hittite," in Drews, *Greater Anatolia and the Indo-Hittite Language Family*, 184–228.

10. Excavators found a sealed envelope of a letter of this king in level II of *kārum* Kanes.

11. For a discussion of the need to import tin to Anatolia in the Middle Bronze Age despite the prior existence of tin sources in the Taurus Mountains, see Aslihan Yener, *The Domestication of Metals* (CHANE 4; Leiden: Brill, 2000), 71–76.

12. Sargon, King of Battle. Although this text copy dates to the Late Bronze Age, stories about the kings of Akkad circulated in Anatolia at least as early as the Assyrian Colony period. For a school text recently discovered at Kültepe dealing with Sargon's suppression of a revolt, see Cahit Günbatti, "Kültepe'den Akadlı Sargon'a Ait Bir Tablet," *Archivum Anatolicum* 3 (1997): 131–55. For lists of deified Sargonic kings in Hurrian omina and magical rituals, see Annelies Kammenhuber, "Historisch-

ever, it is only with the twenty thousand letters and economic documents, written in an Old Assyrian dialect of Akkadian, that the merchants left behind that Anatolia emerges from prehistory, and we are allowed a glimpse of life in central Anatolia in the three centuries prior to the foundation of the kingdom of the Hittites.

In fact, Kanes was only one of several such colonies in Anatolia. The colony network stretched six hundred miles east to west, from Assur to the Salt Lake in the Konya Plain, and comprised eleven major trading posts, or *kārū* (singular *kārum*), in central Asia Minor, with ten other subsidiary posts, called *wabartū* (fig. 2.1).[13] Only three trading posts have been excavated, at Kültepe-Kanes, Hattus (later to become the Hittite capital Hattusa), and Ališar (ancient Ankuwa).[14] These *kārū* were attached to the major indigenous kingdoms of Anatolia. Although the fact that most of the documents come from Kültepe-Kanes means that we have a somewhat one-sided view of the *kārum* period, it is clear that it was the political and economic center to which the other ten *kārū* deferred.[15]

The site at Kültepe-Kanes consists of an upper and a lower city. From the city mound, with its huge palace and administrative buildings, the local ruler (Akkadian *rubāʾum*) administered his holdings, called *mātū* "countries" in Akkadian. To the east and northeast, a terraced lower town stretched

---

geographische Nachrichten aus der althurrischen Überlieferung, dem Altelamischen und den Inschriften der Könige von Akkad für die Zeit vor dem Einfall der Gutäer (ca. 2200/2136)," *Acta Antiqua Academiae Scientiarum Hungaricae* 22 (1974): 157–60, 165–68. For a general discussion of the Sargonic traditions in Anatolia, see Gary Beckman, "Sargon and Naram-Sin in Ḫatti: Reflections of Mesopotamian Antiquity among the Hittites," in *Die Gegenwart des Altertums: Formen und Funktionen des Altertumsbezugs in den Hochkulturen der Alten Welt* (ed. Dieter Kuhn and Helga Stahl; Heidelberg: Edition Forum, 2001), 85–91.

13. The word *kārum* derives from Sumerian kar "quay" and comes to refer to a "harbor district (of a city)," "trading station," "community of merchants," "merchant administration." *Wabartum* derives from Akkadian ubāru "resident alien." The *kārū* included Burushattum, Durhumit, Hahhum, Hattus, Hurama, Kanes, Nihriya, Tawiniya, Ursu, Wahsusana, and Zalpa. The *wabartum* were Badna, Hanaknak, Karahna, Mama, Salatuwar, Samuha, Tuhpia, Ulama, Washania, and Zalpa south.

14. Ališar (ancient Ankuwa) contains Old Assyrian materials and tablets but is not among the trading posts mentioned in the texts.

15. The ruler of Burushattum (on the southern end of Salt Lake) was the only Anatolian ruler called great prince (*rubaʾum rabi ʿum*). The other rulers are called only prince or even *šarru*, which was of subordinate rank, suggesting that Burushattum enjoyed a special status. Burushattum may have owed its importance to controlling a large part of the production of silver, which was in demand by the Assyrians.

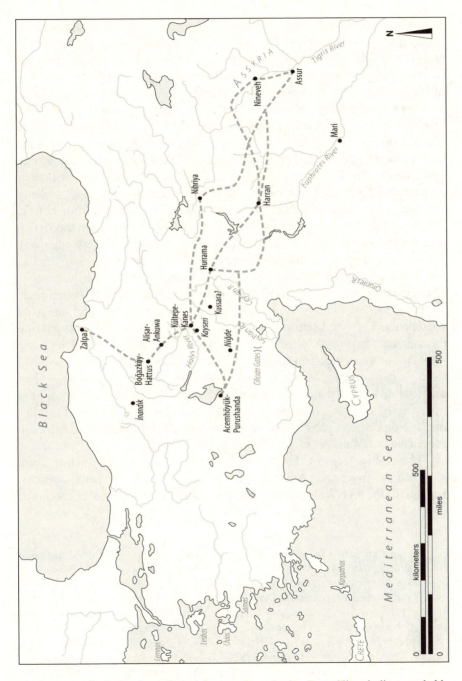

Fig. 2.1. Anatolia during the period of the Assyrian colonies. Dotted lines indicate probable caravan routes.

around the city mound. The extent of the lower town is not yet known, but it may have been as much as 30 hectares (80 acres). The *kārum* was situated at its center, in an area encompassing about 4 hectares (10 acres). Friedrich Hrozný, the decipher of Hittite, conducted a one-season excavation at the site in 1925, recovering one thousand tablets. Since 1948 the site has been excavated continuously by Tahsin and Nimet Özgüç, who have identified four levels, IV through I. The levels that correspond to the Assyrian occupation of the *kārum* are II (ca. 1940–1850 B.C.E.) and Ib (ca. 1850–1775). When the inhabitants left, they took their valuables but little else. As a result, the houses in the *kārum* provide a snapshop of life in the Middle Bronze Age, with their inventories of furniture, richly decorated pottery, and approximately seventy archives, some large and others small, that recorded the transactions of the individual family-run businesses. Were it not for these documents, the Assyrians would be invisible in the archaeological record, since in every other way they shared the material culture of their Anatolian hosts.

Although no complete treaties have been found that outline the specific arrangements between the local Anatolian princes and the Assyrian merchants,[16] their stipulations are not difficult to reconstruct from the surviving documents. The Anatolian rulers retained the right to tax caravans passing through their territory,[17] were given first option to purchase Assyrian goods, were free to impose certain restrictions on the trade in luxury items, and had the right to punish any Assyrian who violated these rules. In exchange, they granted the Assyrians alien-residence status and the right of extraterritoriality (i.e., the right to govern themselves) and guaranteed protection and right of passage on the roads. Self-governance meant a centralized administration conducted out of the *bit kārim* "*kārum* office."

The eighty years of the *kārum* II period were politically stable ones, in which the five major Anatolian powers, or *mātū* (Zalpa, Hattus, Kanes, Burushattum, and Wahsusana), maintained relatively peaceful relations,

---

16. Two partially preserved treaties have been recovered, one from Tell Leilan (Jesper Eidem, "An Old Assyrian Treaty from Tell Leilan," in *Marchands, diplomates et empereurs: Études sur la Civilisation Mesopotamienne offerts à Paul Garelli* [ed. Dominique Charpin and Francis Joannès; Paris: Éditions Recherche sur les Civilisations, 1991], 185–207) and one from Kültepe, on which some treaty stipulations are preserved (Emin Bilgiç, "Ebla in Cappadocian Inscriptions," in *Hittite and Other Anatolian and Near Eastern Studies in Honor of Sedat Alp* [ed. Heinrich Otten, H. Ertem, E. Akurgal, and A. Süel; Ankara: Türk Tarih Kurumu Basımevi, 1992], 61–66).

17. Attempts to avoid taxes by smuggling goods both into and out of Anatolia via side roads that avoided towns imposing tolls were a dangerous, but not uncommon, undertaking.

recognizing that it was in their own best interests to do so. This stabililty encouraged and facilitated the activities of the Assyrian merchant system in the region, which in turn promoted closer links between the various *mātū*. The eventual result, however, was an increase in territorial rivalry and a growing desire on the part of the smaller states to establish their independence in order to deal with the merchants in their own right. In the final years of the *kārum* II period, signs of serious unrest and conflict arose among a number of the Anatolian states, culminating with the burning of the *kārum* at Kanes around 1830. The perpetrator of this attack may have been Uhna, king of Zalpa, whose conquest is mentioned in a later text and who may have had the help of the *mātum* of Hattus, which was also hostile to Kanes.

A generation passed before the Assyrians returned to Anatolia. This time they came in smaller numbers, perhaps due to continuing unrest in the area. Under King Inar, Kanes came back into prominence in this period. A letter that Anumhirbi, king of Mama, wrote to Inar's son, King Warsama, hints at continuing conflict and fragmentation both between and within the various kingdoms.[18] It was a period of shifting alliances and political rivalries in which vassals were chafing against the yoke of their overlords. In the midst of this growing fragmentation, the king of Kussar, Pithana, set out to take Kanes away from Warsama and make it his city.

The conquests of Pithana and his son Anitta were recorded in the earliest historical document found in the Hittite archive, the Anitta Chronicle. Originally composed in either Hittite or Akkadian by Anitta himself, the document was later copied and preserved by Hittite scribes. Anitta's residence at Kanes was verified in dramatic fashion by the 1954 discovery in a large building on the city mount of a spearhead bearing the inscription "the palace of Anitta the Prince." In addition, a number of documents from *kārum* Ib record transactions that are notarized by Anitta "prince" or his father, Pithana, also titled "prince." Finally, a large tablet found in a building in the center of the *kārum* lists six native kings, including Inar, Warsama, and Anitta.[19]

Pithana's conquest of Kanes may have been only the essential first step in a grand plan to gain control over the trade networks. His son continued his ambitions in this direction by subduing the entire region within the basin of the river known in classical sources as the Halys (the modern Kızıl Irmak

---

18. It also reveals that the later Hittite system of parity and vassalage was already well developed at this time. The letter further indicates that an Anatolian prince (*ruba'um*) could conduct diplomatic negotiations independently of the Assyrians, controlled vassals in his own right, and was free to make alliances with other princes.

19. See Machteld J. Mellink, "Archaeology in Asia Minor," *AJA* 67 (1963): 175.

"red river" and Hittite Marassantiya). But soon after his initial successes, Anitta was challenged by an alliance of Hattus, under King Piyusti, and Zalpa, under King Huzziya.[20] Anitta succeeded in defeating Zalpa and bringing its king back to Kanes. He laid siege to Hattus until it was starved out and then attacked and laid waste to the city, cursing anyone who would resettle it: "Whoever after me becomes king and resettles Hattusa, [let] the Stormgod of the Sky strike him."[21] His final victories were in the south, against Salatiwara and then Burushattum, whose king voluntarily subjugated himself to Anitta.[22]

After the events described in the Anitta text, our documentation ends. The *kārum* level Ib was destroyed around 1775 B.C.E. at the hands of an unknown enemy. The merchants packed their things and returned to Assur. Although Anitta's empire probably disintegrated within a generation of his death, his impact was long-lasting. He unified for the first time the whole of the Halys basin up to the Black Sea and the region south of the Halys down to Burushattum, with Kanes as its focal point. In so doing, he began a new political age in Anatolia. The old kingdoms were either totally broken up (as at Hattus) or placed under the immediate control of local rulers appointed by Anitta.[23] Most of the ruling cities of the period never regained their importance. Although no Hittite king claims him as an ancestor and neither his name nor his father's is demonstrably Hittite, Anitta was, in many respects, the forerunner of the Hittite monarchy.

A NOTE ON ETHNICITY

Four different ethnolinguistic groups can be distinguished in the Old Assyrian texts: Assyrians, Hattians, Hurrians, and Indo-Europeans (comprising Hittites,

---

20. Itamar Singer ("Hittites and Hattians in Anatolia at the Beginning of the Second Millennium B.C.," *JIES* 9 [1981]: 119–34; idem, "Our God and Their God,"in *Atti del II Congresso Internazionale die Hittitologia* [ed. Mauro Giorgieri, Onofrio Carruba, and Clelia Mora; Studia Mediterranea 9; Pavia: Gianni Iuculano, 1995], 343–49) suggests that at the time of Anitta's unification of the land, Anatolia was divided into ethnocultural zones distinguishable by their onomasticon, pantheon, and material culture, the two main divisions being between the Halys basin, with its largely Hattian population, and the Hittite region extending from Kanes eastward. The coalition between the kings of Zalpa and Hattus, then, would represent a concerted Hattian opposition to Hittite control.

21. "Proclamation of Anitta of Kuššar," translated by Harry A. Hoffner Jr. (*COS* 1.72:183, §12).

22. Trevor Bryce, *The Kingdom of the Hittites* (2nd ed.; Oxford: Oxford University Press, 2005), 39.

23. Ibid., 39–40.

Luwians, and Palaians). The Hattians are believed to make up the indigenous population of central Anatolia prior to the arrival of Indo-European speakers. At the beginning of the second millennium, the Hattians inhabited the Kızıl Irmak basin in north-central Anatolia, including towns such as Hattus and Zalpa, while the Hittites were centered to their south in Cappadocia in the vicinity of Kanes and Kussar.[24] The Hattian language of this indigenous people is among the eight first identified by Emil Forrer as being represented in the Hittite archives, where it is preserved primarily in records of religious ceremonies. The term *Hittite*, which is used in the Bible and is the source of our modern terminology, derives from the indigenous name that the Hittites used when referring to their own land: Hatti. The Hittites referred to their own language not as Hattian, however, but as Nesite, after Kanes (also called Nesa), the town they considered their ancestral home. The eventual disappearance of Hattian speakers in favor of Hittite occurred not necessarily because the latter outnumbered and outcompeted them, but more likely because it was in the interests of the Hattian speakers to adopt the Hittite language.[25] In any case, the Hattian language was not simply overpowered but continued to be used in religious festivals and rituals for some time.[26]

Palaic was spoken in Pala, a territory perhaps corresponding to the Roman province of Paphlagonia, north of the Hittite heartland. Both the land and the language appear to have become extinct relatively early in the Old Kingdom period. The language is preserved in only a handful of early cultic texts. Luwian, in contrast, was widely spoken throughout Anatolia by the Late Bronze Age. In the latter half of the millennium, Luwian speakers comprised the dominant population group in Anatolia. The Hittite documents allow us to follow the continuing migration of Luwian as a spoken language from its base in the Arzawa lands of western Anatolia to the southern coast, including, from west to east, Lycia, Tarhuntassa, and Kizzuwatna.[27] The region in the west that formed the core of the Luwian

---

24. On the probable location of Kussar, see ibid., 36 with references.

25. Language change is a self-conscious, intentional social strategy in which individuals and groups compete for social and economic power. Vertical social mobility must exist for people occupying lower-status positions to adopt the speech of the elite; otherwise there is no incentive to do so. See David Anthony, "Prehistoric Migration as Social Process," in *Migrations and Invasions in Archaeological Explanation* (ed. John Chapman and Helena Hamerow; BAR International Series 664; Oxford: BAR, 1997), 28.

26. For a reassessment of the impact of Hattian on Hittite language and institutions, see Melchert, "Prehistory," 15–22.

27. But see Ilya Yakubovich ("Luwian Migrations in Light of Linguistic Contacts," in Collins, Bachvarova, and Rutherford, *Anatolian Interfaces*), who posits a second-

speakers was known as Luwiya, later to become the politically organized Arzawa lands. Tarhundaradu, king of Arzawa, wrote to Amenhotep III in the fourteenth century in Hittite rather than Luwian, Akkadian (the international language of the period), or Egyptian, because that was the only court language common to both, Arzawa being by international standards a relative backwater. Although the hieroglyphic script was developed for writing the Luwian language, it never became the official language of diplomacy. A seal discovered at Troy (level VIIa) belonged to an individual with a Luwian name and may be the first evidence of the language of the Trojans. Notably, the Lukka lands (modern Lycia) in southwestern Anatolia also spoke Luwian. According to Homeric tradition, the Lycians were the Trojans' closest ally, a bond that would have been easier to form if they shared a common tongue.

The Old Assyrian texts reveal the presence of Hurrian traders in central Anatolia already at the beginning of the second millennium, but the center of Hurrian settlement in the Near East was in northern Mesopotamia. The origins of the Hurrians is unclear, but they may have come from the east, perhaps Transcaucasia, sometime in the third millennium. This population coalesced for a time into a political entity known as Mitanni, a kingdom that would be the Hittites' nemesis for many years. The first Hittite kings were clearly conscious of the potential threat posed by the Hurrians, who were already well-established in northern Syria. The inevitable clash of Mitannian and Hittite ambitions in the Euphrates region eventually led to the conquest and annexation of the Hurrian province of Kizzuwatna to the Hittite kingdom and the influx of Hurrian cultural elements, particularly in the area of religion, on the Hittite state. Although the military victory was Hatti's, the cultural one appears to have belonged to the Hurrians, as Hurrian cults and practices infiltrated deep into the Hittite heartland.

FROM KINGDOM TO EMPIRE

Despite Anitta's curse, Hattus, now Hattusa, was resettled perhaps within only a generation.[28] A modern visitor to the site of Boghazköy is immedi-

---

millennium Luwian homeland in central Anatolia (the Konya Plain), thus rejecting the popular view of a Luwian eastward expansion from western Anatolia in the Middle Bronze Age.

28. See Jörg Klinger, *Untersuchungen zur Rekonstruktion der hattischen Kultschicht* (StBoT 37; Wiesbaden: Harrassowitz, 1996), 122 and n. 168, citing Peter Neve, "Ein althethitischer Sammelfund aus der Unterstadt," in Kurt Bittel et al., *Boğazköy* (6 vols.; Berlin: de Gruyter, 1935–84), 6:89; also Richard Beal, "The Predecessors of Ḫattušili I," in *Hittite*

ately struck by the isolation of the Hittite capital. The winters can be bitterly cold, and the summers are hot and dry. Even if one casts one's mind back to an era when trees covered the hillsides and clusters of habitations dotted the landscape, it is difficult to understand why this city was chosen for the site of the new capital and why future kings remained here in spite of the hardships and despite other, more hospitable, options. Its natural advantages—it was easily defensible and had a year-round water supply—may have been important factors, but ideological and strategic factors probably lay behind the decision to locate the capital at Hattusa.

HATTUSA, A CITY FIT FOR GODS AND KINGS

Hattusa is located at the southern end of the Budaközü Valley adjacent to the stream of the same name, which has cut a large cleft into the rocks to form a natural citadel that was settled already at the end of the Early Bronze Age (fig. 2.2). Easily defensible, the citadel commanded a view of the entire Late Bronze Age city. Called Büyükkale today, the citadel is only one of many rocky outcroppings incorporated into the city plan. Here were located the palace, which was the residence of the king, his family, and their retinue, and, adjacent to it, the administrative buildings, including an extensive library and chancellery.

The oldest part of the city is located in the Lower City to the north, in the area around and including the Great Temple. In this temple, priests saw to the needs of the Storm-God and Sun-Goddess, the divine couple who ruled the Hittite pantheon. Surrounded by storerooms that housed the temple's wealth (fig. 3.3), workshops, kitchens, and a residential quarter for the temple staff and dependents, the Great Temple was as much the heart of the city's commercial enterprises as it was its religious center.[29]

The Upper City, so-called because of the gentle rise in elevation one experiences as one moves southward through the city, served primarily as

---

Studies in Honor of Harry A. Hoffner Jr. on the Occasion of His 65th Birthday (ed. Gary Beckman, Richard Beal, and Gregory McMahon; Winona Lake, Ind.: Eisenbrauns, 2003), 25; Dietrich Sürenhagen, "Verwandtschaftsbeziehungen und Erbrecht im althethitischen Königshaus vor Telipinu—ein erneuter Erklärungsversuch," *AoF* 25 (1998): 83 n. 39.

29. For more on the Great Temple, see Peter Neve, "The Great Temple in Boğazköy-Ḫattuša," in *Across the Anatolian Plateau: Readings in the Archaeology of Ancient Turkey* (ed. David C. Hopkins; AASOR 57; Boston: American Schools of Oriental Research, 2002), 77–98; Itamar Singer, "A City of Many Temples: Ḫattuša, Capital of the Hittites," in *Sacred Space: Shrine, City, Land* (ed. Benjamin Z. Kedar and R. J. Zwi Werblowsky; Washington Square: New York University Press, 1998), 33–34.

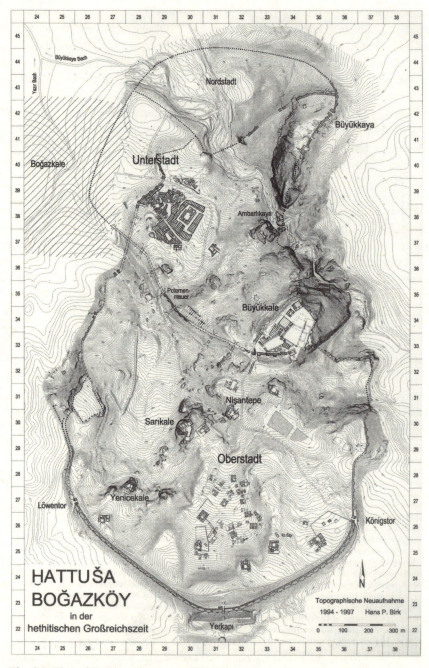

Fig. 2.2. Plan of Hattusa. Courtesy of the Bogazköy-Archive, Deutsches Archäologisches Institut.

a temple district. To date, thirty temples have been excavated in this area, each following a common architectural plan (fig. 4.1). Several of the temples (e.g., nos. 2, 3, and 4) were already a part of the city's landscape in the Old Kingdom. Others were constructed later, as new kings sought to curry divine favor and/or enhance the city's (or their own) prestige.[30] All that remains today of these buildings are the bottom-most portions of the foundations—such was the damage inflicted by its enemies.

Completing the impression that one is in a truly imperial city are the extensive fortifications, which are punctuated in the south by three monumental gates. Each of the three gates is decorated with elaborate sculpture that helps to define their separate uses. From an artificial embankment at the highest and southernmost point of the city, known as Yerkapı, two carved sphinxes once looked down protectively upon the temple quarter. The gate was accessible from the outside only by two steep, narrow staircases and so is unlikely to have been a regular point of entrance to the city. Its narrow open gateway has a shrine-like feel, and it may have served primarily as the stage for religious celebrations. The Lion Gate to the southwest (fig. 2.3), so-called because of the two massive lions in stone designed to impress those entering the city, probably served as the city's formal entrance for dignitaries and other important visitors, while a deity carved in high relief on the King's Gate bid farewell to those exiting on the southeast.

Stone was sacred to the Hittites, and the numerous rocky outcroppings within the city thus took on special importance. Some, such as Kızlarkaya, Yenicekale, Sarıkale, and Nişantaş, were enhanced with architectural structures and probably served as the seats of religious institutions, perhaps the "rock-crest" structures (*hekur*) referred to in the Hittite texts as being connected with the cults of dead kings (see ch. 4). Equally important to Hittite religious beliefs, water was also incorporated into the city plan. Two large pools served as a reservoir for the adjacent citadel. The two stone chambers built into the corners of one of these, one of them with the Sun-God and king carved in relief and a shallow depression for offerings, provided another venue for cultic activity.

Separated from the citadel by the deep gorge formed by the Budaközü stream is the enclosed ridge called Büyükkaya, which was a part of the city plan from its early settlement in the thirteenth century. Here the Hittites built

---

30. On the revised dating of the temples in the Upper City, see Jürgen Seeher, "Chronology in Ḫattuša: New Approaches to an Old Problem," *BYZAS* 4 (2006): 197–213. For a more detailed description of the temples in the Upper City, see Singer, "A City of Many Temples," 36–40.

Fig: 2.3. One of the lions flanking Hattusa's Lion Gate, located on the southwest of the fortifications of the Upper City. This gate probably served as the city's main entrance. Photo by the author.

an extensive granary comprising rectangular cellars dug into the earth, with a capacity to store some four to six thousand tons of grain total.

New excavations in the western part of the Upper City, dominated by Sarıkale, have revealed that the area was settled already in the sixteenth century. The square structures dating to this period are thought to have been barracks for military troops, thus clearing up the mystery of where Hattusa's defenders resided. Later, before the thirteenth century, the area seems to have been used for workshops and urban habitations.

THE OLD KINGDOM

Our information about the period following the departure of the Assyrians is sketchy at best, but Hattusili, the first king for whom we have contemporary historical evidence, could trace his genealogy back at least two generations. Like Anitta, he was from Kussar and was probably a member of its extended ruling family, perhaps even a distant relative of Anitta. About Hattusili's predecessors, we know very little (fig. 2.4). His grandfather may have been a Huzziya, whose name appears in fragmentary form on a cruciform seal from Hattusa as the predecessor of Labarna.[31] His father and immediate predecessor was Labarna, whose royal name would be adopted by future Hittite kings (including Hattusili himself) as a title, as Caesar was used by Roman kings. Whatever success his forebears may have had in strengthening their position in central Anatolia, Hattusili is the first king to whom we can attribute historical records. It was he who likely moved the dynastic seat to Hattusa, who united the plateau under a centralized government and sought to expand his interests beyond the Euphrates, and, most importantly, who laid the groundwork for the administrative and cultural infrastructure that would define the state until its last days.

Hattusili was quick to recognize the importance of Syria in Anatolia's increasing need for control of the Near Eastern trade routes.[32] After securing control of the north, he directed his attention to the southeast, with the intention of gaining access to the outlets to the Mediterranean Sea. Although he succeeded in destroying Alalakh, Halpa (Aleppo)'s port city, his initial campaigns against the cities of the Syrian kingdom of Yamhad were cut short by events in Anatolia. Skirmishes along the border with the Arzawa lands, a coalition of kingdoms, threatened to destabilize the balance of power in the western part of the peninsula. Hattusili appears to have been successful

---

31. See A. M. Dinçol, B. Dinçol, J. David Hawkins, and Gernot Wilhelm, "The 'Cruciform' Seal from Boğazköy-Hattusa," *IstMitt* 43 (1993): 87–106, esp. 104–6. Massimo Forlanini ("La nascita di un impero: Considerazioni sulla prima fase della storia hittita: Da Kaniš a Hattuša," *Or* 73 [2004]: 363–89) attempts to connect Huzziya on the cruciform seal dynastically with Huzziya, king of Zalpa and enemy of Anitta. Richard Beal ("Predecessors of Ḫattušili I," 31–32) suggests that Huzziya was the founder of the Hittite dynasty and that Hattusili's grandfather was either Tudhaliya or PU-Sarruma, mentioned in the offering list *KUB* 36.121 + *KUB* 11.7 + *KUB* 36.122. Many Hittitologists consider these last two names to be misplaced in the list and therefore not relevant to Old Kingdom history.

32. He may also have been after new sources of tin, since the dissolution of the Assyrian trade a few decades before must have severely curtailed access (Bryce, *Kingdom of the Hittites*, 82).

Approximate Date of Accession	Throne Name (Birth Name)	Relationship to Previous King
	Old Kingdom	
1690	Huzziya I	
1670	Labarna	son
1650	Hattusili I	son
1620	Mursili I	grandson
1590	Hantili I	brother-in-law
1560	Zidanta I	son-in-law
1550	Ammuna	son
1530	Huzziya II	nephew by marriage
1525	Telipinu	son-in-law of Ammuna
1500	Alluwamna	son-in-law of Telipinu
	Tahurwaili	none
	Hantili II	son of Alluwamna
	Zidanta II	son?
	Huzziya III	son?
	Muwatalli I	none
	Empire	
1400	Tudhaliya II	grandson of Huzziya II?
	Arnuwanda I	son-in-law
	Hattusili II?	son?
	Tudhaliya III	son of Arnuwanda?
1350	Suppiluliuma I	son
1322	Arnuwanda II	son
1321	Mursili II	brother
1295	Muwatalli II	son
1272	Mursili III	son
1267	Hattusili III	uncle
1237	Tudhaliya IV	son
1209	Arnuwanda III	son
1207	Suppiluliuma II	brother

Fig. 2.4. The kings of the Hittites. The dates provided here follow Bryce, *Kingdom of the Hittites*, xv.

in eliminating this threat, at least for the time being. But while his back was turned, the Hurrians attacked the east, perhaps in retaliation for Hattusili's own attacks on Hurrian-held territory on his way back to Anatolia from his initial forays in Syria.[33] In any case, Hattusili was forced to reestablish control over his power base, in the process finally conquering Sanahuitta, the renegade city that had thus far withstood his efforts at unification.[34] Toward the end of his reign, Hattusili again crossed the Taurus to campaign against Halpa, although he did not succeed in conquering its capital.

Hattusili's activities in Syria were undoubtedly more extensive than the meager records from Hattusa reveal. A letter—the only one of its kind to survive from the Hittite Old Kingdom—that he wrote in Akkadian to Tunip-Teshub (Tuniya) of Tikunani, a minor ruler in northern Mesopotamia, urges Tuniya to remain firmly on Hattusili's side in his impending campaign against Hahhum on the Upper Euphrates.[35]

> My campaign has begun. So you should be a man with respect to the man of Hahhu. Eat up his grain ration like a dog. The oxen that you take away will be yours. The sheep and goats that you take away will be yours too. Be a man with respect to him. I from this side and you from that side…. And do not listen to the hostile words that he speaks. Keep to the bull's horn (!) and keep to the lion's side and do not take the side of the fox, who always does hostile things. Just as I have treated Zalpa, I will treat him likewise. Do not listen to words from any (other) side. Keep to my words. (lines 8–15, 31–41)

Hattusili addresses Tuniya as a subordinate, calling him "my servant" and offering his protection, an indication that he wielded some authority and influence beyond the borders of his own kingdom.[36]

On the home front, Hattusili's accomplishments were even more impressive, although they have received much less attention. The achievements

---

33. Hattusili I's generals had laid seige to Urshu, a city on the old trade route from Assur, perhaps in order to secure the supply routes (ibid., 82–83).

34. The city was under the control of Papahdilmah, a renegade member of the royal family.

35. Mirjo Salvini, "Una Lettera di Hattusili relativa alla spedizione contro Hahhum," *SMEA* 34 (1995): 61–80.

36. Further evidence that Hittite involvement across the Euphrates in Hattusili's reign may have been greater than previously suspected are the texts from Terqa (a part of the kingdom of Mari in the Middle Euphrates region) that mention clashes with troops of Hatte/Hattu. Excavators also found an Old Hittite stamp seal at this site. See Itamar Singer, review of Horst Klengel, *Geschichte des hethitischen Reiches*, BiOr 57 (2000): 638–39; Klengel, *Geschichte des hethitischen Reiches*, 66.

of his reign include a rich literature comprising myths, historiography, and rituals that demonstrate a keen interest in using the scribal arts for more than simply administrative needs. Hittite literature would never again match the aesthetic quality that was achieved in Hattusili's reign (see ch. 4). Inspired by the achievements of the kings of Mesopotamia, Hattusili saw himself as on a par with Sargon of Akkad, who had also crossed the Euphrates in his quest for empire. Hattusili's interest in preserving a memory of the past and in recording current events for posterity suggests that he was an intelligent and complex ruler. He also formulated the Hittite law code and established the *pankus* "assembly," an ad hoc judicial body composed of members of the state bureaucracy whose role was to witness and enforce agreements and royal proclamations and to try criminal offenders of particularly high status.

The greatest challenge to Hattusili's reign was the securing of a suitable heir. His sons and daughter (whose husband would have been eligible to succeed to the throne) each in turn had betrayed him and, as a result, had been deposed or banished. At the end of his life, Hattusili also deposed his nephew, adopting instead his young grandson, Mursili I, as his heir, and adjured the *pankus* to accept the appointment. Tired and disillusioned, or so it seems from the tone of his Edict, Hattusili died in his hometown of Kussar shortly after the succession was secured.

The *pankus* apparently honored Hattusili's last request, and a young Mursili I ascended the throne of Hatti. Mursili shared his grandfather's military ambitions, if not his domestic ones. He finally succeeded in destroying the kingdom of Yamhad and its capital Halpa, but his ambitions did not stop with taking care of Hattusili's unfinished business. He continued to Babylon, sacking the city (ca. 1595 B.C.E.) and bringing an end to the Old Babylonian dynasty that Hammurabi had established two hundred years earlier. The incentives for Mursili's raid are unclear, although the rich spoils were no doubt a part of it, perhaps combined with a desire to exceed his predecessor's accomplishments. History would certainly remember the raid as one of Hatti's most glorious moments. It may also be that Mursili had allied himself with the Kassites, who established a dynasty in Babylon shortly thereafter, in order to confine the growing threat from the Hurrians who inhabited the territory between.[37]

In any case, his attention might better have been directed toward securing his position at home than overextending Hatti's limited military might. Sometime after his return to Hattusa, he was assassinated by his brother-in-

---

37. Bryce, *Kingdom of the Hittites*, 99.

law Hantili, who assumed the throne. Given the hubris that the raid upon Babylon exhibited, Hantili may well have felt that Mursili's murder was in the best interests of the kingdom. Such is hinted at in the fragmentary documents from his long reign. Even so, Hantili's reign began a period of instability within the royal family and the kingdom as a whole. His wife and sons were captured and murdered by the Hurrians, with whom he was at war at the time. In his old age, his remaining heirs were murdered by his one-time ally Zidanta (I), who assumed the throne. Zidanta's reign was short, however, as he in turn was assassinated by his own son Ammuna. Ammuna, who left a record of his military campaigns, died of natural causes, although his sons were not so fortunate. They were murdered by an ambitious in-law of Ammuna named Huzziya (II), who took the throne. According to the moralizing edict issued by King Telipinu after the fact, for their sins the reigns of Hantili and Ammuna were both beset by threefold disaster: drought resulting in the failure of the crops and livestock; invasion from hostile forces; and the assassination of their families. Each of these early kings fought with limited success to keep the kingdom from distintegrating altogether in the face of incursions by Kaskeans, Hurrians, and the Arzawa lands. It seems that Hattusili's fragile kingdom came perilously close to collapse within only a century of its foundation.

Telipinu himself came to the throne in a bloodless coup against Huzziya II, but he had had enough of murder and mayhem and committed himself to instituting the reforms needed to eliminate infighting in the Hittite court. Telipinu is unique as a throne name and may have been selected deliberately to symbolize the restoration of order, as the agricultural deity Telipinu did in the myth of his disappearance and return (see ch. 4).[38] The rules he established were hardly revolutionary: a son of the first rank (i.e., a son of the king's primary wife) should succeed him; if there was no first-rank son, a son of the second rank (i.e., the son of a concubine) could succeed; in the absence of a second-rank son, a son-in-law could be chosen. Notably, the king still had flexibility in his selection, as the succession did not automatically go to the eldest son. Ironically, despite Telipinu's efforts to secure a process for dynastic succession, he failed to provide himself with an heir (his one son had been murdered), thus setting the stage for another century of political infighting. His reign was followed by a series of kings who left little or no lasting impression on the monarchy.

Telipinu's more enduring contribution was the concluding of Hatti's first treaty agreement, with Isputahsu, ruler of the newly formed kingdom of Kiz-

---

38. Harry A. Hoffner Jr., personal communication.

zuwatna.[39] Telipinu's campaigns to reclaim some of Hatti's lost territories had taken him to the southeast, to the towns in the region bordering on Kizzuwatna. By formalizing the border between the two kingdoms, this treaty ensured the security of Hatti's southern border without further conflict.

Telipinu's immediate successors appear to have continued his diplomatic policy with Kizzuwatna. In other arenas, however, diplomacy was not an option. Hantili II (early fifteenth century) is attributed with extending the fortification wall around Hattusa's Lower City, a step perhaps designed to protect the city from incursions by the Kaska, an unruly alliance of mountain-dwelling tribes from the Pontic region along the southern coast of the Black Sea, who first make their appearance in the texts in his reign. These tribes succeeded in overrunning Nerik, one of the kingdom's most sacred cities, and would continue to represent a clear and present danger to the Hittite capital and all points north until its last days.

PRELUDE TO EMPIRE

Hatti's fortunes finally changed for the better with the accession to the throne of an individual named Tudhaliya (II).[40] The assassination of the usurper Muwatalli I and the subsequent bloody battle over the succession finally ended when Tudhaliya II's supporters (including his father Kantuzili) succeeded in placing him on the throne.[41] Tudhaliya II was a member of the Hittite ruling dynasty, as his annals mention a grandfather who was also a king. This grandfather was probably Huzziya III,[42] the predecessor of Muwatalli, and if so, Tudhaliya II's reign marks the restoration of Hattusili I's dynasty on the throne of Hatti. It also marks the beginning of a new era for the kingdom. Indeed, Tudhaliya II may justifiably be credited with founding the Hittite Empire.[43]

---

39. The Old Kingdom rulers presumably also established diplomatic relations with the western territories, as suggested by the laws governing the return of fugitives from Luwiya (Arzawa). See Harry A. Hoffner Jr., *The Laws of the Hittites: A Critical Edition* (DMOA 23; Leiden: Brill, 1997), 31–32, 180–81 (§§22–23).

40. Whether Tudhaliya is labeled I or II depends on whether one accepts the existence of a King Tudhaliya at the beginning of the dynasty (see n. 31). To avoid confusion, many Hittitologists refer to Tudhaliya I/II. For the sake of simplicity, I refer to him here as Tudhaliya II.

41. See Heinrich Otten, "Ein Siegelabdruck Duthalijas I.(?)," *AA* 2000 (2000): 375–76, for a seal naming Kantuzili, probably to be identified with the Kantuzili who is named as one of the conspirators, as Tudhaliya's father.

42. Bryce, *Kingdom of the Hittites*, 122.

43. For a reconstruction of this period, see Jacques Freu, "La 'révolution dynas-

According to his annals, Tudhaliya II's first military expeditions as king took him deep into western Anatolia. He was the first king actively to concern himself with the west since Hattusili I two centuries earlier. The western lands had a tendency to form coalitions, which could ultimately prove very dangerous for the Hittite kingdom, and Hittite interests in the region seem to have been restricted to limiting such a threat. Tudhaliya II claims to have brought back to Hattusa ten thousand infantry and six hundred chariotry of the enemy, a policy designed to eliminate any further threat in the region. But his initial successes in the west, directed particularly against the Arzawa lands, had the unintended effect of bringing the western kingdoms into even closer cooperation. They formed an alliance of twenty-two countries, known as the Assuwan confederacy, to fight the Hittite enemy. This is the first time we encounter the geographical term Assuwa, the name from which the designation of the Roman province of Asia was later derived. Tudhaliya II's defeat of the confederacy was decisive. Among the spoils from the campaign was a bronze sword of western Anatolian manufacture, which he had inscribed with a dedication in Akkadian to the Storm-God to commemorate his victory over Assuwa. Nevertheless, Hittite conquests in the west, while apparently successful for the moment, had little long-term effect.

As with Hattusili I before him, Tudhaliya II's presence in Arzawa left the kingdom vulnerable from the north and the east. The Kaska immediately took advantage of his absence to invade Hatti's northern border. The letters from the archive at Tapikka (modern Maşat), on the northern frontier, document the serious problem the Kaska represented for Hatti in the reigns of Tudhaliya II and his son-in-law Arnuwanda.[44] Tudhaliya II succeeded in pushing them out of Hittite territory, only to be confronted by another threat in the east.

In the years between the reigns of Telipinu and Tudhaliya II, the power of the kingdom of Mitanni had spread over the whole of northern Syria, including Alalakh and Aleppo. Mitanni had been encouraging dissension in Isuwa, a Hittite subject state in the upper Euphrates, which took up arms against Tudhaliya II. Although Tudhaliya II was successful in this arena as

---

tique' du Grand Roi de Hatti Tuthalia I," *Hethitica* 13 (1996): 17–38; idem, "Le grand roi Tuthaliya, fils de Kantuzzili," in *Mélanges offerts au professeur René Lebrun* (ed. Michel Mazoyer and Olivier Casabonne; 2 vols.; Collection Kubaba, Série Antiquité 5–6; Paris: L'Harmattan, 2004), 1:271–304.

44. For a dating of the correspondence from Maşat-Tapikka to the reigns of Tudhaliya II and Arnuwanda I, see Jörg Klinger, "Das Corpus der Maşat-Briefe und seine Beziehungen zu den Texten aus Hattusa," *ZA* 85 (1995): 74–108; cf. Bryce, *Kingdom of the Hittites*, 145, who follows a dating of this corpus to the reign of Tudhaliya III, Arnuwanda's successor (see p. 425 n. 25 for literature).

well, once again it was only a temporary victory, as Isuwa remained sympathetic to Mitanni and would later have cause once again to rise up in arms against Hatti. In preparation for further confrontations with Mitanni in Syria, Tudhaliya II concluded a new treaty with Sunashshura of Kizzuwatna, who had broken his alliance with Mitanni. With his buffer thus secured, Tudhaliya II took his troops into Syria, destroying Halpa and making major inroads against other Mitannian territories. Shortly after these events, Kizzuwatna was annexed and placed under direct Hittite rule.

In his domestic policy, Tudhaliya II did manage to avoid one pitfall. By making his son-in-law Arnuwanda his co-regent while he still lived, he ensured that power was already firmly in his successor's hands when the time came for the transition to a new king. However impressive Tudhaliya II's military successes may have appeared, they were a house of cards. During the reign of Arnuwanda, Mitanni's new king, Artatama, came to an agreement with Tuthmosis IV of Egypt, effectively halting Hittite ambition in Syria. In the north, the Kaska were once again threatening the borders. They ravaged many of the Hittite holy cities that lay along its northern frontier and carried off all their personnel, from priests to gardeners. The result was a complete cessation of the religious cult in these northern lands. Arnuwanda attempted to bind the tribal Kaska by treaty and took other measures to ensure the safety of the frontier, but with limited success.

Since Tudhaliya II's defeat of the Assuwan confederacy, the situation in the west had remained unstable, primarily as a result of the enterprises of a man named Madduwatta.[45] Having in some way made a mortal enemy of Attarsiya, the "man of Ahhiyawa" (that is, a Mycenaean Greek), Madduwatta fled to Hattusa, where he sought asylum in Tudhaliya II's court. He was clearly a man of some importance in the land from which he was expelled, since he traveled about with an extensive retinue, and Tudhaliya II set him up as a minor king in the mountain country of Zippasla.[46] But through a series of duplicities played out in the reigns first of Tudhaliya II and then of Arnuwanda, Madduwatta managed to acquire for himself most of the southwest of Anatolia, including Arzawa, as well as Alasiya (Cyprus). Although Arnuwanda's indictment against Madduwatta affects a tone of righteous indignation, the king appears not to have punished him, perhaps

---

45. The main source for the situation in the west in this period is the so-called Indictment of Madduwatta, which is written in the form of a letter from the Hittite king Arnuwanda I to Madduwatta. It relates events in the reigns of both Arnuwanda and of his father-in-law, Tudhaliya II. For a translation, see Gary Beckman, *Hittite Diplomatic Texts* (2nd ed.; SBLWAW 7; Atlanta: Scholars Press, 1999), 153–60.

46. Bryce, *Kingdom of the Hittites*, 130.

because Madduwatta's destabilizing influence indirectly played to Hittite interests.[47] Hittite policy in dealing with the west at this time generally was not to risk Hittite security on other fronts by intervening militarily.[48] So long as Madduwatta posed no direct threat to Hatti itself, the Hittite kings could afford to let him satisfy his ambition in the west.

Arnuwanda's son Tudhaliya (III) succeeded him on the throne.[49] A later text recalls the sad state of affairs in Hatti during Tudhaliya III's reign:

> Previously the lands of Hatti were destroyed by enemies. The Kaskan enemy came and destroyed the territories of Hatti and made the city of Nenassa its border. The Arzawan enemy came from the Lower Land, and it, too, destroyed Hittite territories and made the cities Tuwanua and Uda its border. The Arauwanan enemy [ca]me from afar and destroyed the entire land of Gassiya. The Azzian enemy came from afar and destroyed all of the Upper [Land]s and made Samuha its border. The Isuwan [enemy] came and destroyed the [land] of Tegarama. The Armatanan enemy [came] from afar, and it also destroyed the territories of Hatti, and it [made] the city of Kizzuwatna [its border]. The city of Hattusa was also burned down.[50]

The kingdom was attacked from every side in an episode that has come to be known as the "concentric invasion." Excavations have confirmed that Hattusa was burned at this time, as was the regional center at Tapikka (modern Maşat). Clearly, things had reached yet another low point for Hatti. When the Egyptian pharaoh Amenhotep III corresponded with the king of Arzawa, Tarhundaradu, at about this time, he wrote, "I have heard that everything is finished, and that the country Ḫattuša is paralyzed."[51] He also requested Kaskean slaves from the Arzawans, which would have been possible only

---

47. His indictment of another disloyal vassal, Mita, ruler of Pahhuwa, a town on the upper Euphrates, seems to have been more strict. See Bryce, *Kingdom of the Hittites*, 143–44; Klengel, *Geschichte des hethitischen Reiches*, 124; Beckman, *Hittite Diplomatic Texts*, 160–66.

48. Bryce, *Kingdom of the Hittites*, 138.

49. This Tudhaliya is attested on a bulla as the father of Suppiluliuma. See Klengel, *Geschichte des hethitischen Reiches*, 129 [B1]. For the problem of where in the sequence of kings in the period to place the otherwise unattested king Hattusili (II) mentioned in the Aleppo Treaty, see Bryce, *Kingdom of the Hittites*, 141; Klengel, *Geschichte des hethitischen Reiches*, 125–26.

50. *KBo* 6.28 + KUB 26.48 (*CTH* 88) obv. 6–15, composed by Hattusili III (r. ca. 1267–1236 B.C.E.).

51. EA 31, translated by Volkert Haas in William Moran, *The Amarna Letters* (Baltimore: Johns Hopkins University Press, 1992), 101; however, on the translation "paralyzed" for *egai-* instead of Haas's "shattered," see Jaan Puhvel, *HED* 2:257, s.v. *eka-*.

if the Kaska had penetrated into the center of the Hittite kingdom. Arzawa was now in control of the Lower Land, giving it direct access to the Hittite heartland and the Kaska. The pharaoh's interest in a marriage alliance with Arzawa suggests that Egypt thought Arzawa might become the new power in Anatolia. However, despite the extent of the uprising, the Hittite king and his court somehow managed to survive the calamity. The regime had temporarily abandoned the capital to its fate and resettled somewhere else, perhaps in Samuha, the base from which Tudhaliya III and his son, Suppiluliuma, would begin the task of rebuilding the kingdom.[52]

FROM KINGDOM TO EMPIRE

Not for the first time, a Hittite king was forced to reconquer Anatolia (fig. 2.5). From Samuha, and with the help of his son, Tudhaliya III took the battle to the enemy, attacking the Kaska and the territory of Azzi-Hayasa in the northeast. Once the threat from these lands was contained, Tudhaliya III sent Suppiluliuma to the west to do battle with Arzawa. But the Arzawan enemy resisted the offensive with equal determination, and the struggle to regain control in the west would remain incomplete for another twenty years. During this period, Tudhaliya III's repeated bouts of illness meant that Suppiluliuma often acted as his military representative, fortifying cities previously ravaged by the enemy and repopulating them. Despite his poor health, however, Tudhaliya III continued to lead armies into battle until his death in Samuha.

Although Suppiluliuma had been his most trusted advisor and general, he was not Tudhaliya III's chosen heir. Rather, Tudhaliya had appointed another, probably older, son, referred to in the texts as Tudhaliya the Younger, perhaps believing that the kingdom was best served by continuing the arrangement he enjoyed in his own reign, that is, with Suppiluliuma playing a vital supporting role. Not everyone in his court had faith in this arrangement, however, and Suppiluliuma himself must have been dissatisfied with it. Perhaps motivated by the dire circumstances in which the kingdom

---

52. Samuha is the same city—lying east of Hattusa in the region of the Turkish city of Sivas somewhere on the Halys River, in the direction of Malatya—to which Tudhaliya II introduced the cult of the Kizzuwatnean "goddess of the night." As early as Telipinu's reign in the Old Kingdom, the city had housed one of the regional royal storehouses, so it was a major administrative center. More important, the city was a major religious center hosting an array of cultic centers, including those of a number of Ishtars, several storm-gods, the usual assortment of mountain and river deities, and even a few gods and goddesses of Aleppo.

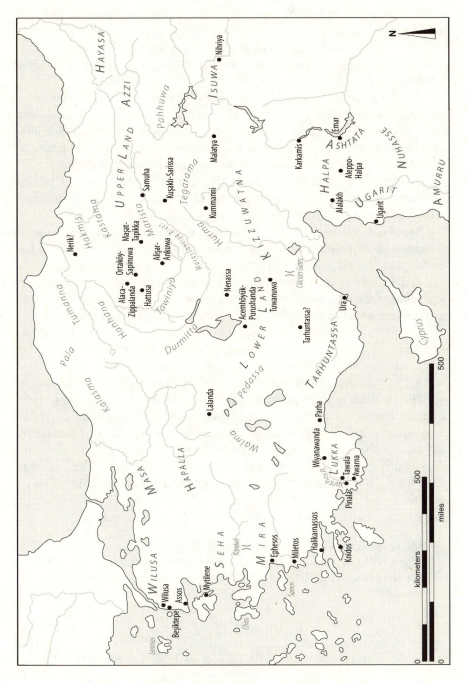

Fig. 2.5. Hatti and its vassals in the Late Bronze Age.

found itself at the end of the reign of Tudhaliya III and the conviction that only Suppiluliuma, a proven military leader, could successfully bring Hatti out of the crisis intact, a group of army officers, apparently with Suppiluliuma's knowledge and consent, assassinated the heir apparent and installed Suppiluliuma on the throne of Hatti.

Shortly after seizing the kingship, Suppiluliuma turned his attention to the south and east with a view to recovering the lost territory of Kizzuwatna and retaking the city of Tegarama, which had been overrun by Isuwa, now allied to Mitanni. In preparation for the inevitable conflict with Mitanni that would result from these incursions, Suppiluliuma sought to undermine its king, Tushratta, by cultivating a rival claimant to his throne, a man named Artatama. Perhaps for the same reason, Suppiluliuma also sought to establish relations with Egypt, which had been on good terms with Mitanni.[53]

Suppiluliuma began his first Syrian campaign east of the Euphrates, with the conquest of Isuwa. He then turned south to march against Mitanni but arrived at Wassukkanni, the Mitannian capital, only to find that Tushratta had fled. Unable to confront its king, he turned his army westward into Syria and conquered all the kingdoms of northern Syria in a single campaign, transporting their kings and their families to Hattusa. Only Karkamis remained.

Suppiluliuma's war now entered a new phase, one that would take several years to complete. The conquest of Karkamis, the final stage in his subjugation of Mitanni, was left to his son Telipinu, whom he had installed as king of the land of Aleppo. But a Hurrian counterattack forced Suppiluliuma to make another personal appearance in Syria. While his general Lupakki fought off an Egyptian bid to retake the city of Qadesh in Amka, Suppiluliuma laid siege to Karkamis. It was while he was camped outside the city that an envoy from Egypt arrived in the Hittite camp with a letter from the Egyptian queen asking for a Hittite prince in marriage. The year was 1327 B.C.E., and the narratives that recount this episode affirm that it was a remarkable occurrence even for those who lived it; it seems no less so today. The queen, Ankhesenamun,[54] widow of Tutankhamun, wrote,

> My husband has died, and I have no son. They say you have many sons. If you will give me one of your sons, he will become my husband. I do not wish to choose a subject of mine and make him my husband. I am afraid.[55]

---

53. Bryce, *Kingdom of the Hittites*, 159.

54. She is called simply *dahamunzu* "the king's wife" in the Deeds of Suppiluliuma, and not all accept her identification with Ankhesenamun.

55. "Deeds of Šuppiluliuma," translated by Harry A. Hoffner Jr. (*COS* 1.74:190).

Suppiluliuma's response was understandable and very human: "Nothing like this has ever happened to me in my whole life!" Naturally suspicious, he sent an envoy to Egypt to verify the communication and in the meantime devoted his attention to the siege of Karkamis. In the time it took the envoy to make the round trip between the two courts, several months had passed. Suppiluliuma had captured Karkamis, installed his son Piyassili (Sharri-Kushuh) as its king, and returned to Hattusa, where he received the queen's angry retort:

> Why did you say "they deceive me" in that way? If I had a son, would I have written about my own and my land's embarrassing predicament to a foreign land? You did not believe me and have dared to speak this way to me.[56]

Reassured by the queen's emissary Hani that the offer was sincere, Suppiluliuma made arrangements for his son Zannanza to travel to Egypt. For a brief moment in time, the Hittites were poised for world domination. Such was not to be, however, as the next messenger to the Hittite court would come bearing the news of Zannanza's murder en route to Egypt.

Dismissing the protestations of innocence from the new pharaoh Ay,[57] a bereaved and angry Suppiluliuma immediately took punitive action, sending Hittite troops into the Egyptian-held territories. Ironically, the Egyptian prisoners whom they transported back to Hatti from these campaigns were blamed for the plagues that wreaked havoc in the Hittite heartland for the next two decades. Six years after his conquest of Karkamis, Suppiluliuma died, probably from this very plague. His son and successor, Arnuwanda II, also succumbed to it after little more than a year on the throne.

As impressive as Suppiluliuma's conquests were, his most important legacy was in the formation of series of alliances secured by treaty that brought the vassals and appanage kingdoms firmly under the control of the Hittite king. Whatever successes his predecessors may have had, through this system of alliances and the appointment of his sons Sharri-Kushuh and Telipinu to administer his Syrian holdings, which now included Ugarit, Nuhasse, Qadesh, and Amurru, Suppiluliuma went beyond mere conquest to establish for the first time a sustainable Hittite empire.

---

56. Ibid.

57. On Ay's innocence in the matter, see Bryce, *Kingdom of the Hittites*, 183; for the letter from Suppiluliuma to Ay (*KUB* 19.20 + *KBo* 12.23+154/s; *CTH* 154) in which the latter is quoted as having disclaimed any responsibility (obv. 24–25), see also Theo P. J. van den Hout, "Der Falke und das Kücken: Der neue Pharao und der hethitische Prinze?" *ZA* 84 (1994): 60–88.

As we have seen, royal transitions bring instability. With the news of
Suppiluliuma's illness and then that of Arnuwanda, the Hittite vassals
became restive. Suppiluliuma's youngest son, Mursili, was still a youth when
he assumed the kingship in 1321 B.C.E. after his brother's unexpected death.
According to him, the enemies of Hatti maligned him, saying,

> His father, who was king of the land of Hatti and a hero-king, held sway
> over the enemy lands. And he became a god. His son who ascended to
> his father's throne had been a great warrior, but he fell ill, and he too has
> become a god. But he who has recently ascended to his father's throne is a
> boy. He will not preserve the land of Hatti and its borders.[58]

With Mursili's older brothers Sharri-Kushuh and Telipinu effectively deter-
ring any immediate threat from Assyria and Egypt from their viceregal seats
at Karkamis and Aleppo, respectively, the Kaska presented the most immediate problem for the new king, and he turned his attention first to halting
their reign of terror in the north. Soon, however, developments in the west
would again take center stage. Here Mursili faced a new coordinated offensive initiated by the king of Arzawa, Uhhaziti, in collaboration with the king
of Ahhiyawa and the city of Millawanda (Miletos). Joined by his brother
Sharri-Kushuh and confident that the gods were firmly on his side, Mursili vanquished the forces of Arzawa and transported its population to the
Hittite heartland and perhaps elsewhere. Uhhaziti fled to the islands off the
coast, where he died in exile. With the elimination of Arzawa, its constituent
parts—Hapalla, Mira, and the Seha River Land—hastened to acknowledge
Hatti as their overlord. In the case of the Seha River Land, Mursili II was
persuaded (according to his own account) to spare the life of the disloyal
vassal only after he sent his elderly mother to Mursili's camp to beg for his
life! Mursili II gave Mira-Kuwaliya to Mashuiluwa, the Seha River Land and
Appawiya to a rehabilitated Manapa-Tarhunda, and Hapalla to Targasnalli.[59]
The west was finally under Hittite control.

For the next two years, Mursili focused his attention again on the northern frontier, where the Kaska had organized themselves under Pihhuniya.
Although Mursili defeated his forces and brought him back to Hattusa, the
situation in the north was far from calm when in this ninth year he made the

---

58. Ten-Year Annals of Mursili II, *KBo* 3.4 (*CTH* 61) i 10–15.

59. For their status as lords rather than minor kings, see J. David Hawkins,
"Tarkasnawa King of Mira," *AnSt* 48 (1998): 15; and Susanne Heinhold-Krahmer,
Arzawa: Untersuchungen zu seiner Geschichte nach den hethitischen Quellen (THeth 8;
Heidelberg: Winter 1977), 127–29.

journey to Kummanni in Kizzuwatna to celebrate the festival of Hebat, a cult that his father had neglected.

An ailing Sharri-Kushuh made the trip from Karkamis to Kummanni for a meeting with the king during his stay in the city. Both brothers had been engaged for the past two years in quelling rebellions in Nuhasse, which had the support of Egyptian forces, and Qadesh. With Sharri-Kushuh's sudden death in Kummanni during that visit, and Telipinu's earlier that year,[60] the rebellion strengthened. Assyria, which had been waiting for an opportunity to fill the vacuum left by the destruction of the kingdom of Mitanni, invaded and occupied the kingdom of Karkamis. Azzi-Hayasa, too, took advantage of the situation by overrunning the Upper Land. With the help of his generals, Mursili was able to withstand the threats on all fronts. Assyria was driven out of Karkamis, and Mursili was able to install the sons of Sharri-Kushuh and Telipinu as viceroys in Karkamis and Aleppo, respectively.[61]

While in Kummanni, Mursili had prayed for the well-being of his family, in particular for his wife Gassulawiya, who had for some time been the target of the animosity of the reigning queen, the Babylonian princess called Tawananna, who was Suppiluliuma's last wife. Mursili suspected Tawananna of several serious abuses of her power. She had even dared to interpret a solar eclipse that occurred while Mursili was away campaigning in Azzi-Hayasa in his tenth year (1312 B.C.E.) as predicting the king's death. Perhaps she hoped that her own son might replace him as king.[62] Mursili could endure all her offenses, but when Gassulawiya died despite his urgent appeals to the gods to spare her life, he knew that Tawananna's sorcerous invocations had been behind it: "She stands day and night before the gods and curses my wife before the gods … and she wishes for her death saying: 'Let her die!' "[63] Oracular inquiry confirmed the queen's guilt in the matter, and the gods authorized the king to take her life. In a display of restraint, however, he opted instead to depose her and banish her from the capital.

The queen was not the only problem that Mursili had inherited from his father. The plague that Suppiluliuma had brought home from his conquests in Syria continued to rage unabated throughout the kingdom well into the latter half of Mursili's reign. There was no question that this scourge had

---

60. So Bryce, *Kingdom of the Hittites*, 203.

61. On Telipinu's religious (as "Great Priest" of the Storm-God of Aleppo) and judicial role in Syria compared with Sharri-Kushuh's military one, see ibid.,187–88.

62. Itamar Singer, *Hittite Prayers* (SBLWAW 11; Atlanta: Society of Biblical Literature, 2002), 75.

63. "Mursili's Accusations against Tawananna," *CTH* 70; translated by Singer, *Hittite Prayers*, 76 (no. 17, §4').

been brought on by an angry deity, but Mursili had to find the source of its anger. Oracular inquiry identified three possible causes, each attributable to Suppiluliuma. Among the possibilities was a retaliatory attack Suppiluliuma had made on Egyptian-held Amka, which, it turned out, was a violation of an old treaty between Hatti and Egypt.[64] While maintaining that the responsibility for the plague did not rest with him personally, Mursili promptly made restitution for his father's lapses.

At some point in his long and troubled reign, Mursili was en route to a town called Til-Kunnu to celebrate a festival when a thunderstorm broke out. The king suffered a temporary speech loss perhaps induced by shock owing to the severity of the storm. He put the incident out of his mind but years later began to have dreams about it. Then one night the affliction returned, and Mursili was unable to speak. He may have suffered a minor stroke that resulted in partial speech paralysis. The illness was attributed to divine forces, however, and oracular inquiries revealed that the offended deity was the Storm-God of the Kizzuwatnean city of Manuzziya and that the king would have to send an ox as a substitute to be burned as an offering in the temple of the Storm-God in Kummanni, Kizzuwatna's religious center. Whether the elaborate ritual that was performed for the king and simultaneously on his behalf in Kummanni (see ch. 4) provided the needed relief from his suffering is not known, but there is no evidence that the illness ever prevented him from carrying out his royal responsibilities.

The campaigns conducted in the second half of his reign brought Mursili again to the west and north. A new insurrection in the west instigated by the rulers of Mira and Masa to its north ended with the reaffirmation by both kingdoms of their loyalty to the Hittite king.[65] In the north, Mursili's final years were engaged in ongoing campaigns against the Kaska. Although he would have no more success than any other king in finally ending the Kaskean menace, Mursili did achieve a great symbolic, albeit temporary, victory when he wrested the sacred city of Nerik from Kaskean control and became the first Hittite king in two hundred years to worship in its temples.

---

64. The treaty related to the resettlement in Egyptian territory of the residents of the Hittite town of Kurustamma, for which see chapter 5.

65. Mashuiluwa and É.GAL.PAP, respectively. In Mira, Mursili II forced the citizenry to surrender Mashuiluwa, whom he then replaced with Mashuiluwa's adopted son, Kupanta-Kurunta.

Egypt and Hatti

War

Through the reign of Mursili II, Egyptian influence on the international scene had been in abeyance, although Egyptian support of the rebellion in Nuhasse indicates that they had not relinquished interest in regaining their territories in Syria, particularly Qadesh and Amurru. As a result, relations between the two superpowers remained tense. The rise of Egypt's ambitious Nineteenth Dynasty would end this cold war. When the dynamic father of Ramesses II, Seti I (r. 1294–1279 B.C.E.), the second pharaoh of the new dynasty, struck out successfully to reclaim Egypt's lost territories of Qadesh and Amurru, he effectively declared war on the Hittites. In the clash that followed between Mursili II's son Muwatalli II and Seti, the victorious pharoah returned to Egypt with a number of Hittite prisoners. The hostilities between the two superpowers culminated a few years later in an epic battle that would define the reign of Muwatalli II.

First, however, Muwatalli had to deal with yet another renegade vassal in the west, one Piyamaradu, who may have taken control of the loyal vassalage of Wilusa.[66] With the help of his vassals in Mira and the Seha River Land, Muwatalli expelled Piyamaradu, who probably found refuge with the Ahhiyawans, who were always ready to support anti-Hittite efforts in the region, and restored Alaksandu to the throne of Wilusa. Muwatalli also banished the reigning king of the Seha River Land, Manapa-Tarhunda, whose support in the conflict had been less than enthusiastic, and installed his son Masturi in his place. Piyamaradu's career, however, was not yet over, as we will see.

It was some time after his return from this campaign that Muwatalli decided to move his capital to Tarhuntassa, capital of the region by the same name in south-central Anatolia.[67] Hattusa had been the political and religious

---

66. On the probability that Piyamaradu was an ambitious Arzawan prince, see Hawkins, "Tarkasnawa King of Mira," 17. On the difficulty of interpreting the relevant passage in the Manapa-Tarhunda letter, see Trevor Bryce, *The Trojans and Their Neighbors* (New York: Routledge, 2006), 184–85.

67. Although the boundaries of the kingdom of Tarhuntassa are roughly known, the exact location of its capital city is still debated (see Stefano de Martino, "Ura and the Boundaries of Tarhuntašša," *AoF* 26 [1999]: 291–300; Ali M. Dinçol, Jak Yakar, Belkıs Dinçol, and Avia Taffer, "The Borders of the Appanage Kingdom of Tarhuntašša: A Geographical and Archaeological Assessment," *Anatolica* 26 [2000]: 1–29). Without its royal library and the historical and religious documents no doubt still protected within it, Muwatalli's reign remains among the most enigmatic.

heart of the Hittite kingdom for the past 350 years, and Muwatalli's reasons for abandoning it must have been compelling ones. He may, for example, have wanted to move the capital farther from the threat of Kaskean incursions and closer to the scene of the upcoming confrontation with Ramesses II in Syria. Muwatalli brought to the new capital the statues of the gods of Hatti and the manes (venerated spirits) of the ancestors,[68] a sign that the move was intended to be permanent.[69] Hattusili III would later write that his brother's relocation of the capital had been at the command of his personal god, the Storm-God of Lightning. Perhaps Muwatalli's motivation was purely religious.[70] The neglect of the cults in the south in favor of the sacred cities of the north was not a new problem, but Muwatalli may have felt an urgent need to correct the chronic inattention of his predecessors. After all, he would need the Storm-God's support in the coming war with Egypt.

Still, Muwatalli could not simply abandon the north to its fate. Despite repeated successes against the Kaska, Muwatalli's predecessors had not succeeded in containing them for any length of time, so Muwatalli decided to attempt a new strategy. He appointed his brother Hattusili, who had served as chief of the royal guard and governor of the Upper Land, king in Hakpis and gave him control over the northern half of the kingdom, including the Marassantiya (Halys) River basin. Notably, the city of Hattusa itself was left in the hands of Muwatalli's trusted official Mittannamuwa. With Muwatalli in Tarhuntassa, the situation in the north deteriorated, despite Hattusili's best efforts, but with the help of his patron goddess Shaushga, Hattusili reestablished control of the north despite, according to him, having been left with too few troops by Muwatalli.

The vast bulk of Muwatalli's troops were, in fact, amassing in Syria for the long-anticipated showdown with Egypt. Ramesses II (r. 1279–1212 B.C.E.) was now pharaoh of Egypt and every bit as intent as his father on establishing Egyptian hegemony over Syria-Palestine. A major clash was unavoidable. The scene of the battle would be Qadesh, now in Hittite control. The other contested state, Amurru, under its king, Benteshina, remained for the moment a loyal vassal of Egypt. According to the Egyptian sources, the Hittite forces numbered 47,500 troops, including 3,500 chariotry, regular troops, contingents gathered from all over the empire, and mercenaries. Hat-

---

68. "Apology of Ḫattušili III" (trans. van den Hout, *COS* 1.77:200, §6).

69. Itamar Singer ("From Hattuša to Tarhuntašša: Some Thoughts on Muwatalli's Reign," in *Acts of the IIIrd International Congress of Hittitology, Çorum, September 16–22, 1996* [ed. S. Alp and A. Süel; Ankara: Uyum Ajans, 1998], 535–41) compares Akhenaton's choice of Akhetaton as his new capital.

70. As argued by Singer, "From Hattuša to Tarhuntašša," esp. 539.

tusili also took part in the campaign, leading the Hittite contingents levied from the areas in the north over which he ruled in addition to the regular infantry and chariotry at his disposal as king of Hakpis. The Egyptian forces, which consisted of four divisions—Ra (from Heliopolis), Ptah (from Memphis), Amun (from Thebes), and Seth (from Tanis)—set out single-file in the spring of 1275 B.C.E. from Pi-Ramesse in the eastern Delta for the month-long march to Qadesh.

At a ford in the Orontes near Shabtuna, Ramesses met two Shasu bedouins who claimed to be defectors from the Hittite army, which they reported was far to the north in Aleppo. Unaware that the bedouins were spies sent by Muwatalli, Ramesses failed to check out the story or do any kind of reconnaisance and forged on to Qadesh. As the division of Amun began to set up camp to the northwest of the town in preparation for a siege the following day, the Egyptians captured two Hittite scouts who had been sent to find out the Egyptian position and compelled them to reveal the true position of the Hittite army. Muwatalli's troops, it turned out, were concealed behind the town on the other side of the river!

As Ramesses rushed dispatches to try to hurry the other divisions, the Hittites attacked, surrounding the forces of Amun, who scattered in a panic. Ramesses II stood his ground and mounted a counterattack. Despite Egyptian claims of victory, Ramesses II's forces were probably saved only by the timely arrival of reinforcements from Amurru.[71] The Hittites no doubt suffered heavy losses, as indicated by the lists of names of dead Hittite officers in the account of the battle carved on the walls of the Ramesseum in Thebes. In one relief, the prince of Aleppo is depicted up-ended to empty him of the water he swallowed while swimming the Orontes in retreat!

Despite these claims of victory, Ramesses had failed in his goals, and Muwatalli was able to pursue the retreating Egyptian troops south into Egyptian-controlled Aba. Hattusili would remain behind to oversee Hittite interests in that region for another year. A more important outcome of the battle was the return of Amurru to Hittite overlordship. Ultimately, however, the border between Hittite and Egyptian control in the region was reestablished where it had been for generations past.

On his return from Aba a year after the battle, Hattusili stopped over in Lawazantiya in Kizzuwatna to pay homage to Ishtar. There he met and married a woman named Puduhepa, the daughter of a powerful priest of Ishtar.

---

71. This is not preserved in the written accounts, but the illustrations of the battle seem to indicate it.

At the behest of the goddess I took Puduḫepa, the daughter of Pentipšarri, the priest, for my wife: we joined (in matrimony) [and] the goddess gave [u]s the love of husband (and) w[i]fe. We made ourselves sons (and) daughters. Then the goddess, My Lady, appeared to me in a dream (saying): "Become my servant [with] (your) household!" so the goddess' [serv]ant with my household I became. In the house which we made ourselves, the goddess was there with us and our house thrives.[72]

On his return to the Upper Land, Hattusili was faced with rebellion in Hakpis. Muwatalli's appointment of Hattusili to the governorship of the Upper Land had meant the displacement of Arma-Tarhunda, its previous governor and member of the royal clan. Arma-Tarhunda did not take the demotion lying down; with his own base of support behind him, he brought charges against Hattusili on two separate occasions. On the first occasion, Hattusili underwent an ordeal by divine wheel (a kind of judicial procedure) to determine his guilt or innocence and was exonerated. In the second instance, following his return from Syria, Muwatalli decided in favor of Hattusili, and the unfortunate Arma-Tarhunda, himself convicted of sorcery, was exiled to Cyprus.

Muwatalli died a few years after the battle of Qadesh. For reasons unknown, toward the end of his reign his queen, Danuhepa,[73] had lost his favor and was tried and expelled from the capital with her son. Either because of the scandal or because their son was still a child, he had chosen a second-rank son, Urhi-Teshub, as his heir.[74]

Urhi-Teshub adopted the throne name Mursili III, which is attested on a number of seal impressions. Outside of the seals, we are forced to view Mursili's reign through the hostile eyes of his uncle Hattusili, who would usurp his throne in a bitter civil war a few years later. Initially, however, Hattusili, claims to have supported the succession, even taking credit for installing Urhi-Teshub in kingship:

---

72. "Apology of Ḫattušili III," translated by van den Hout (*COS* 1.77:202, §9).

73. I follow Itamar Singer in attributing Danuhepa to Muwatalli rather than Mursili II. For his arguments, see "Danuḫepa and Kurunta," *Anatolia Antica: Studi in Memoria di Fiorella Imparati* (ed. Stefano De Martino and Franca Pecchioli Daddi; Eothen 11; Firenze: LoGisma editore, 2002), 739–51.

74. Ibid., 746; see also idem, "The Fate of Hattusa during the Period of Tarhuntassa's Supremacy," in *Kulturgeschichten: Altorientalistische Studien für Volkert Haas zum 65. Geburtstag* (ed. Thomas Richter, Doris Prechel, and Jörg Klinger; Saarbrücken: Saarbrücker Druckerei, 2001), 403.

[T]herefore sin[ce] my brother did not have a [l]egitimate son, I took up Urḫitešup, son of a concubine. [I put] him into lordship over [Ḫa]tti Land and laid all of [Ḫattuša] in (his) hand.[75]

Since Mursili III's queen on his official seals was also Danuhepa, one of his first acts must have been to reinstate her as Tawananna. This was only one of a number of reversals of Muwatalli's decisions that Mursili III implemented. Most significant was the transfer after Muwatalli's death of the seat of government back to Hattusa. Whether he had disagreed with his father's decision to transfer the capital to Tarhuntassa or was under pressure from members of the court to return to the status quo, Mursili III brought the statues of the gods back to Hattusa.[76] Tarhuntassa was demoted to the status of a regional center, albeit an important one. This decision appears to have had the support of Hattusili and no doubt was a popular one generally.

On the political front, Mursili III allowed the return from exile of Manapa-Tarhunda, the old king of the Seha River Land whom Muwatalli had deposed, and gave his aunt Massanauzzi in marriage to Masturi, its current king.[77] In Syria, he reinstalled Benteshina as king of Amurru. Muwatalli had deposed Benteshina after his defection to the Egyptian side and had sent him to live in Hakpis under Hattusili's protection. Hattusili may well have been instrumental in his reinstatement. Hattusili's influence with his nephew is evident in one policy decision he did not support. When Mursili III replaced Mittannamuwa's son as chief scribe, a post that Mittannamuwa had held before Muwatalli placed him in charge of Hattusa, Hattusili successfully intervened with his nephew on behalf of Mittannamuwa's family.

It was also during Mursili III's reign that Hattusili rebuilt the holy city of Nerik, which had lain in ruins since the days of Hantili II. Hattusili was a devout servant and priest of the Storm-God of Nerik, with a record of service of which Puduhepa, his queen, would not hesitate to remind the gods later in Hattusili's life. He even named one of his sons Nerikkaili ("man of Nerik") in honor of the holy city.

Diplomatic relations with Assyria during Mursili III's reign were strained. Adad-nirari had succeeded in making Hanigalbat, the remnant of the former Mitannian kingdom, a vassal of Assyria. Mursili III's failure to

---

75. "Apology of Ḫattušili III," translated by van den Hout (*COS* 1.77:202, §10a).

76. *KUB* 21.15 (*CTH* 85.I.B) i 11–12.

77. Masturi would later support Hattusili against Mursili III in the civil war. Ironically, Hattusili's son and successor, Tudhaliya IV, who obviously benefited by Masturi's rebellion against Urhi-Teshub, later held him up as an example of a vassal who had broken his oath of loyalty.

support a new rebellion in Hanigalbat, led by its king Wasashatta, resulted in the final annexation of the territory to the Assyrian Empire and effectively eliminated any buffer between the lands controlled by Hatti and Assyria. Mursili III's displeasure with the situation is evident in the tone he takes in a letter to Adad-nirari in which he refuses to acknowledge the Assyrian king as his "brother," that is, as a king with whom he enjoyed good diplomatic relations.[78] Hattusili would later have occasion to remind the Assyrian king Shalmaneser I of how poorly Assyrian ambassadors had been treated at Mursili III's court.[79] In the end, Mursili III's inability to find a diplomatic means for dealing with the Assyrian problem may have been the one significant failure of his short reign.

Hattusili's Apology, a document composed to justify his usurpation and to secure the line of succession, blames Mursili III, to whom he refers disrespectfully by his birth-name Urhi-Teshub, for initiating the hostilities that led to the civil war by systematically dismantling his base of power and demoting him from office. The text claims that the goddess Shaushga sent dreams to Hattusili's wife Puduhepa promising him the kingship. If word of the goddess's promise (and the ambition it implied) had gotten back to the reigning king, then his attempts to limit Hattusili's power would hardly be surprising. Shaushka also allegedly appeared in dreams to generals whom Mursili III had exiled and won them to Hattusili's side with promises of victory. In fact, these members of the elite may have thrown their hats in with Hattusili as the more likely victor in the coming civil war.

Despite his diminished powers, Hattusili still retained the important cities of Nerik and Hakpis—the seats of his religious and political power, respectively—because an oracle had forbidden Mursili III from taking them from him. Hattusili wrote that he "sought my destruction at divine and human behest,"[80] meaning that he solicited the advice of both the gods (through oracular inquiry) and men on how to limit him. Hattusili claims to have submitted to these humiliations and provocations for seven years before

---

78. *KUB* 23.102 (*CTH* 171) i 1–19, for which see Beckman, *Hittite Diplomatic Texts*, 146–47 (no. 24A). Against the generally accepted view that Mursili III (Urhi-Teshub), not Hattusili III, authored the letter, see Theo P. J. van den Hout, "Khattushili III, King of the Hittites," in *CANE*, 1114–15. For this nuance of the diplomatic use of the term "brother," see Trevor R. Bryce, *Letters of the Great Kings of the Ancient Near East: The Royal Correspondence of the Late Bronze Age* (London: Routledge, 2003), 74–78.

79. *KBo* 1.14 (*CTH* 173) rev. 11'–19' (§5), translated by Beckman, *Hittite Diplomatic Texts*, 149 (no. 24B).

80. "Apology of Ḫattušili III," translated by van den Hout (*COS* 1.77:203, §10).

rebelling. When Urhi-Teshub finally took Nerik and Hakpis from him, Hattusili declared war, writing to the king,

> You opposed me. You (are) Great King, whereas I (am) king of the single fortress that you left me. So come! Ištar of Šamuḫa and the Stormgod of Nerik will judge us.[81]

Mursili III set out from Marassantiya and took the fight to Hattusili in the Upper Land. When Muwatalli had exiled Arma-Tarhunda, the latter's son, Sippaziti, had been allowed to remain in Hatti, and he now allied himself to Mursili III by recruiting troops for him in the Upper Land. Sippaziti's help notwithstanding, Mursili's superior resources were minimized in this region full of faithful allies of Hattusili. In taking the fight into Hattusili's territory, Mursili III had made a fatal strategic error. Hattusili used his connections to enlist the Kaska tribesmen to fight with him. Able fighters at home in mountainous areas, they proved to be more than a match for Mursili III's troops. Mursili III retreated to the city of Samuha, which Hattusili placed under siege. From within the city, traitors stole out to Hattusili's camp nearby in Suluppa and offered to bring him the king's head, but Hattusili refused. Mursili III in any event was trapped "like a pig in a sty." The city fell to Hattusili, and the king was led out of the city in bonds. Divine judgment had obviously decided in Hattusili's favor: "If he had in no way opposed me, would they (the gods) really have made a Great King succumb to a petty king? Because he has now opposed me, the gods have made him succumb to me by (their) judgement."[82]

PEACE

Hattusili wrote of the universal welcome his enthronement allegedly received as follows:

> The kings (who were) my elders (and) who had been on good terms with me, they remained on just those good terms with me, and they began to send envoys to me. They began to send gifts to me, and the gifts they ke[ep] sending me, they never sent to any (of my) fathers and grandfathers. The king supposed to respect me, respected me, and the (countries) that had been my enemies, I conquered them. For the Ḫatti Lands I [a]nnexed territory upon territory. (Those) who had been enemies in the days of my fathers (and) grandfat[her]s concluded peace with me.[83]

---

81. Ibid.
82. Ibid.
83. "Apology of Ḫattušili III," translated by van den Hout (*COS* 1.77:204, §12b).

In actuality, the reaction of friend and foe alike appears to have been mixed. Within Hattusa itself, as is evident from a proclamation that Hattusili made to its citizens right after his accession, there were fences to mend.[84]

The deposed king was to remain a thorn in Hattusili's side for the next several years. At first Hattusili sent Urhi-Teshub into exile in Nuhasse, where he was given fortified cities to govern. But soon Urhi-Teshub was caught trying to escape to Babylonia,[85] whereupon Hattusili transferred him to a more secure location, probably in one of the coastal kingdoms firmly in the Hittite orbit.[86] It was apparently not secure enough, however, for Urhi-Teshub soon removed himself to Egypt and the protection of Ramesses II, his father's nemesis.

As a prince of the realm, Hattusili had been a successful military leader. As king, he became a consummate diplomat. Given his unconventional route to the throne, it was essential that he establish good relations with vassals and foreign powers alike. Treaties with Amurru, Babylon, and Egypt were reinforced by diplomatic marriages between his children and the rulers of Amurru, Isuwa, Babylon, and Egypt.[87] He no doubt pursued all of these alliances with a view to reinforcing the legitimacy of his rule in the eyes of the international community.

With Assyria, Hattusili tread softly. Adad-nirari had not recognized his legitimacy, initially failing to send a gift on the occasion of Hattusili's enthronement and remarking to him that "you are (but) a substitute for the Great King."[88] When the king of Hanigalbat, Shattuara II, rebelled against

---

84. *KUB* 21.37 (CTH 85.2); edited by Alfonso Archi, "The Propaganda of Ḫattušiliš III," *SMEA* 14 (1971): 203–8; for a discussion of the text, see Singer, "The Fate of Hattusa," 399–402).

85. Klengel, (*Geschichte des hethitischen Reiches,* 232) notes that Urhi-Teshub might have unsuccessfully sought the support of the king of Ahhiyawa before turning to Babylon.

86. He was sent A.AB.BA *tapuša* "beside/across/alongside the sea" (Apology §11). Thus, Mira in western Anatolia, Ugarit and Amurru in Syria, and the island of Cyprus have all been proposed.

87. In the case of Amurru, Hattusili's son Nerikkaili took Benteshina's daughter as wife. This was one of two marriage alliances between Amurru and Hatti. A third marriage was made in Tudhaliya IV's reign.

88. As reported in a letter from Ramesses (*KBo* 8.14 [*CTH* 163] obv. 10'; see Elmar Edel, *Umschriften und Übersetzungen* (vol. 1 of *Die ägyptisch-hethitische Korrespondenz aus Boghazköy in babylonischer und hethitischer Sprache*; Abhandlungen der Rheinisch-Westphälischen Akademie der Wissenschaften 77; Opladen: Westdeutscher Verlag, 1994), 24–25, [no. 5]), who records the Assyrian king's statement. The Assyrian king could also have been Shalmaneser (Bryce, *Kingdom of the Hittites,* 466 n. 49).

Adad-nirari's successor, Shalmaneser, the effort went unaided by Hattusili, who acknowledged the Assyrian as a Great King and officially recognized his sovereignty over Hanigalbat. Shalmaneser's response to the rebellion was to obliterate the kingdom of Hanigalbat once and for all. Hattusili's policy of forbearance may have helped to ease tensions between the two powers, at least temporarily.

Hattusili's paramount concern and the motivation behind all these actions was not only to garner international recognition of his kingship while building up his base of support at home but to ensure that the right of succession to the throne of Hatti remain with his line. It was for these same reasons that he approached Ramesses II with a proposal for a treaty alliance. A treaty would further ensure that Urhi-Teshub did not have Egyptian support in any bid to reclaim his throne. Whether Urhi-Teshub was living in Egypt already at the time that the treaty was being negotiated is not known. At some point, possibly after the treaty had been concluded, Hattusili asked for his extradition, but Ramesses refused, perhaps believing that Urhi-Teshub's presence gave him a trump card in his dealings with the Hittite king.

For his part, Ramesses II had little to lose by agreeing to the treaty and likely welcomed the opportunity for self-promotional propaganda that it afforded. The treaty was concluded in 1259, Ramesses's twenty-first year. Two virtually identical versions were drawn up in Hattusa and Pi-Ramesse and then exchanged. The version composed in Hattusa was translated into Egyptian and enscribed on the walls of the temple at Karnak, while the Egyptian version, translated into Akkadian, survives in a clay copy of an original silver tablet sent from Egypt. The treaty followed the formula characteristic of Hittite treaties (see ch. 3) and included stipulations of nonaggression, mutual assistance against internal and external enemies, and the extradition of fugitives. The insertion of a clause whereby Ramesses guaranteed the succession of Hattusili's legitimate heir has no corresponding stipulation on the Egyptian side and underscores Hattusili's preoccupation with securing the succession for his heirs.

Both parties honored the conditions of the treaty. When Kupanta-Kurunta, king of Mira, wrote to Ramesses regarding Urhi-Teshub's situation, Ramesses simply referred him to the treaty and endorsed Hattusili's handling of the matter.[89] Requests for the services of the highly respected Egyptian physicians also came through the mail. In a letter to Ramesses, the Hittite king asked the Egyptian monarch to send a physician to help his sister Massanauzzi bear a child, since she and her husband Masturi, king of Mira, had

---

89. *KBo* 1.24 + *KUB* 3.23 + *KUB* 3.84 obv. 12–13; Edel, *ÄHK*, 74–75 (no. 28).

thus far remained childless. Ramesses agreed to the request against his better judgment. He knew that Massanauzzi was pushing sixty at best and harbored little hope of the physician's success in the matter![90]

The treaty, which both Hattusili and his queen Puduhepa signed, initiated a period of cooperation known as the Egypto-Hittite peace, in which intense contact took place between the two courts. The land and sea routes that passed through the petty kingdoms lying between the two superpowers were well-traveled as envoys, diplomats, merchants, and cultural attachés made the journey from Pi-Ramesse to Hattusa and back again. Thirteen years after the treaty, amidst a flurry of arrangements, the royal couple sent one of their daughters to Egypt to wed the by-now-elderly Ramesses. Among the considerable correspondence between the two courts in this period was a letter from Puduhepa to the pharaoh attributing a delay in the arrangements for the wedding to a lack of resources on which to draw for the dowry:

> [I have indeed withheld my daughter.] You will not disapprove of it; you will approve of it. At the moment [I am not able to give] her to you. As you, my brother, know, the House of Hatti, do I not [know that it is] depleted? And Urhi-Teshup gave what remained to the Great God. Since Urhi-Teshup is there, ask him if this is so or not so.[91]

Ramesses had denied on more than one occasion that Urhi-Teshup was still under his protection. Whether or not Urhi-Teshup had left the Egyptian court after the conclusion of the treaty, Hattusili and his queen clearly believed he was still there.

A second wedding to another daughter of Hattusili and Puduhepa followed some years later, perhaps after Hattusili's death. Puduhepa was instrumental in making those arrangements as well. She continued in her role as queen well into the reign of her son Tudhaliya. In a kingdom in which the Tawananna had considerable power in domestic affairs, particularly within the capital, Puduhepa stands out for having participated on an equal footing with her husband in international matters. On a rock relief at Firaktin, she and Hattusili are shown side by side pouring libations to two divinities (fig. 2.6). The respect and power accorded her as queen both in Hatti and by the international community is unparalleled in the Late Bronze Age Near East.

---

90. On Massanauzzi's age, see Trevor Bryce, *Letters of the Great Kings*, 115.

91. *KUB* 21.38 (*CTH* 176) obv. 8'–12'. See Singer, "From Hattuša to Tarhuntašša," 537–38, for the restoration of [*arha a*]*rnuwan*, for which I prefer the translation "depleted" to Singer's "taken away, transferred." Otherwise, the translation is adapted from that of Beckman, *Hittite Diplomatic Texts*, 132 (no. 22E).

Fig. 2.6. A relief carved into a rock face at Firaktin near the Lower Land shows Hattusili III and Puduhepa offering libations to Teshub and Hebat. A testament to her unique status among ancient Near Eastern queens, Puduhepa is depicted here on an equal footing with her husband. Photo by the author.

Although Ramesses did invite Hattusili to Egypt, and despite the two renderings of Hattusili III accompanying his daughter, one in the marriage scene in the temple at Abu Simbel and the other on the colossal statue of Ramesses at Tanis in the Delta, it is unlikely that the Hittite king ever made the trip. Hattusili had protested the manner in which Ramesses's artists had depicted the battle of Qadesh, and such an invitation could only be construed as serving the purposes of Egyptian propaganda.

Although a consummate diplomat, Hattusili's reign was not entirely free of military activity. While the heir apparent Tudhaliya honed his martial skills on the Kaskean frontier as his father before him had done, Hattusili was faced with growing problems in the west. His annals relate a campaign he undertook in the Lukka lands in southwestern Anatolia to crush a rebellion there, one that appears to have spread to most of southern Anatolia.[92] The rebels found asylum with Tawagalawa, the brother of the king of Ahhiyawa. Hattusili wrote a long letter to the king of Ahhiyawa, the so-called Tawagalawa letter, the main concern of which was the insurrectionist Piyamaradu, who had been harrassing Hatti's western allies since Muwatalli's reign.

In addition to facilitating the rebels' escape, Piyamaradu had ejected Hittite loyalists in Lukka from their homeland. The people of Lukka had brought their complaint first to Tawagalawa, the brother of the Ahhiyawan

92. *KUB* 21.6 (+) 6a (*CTH* 82), for which see O. R. Gurney, "The Annals of Hattusilis III," *AnSt* 47 (1997): 127–39.

king, whose city Millawanda (Miletos) was being used as the base of operations, and then to the Hittite king, their own suzerain. The Hittite king set
out with his troops for the Lukka lands. When he reached the city of Sallapa,
he received a request from Piyamaradu to take him into vassalage, but when
Hattusili sent his crown prince (perhaps Nerikkaili) to bring Piyamaradu
back for installation as a vassal, Piyamaradu refused to come and demanded
a kingdom on the spot.[93] Their troops clashed at Iyalanda.[94] Hattusili pursued
Piyamaradu as far as Millawanda, which was governed by the latter's son-
in-law Atpa. The Hittite king entered the city and demanded that Atpa hand
over Piyamaradu, but the fugitive managed once again to escape by ship to
the protection of the Ahhiyawan king. From the safety of an island refuge, he
continued his raids on Hittite holdings on the mainland, prompting Hattusili's appeal to the king of Ahhiyawa either to extradite Piyamaradu or to put a
stop to his inflammatory activities in the west. There is no evidence that the
king of Ahhiyawa heeded Hattusili's adjuration, and with Ahhiyawa actively
working against Hittite interests in the region, the situation in the west was
doomed to deteriorate.

Hattusili had been sickly all his life. As a child he had fallen prey to a
serious illness and was put into the care of Mittannamuwa, the chief scribe,
the same man who would govern Hattusa during the Tarhuntassa interlude.
The goddess Shaushga of Samuha had caused Hattusili's brother Muwatalli
to appear to their father Mursili II in a dream in which he promised the king
that, if he gave Hattusili to the goddess in priesthood, the boy would recover.
Under the care of the multitalented official and with the assistance of his
goddess, Hattusili recovered. Later in life Puduhepa appealed on numerous occasions to the gods to grant Hattusili relief from inflammation of the
foot and from an eye problem. When Hattusili finally died at a relatively
advanced age, he left behind a large extended royal family and lingering
questions about who had the right to sit on the throne of Hatti.

---

93. Hawkins ("Tarkasnawa King of Mira," 17) suggests that the kingdom he had
in mind was Mira, whose king, Kupanta-Kurunta, had fallen from favor for supporting
Urhi-Teshub.

94. Iyalanda is classical Alinda (Demirci-daresi) in Caria. That Hattusili is the Hit-
tite king of the Tawagalawa letter is now confirmed by a letter (*KBo* 28:28; Edel, *ÄHK*,
188–189 [no. 80]) from Ramesses to Hattusili that refers to the latter's great victory over
Iyalanta. See Itamar Singer, "New Evidence on the End of the Hittite Empire," in *The
Sea Peoples and Their World: A Reassessment* (ed. Eliezer D. Oren; Philadelphia: The
University Museum, 2000), 25.

The End of an Empire

Tudhaliya IV was not Hattusili's initial choice for a successor. One of his brothers, either Nerikkaili or Hesni, served for a time as heir apparent, but the circumstances under which Hattusili replaced him with Tudhaliya IV are not known.[95] Perhaps Puduhepa was influential in promoting her own son's interests above the child of a previous wife.[96] Whatever the reason for the choice, Tudhaliya did bring one obvious advantage to the throne: he may have been the one son who could best guarantee that the succession would not be challenged by a rival claimant.

That rival claimant was Urhi-Teshub's younger brother, Kurunta.[97] While still a child, their father Muwatalli had given Kurunta to his brother Hattusili to raise in Hakpis.[98] Of a similar age, Tudhaliya and Kurunta grew up together and formed a special bond.[99] In a later treaty between the two, Tudhaliya relates these events:

> But when my father deposed my brother whom he had placed in the office
> of crown prince and installed me in kingship and when my father observed
> the respect and affection between Kurunta and myself, my father brought

---

95. Bronze Tablet ii 35–36, 43–44 (§§13, 14). The elder brother is not named in the text. For the identification with Nerikkaili (rather than Kurunta), see Fiorella Imparati, "Apology of Ḫattušili III or Designation of his Successor?" in *Studio Historiae Ardens: Ancient Near Eastern Studies Presented to Philo H. J. Houwink ten Cate on the Occasion of His 65th Birthday* (ed. Theo P. J. van den Hout and Johan de Roos; Leiden: Nederlands Instituut voor het Nabije Oosten, 1995), 151–53. For the possible identification with Hesni, see Nicoletta Tani, "More about the Hesni Conspiracy," *AoF* 28 (2001): 160–62.

If the brother was Nerikkaili, his removal is all the more mysterious, given that he continued to play an important role in the government. His (re)instatement as Tuhkanti, that is, as heir apparent, to Tudhaliya IV may have been yet another concession that this king made during his reign to members of the royal family with pretensions to the crown; see Bryce, *Kingdom of the Hittites*, 302; and below.

96. On the possibility of a first wife for Hattusili, see, e.g., van den Hout, "Khattushili III, King of the Hittites," 1109–11.

97. On the exact relationship between Urhi-Teshub and Kurunta, see Bryce, "The Secession of Tarhuntassa," in *Tabularia Hethaeorum: Hethitologische Beitruage Silvin Košak zum 65. Geburtstag* (ed. Detlev Groddek and Marina Zorman; DBH 25; Wiesbaden: Harrassowitz, 2007), 119.

98. Perhaps this was an attempt to protect him from the political intrigues within the capital, as suggested by Bryce (*Kingdom of the Hittites*, 244–45, 269), or perhaps it was an outcome of a scandal involving the Queen, Danuhepa, as suggested by Singer ("Danuhepa and Kurunta," 746–47).

99. Bryce, "The Secession of Tarhuntassa," 126, suggests that Tudhaliya IV was approximately ten years younger than Kurunta.

us together and had us swear an oath: "Let one protect the other." Thus my
father had us swear an oath, and aside from that we were sworn allies. And
Kurunta protected me and in no way broke the oaths which he had sworn
to me. I, My Majesty, spoke to him as follows: "If the gods recognize
me so that I become king, on my part there will be only good things for
you."[100]

Kurunta had not aided his brother in the civil war with Hattusili. Raised by his
brother's usurper, his loyalties may have been mixed. Immediately upon his
accession to the throne, Hattusili III installed Kurunta as king of Tarhuntassa
and ratified the appointment with a treaty that granted significant concessions to Kurunta.[101] When Tudhaliya IV came to the throne, he renewed his
father's treaty with Kurunta, the original copy of which, engraved in bronze,
was discovered in 1986 beneath the paved area near the south wall (Yerkapı)
of Hattusa. The new treaty bestowed further favors on Kurunta. He now had
the freedom to choose his own successor and was granted a reduction of
the usual taxes and corvée. These considerations, which included placing
Tarhuntassa's king on a par politically with the viceroy of Karkamis, were
designed to ensure Kurunta's loyalty.

Like his father, Tudhaliya, as a second son, had served as chief of the
royal guard. In this capacity, he had successfully conducted campaigns
against the Kaska, as we have seen, and thus was no stranger to military
engagements. In the west, he succeeded in crushing a rebellion in the Seha
River Land following the death of its king Masturi, who had left no heirs
despite the best efforts of Egyptian physicians. He also restored the loyal
vassal Walmu to the throne of Wilusa, from which he had been forcibly
removed. Walmu had taken refuge with Tarkasnawa king of Mira (fig. 2.7),
who, cooperating with the Hittite court, facilitated Walmu's reinvestiture.
As a result of these events, Mira, key to Hittite interests in the west since
the break-up of Arzawa, obtained partial overlordship over Wilusa, a privi-
leged status unprecedented among the Hittite vassals.[102] At the same time,

---

100. Bronze Tablet ii 43–52 (§14), translated by Beckman, *Hittite Diplomatic Texts*,
118 (no. 18C).

101. This assumes that the throne name Kurunta was adopted by Ulmi-Teshub and
that the two are to be identified. There is as yet by no means a concession that such an
identification is justified. For a summary of the sequence of treaties with Kurunta/Ulmi-
Teshub, see Beckman, *Hittite Diplomatic Texts*, 107–8.

102. For this reconstruction of the events related in the so-called Milawata Letter,
see Itamar Singer, "Western Anatolia in the Thirteenth Century B.C. according to the Hittite Sources," *AnSt* 33 (1983): 214–16. For Tarkasnawa as the recipient of the letter, see
Hawkins, "Tarkasnawa King of Mira," 19.

Fig. 2.7. The Karabel relief has only recently been deciphered. Carved high on a hill on an ancient road from Ephesos (Apasa) to Sardis, the figure is now known to represent Tarkasnawa, king of Mira. Photo by the author.

the loyalty of both these kingdoms gave their Hittite overlord some insurance against any further aggression on the part of Ahhiyawa.

Tudhaliya was destined to be less successful on other fronts, however. The tense relations with Assyria had not eased significantly since Mursili III's indelicate attempts at diplomacy. Tudhaliya IV was keen to improve the strained relations with Assyria, and initially its king, Tukulti-ninurta (r. 1233–1197 B.C.E.), seemed open to reaching a peaceful reconciliation, writing to Tudhaliya, "My father was your enemy ... but I am the friend of My Brother."[103] While in the midst of peace negotiations, however, the Assyrians suddenly attacked the Hurrian lands to their northwest that were under Hittite hegemony, ignoring the warning of the Hittite king that such an attack on Hittite territories would bring retaliation. Tukulti-ninurta I thus gained control of the Subari lands, a region north of Hanigalbat, and with it all of the major passes into Anatolia, leaving the Hittite territory of Isuwa dangerously threatened. Tukulti-ninurta I now wished to secure his new northern border against the Nairi lands (Hittite Nihriya) beyond.

---

103. *KUB* 3.73 (*CTH* 216) 10'–11', ed. A. Hagenbuchner, *Die Korrespondenz der Hethiter 2. Teil* (THeth 16; Heidelberg: Winter, 1989), 275–77 (no. 202).

Nihriya had been the seat of a trading colony in the Old Assyrian period and was situated at the end of the Ergani Pass, an important route into Anatolia, making it strategically critical.

In the meantime, Tudhaliya IV ordered a trade embargo against Assyria that forbade Shaushgamuwa of Amurru to allow ships of Ahhiyawa to trade with Assyria via his ports. He also put both Ugarit and Amurru on notice that he expected troops from them in case of an Assyrian attack. A letter from Tukulti-ninurta to Ibiranu king of Ugarit relates the final events leading up to and including the great battle between Hatti and Assyria at Nihriya.[104] The Hittite troops had occupied Nihriya, and the Assyrians were advancing to meet them. Tukulti-ninurta demanded that Tudhaliya withdraw, but the Hittite king refused, rejecting Tukulti-ninurta's overtures of peace. Tudhaliya ordered the attack, and the Assyrians met his troops outside the city. Effectively deserted by his vassals, Tudhaliya's forces were defeated. The loss would cost the Hittite Empire dearly. After the battle, Tudhaliya IV wrote to a faint-hearted ally on whom he had counted for support against the Assyrian king:

> As (the situation) turned difficult for me, you kept yourself somewhere away from me. Beside me you were not! Have I not fled from Nihriya alone? When it thus occurred that the enemy took away from me the Hurrian lands, was I not left on my own in Alatarma?[105]

This unhelpful ally may have been Isuwa in eastern Anatolia, the region that had been a bone of contention with the state of Mitanni in earlier reigns. But the Hittite king found himself in a difficult position after the humiliating defeat at Nihriya, and this disloyal vassal would go unpunished. Tukulti-ninurta reported his great victory over the Hittites to another Hittite vassal, Ibiranu of Ugarit, possibly in an effort to convince him to abandon allegiance to the Hittites. Indeed, Ugarit seems to have become increasingly brazen in its behavior after the Hittite defeat at Nihriya, even making diplomatic overtures to Egypt.[106]

---

104. S. Lackenbacher, "Nouveaux documents d'Ugarit, I: Une lettre royale," *RA* 76 (1982): 141–56.

105. *KBo* 4.14 (*CTH* 123) ii 7–11, translated by Singer, "The Battle of Nihriya and the End of the Hittite Empire," *ZA* 75 (1985): 110.

106. To the extent that the king of Karkamis was compelled to reprimand the king of Ugarit in a letter discovered in the Urtenu archive, for which see Singer, "New Evidence on the End of the Hittite Empire," 21–22.

Early in his reign, Tudhaliya wrote to his mother of his concern about a rebellion in Lalanda[107] and his fear that it might spread throughout the Lower Land. Despite his best efforts, Hattusili III had failed to pacify the region, and the last kings of Hatti would have no better luck containing the growing dissension in the south and southwest. A hieroglyphic Luwian inscription discovered in Yalburt, northwest of Konya, in 1970 sheds light on this period. The inscription, the longest yet found dating to period of the empire, commemorates a campaign that Tudhaliya IV made to the Lukka lands. With the exception of Wiyanawanda, the places mentioned in the text—Talawa, Pinali, Awarna, and Mount Patara—were situated along the Xanthos River in Lycia.[108] Although Tudhaliya's inscription claimed his victory, the Anatolian southwest was now in an irreversible descent into anarchy.

Further evidence of this was the testing of Tudhaliya's martial skills on an entirely new front. Tudhaliya IV's campaign to conquer the island of Cyprus (Alasiya) is the first indication that the Hittites had any ambitions in that direction since Arnuwanda I's claims on the island in the fifteenth century.[109] The entire episode is doubly unusual for being the first sea battle that the land-bound Hittites had attempted, and without doubt Tudhaliya was relying on the naval expertise of his vassals Ugarit and Amurru. Sandwiched between the growing power of Ahhiyawa in the west and Assyria in the east, Tudhaliya may have committed to this endeavor to ensure that the trade routes remained open[110] since a hostile island could easily interfere with Hittite supply routes. Tudhaliya succeeded, at least temporarily, in establishing a new pro-Hittite regime on the island.

On the domestic front, Tudhaliya was dogged by the specter of his father's coup. All the steps that Hattusili had taken to ensure that Tudhaliya would be accepted as king could not put an end to grumblings from branches of the family whose claims to the throne were as strong as, if not stronger than, Tudhaliya's. It turns out that the king had good reason to be concerned.

---

107. Classical Larende/Karaman; see Massimo Forlanini, "Uda, un cas probable d'homonymie," *Hethitica* 10 (1990): 120–21; Singer, "Great Kings of Tarhuntassa," 71 n. 31.

108. Massimo Poetto, *L'iscrizione luvio-geroglifica di Yalburt* (Studia Mediterranea 8; Pavia: Gianni Iuculano Editore, 1993), 75–84. See also Singer, "New Evidence on the End of the Hittite Empire," 26; Trevor R. Bryce, "History," in Melchert, *The Luwians*, 109.

109. See the Madduwatta Indictment §30, translated by Beckman, *Hittite Diplomatic Texts*, 160 (no. 27).

110. Bryce, *Kingdom of the Hittites*, 322.

A failed assassination attempt led by Hesni, another son of Hattusili III,[111] may have prompted this forceful statement to his officials:

> My Sun has many brothers as his father's sons are numerous. The Land of Hatti is full of the royal line. In Hatti, the descendants of Suppiluliuma, the descendants of Mursili, the descendants of Muwatalli, and the descendants of Hattusili are numerous. You must acknowledge no other person with respect to lordship and protect only the grandson, great grandson, and descendants of Tudhaliya. Should at any time evil be done to My Sun because My Sun has many brothers, and you are responsible and you approach another person and speak thus: "The one whom we select for ourselves need not even be a son of our lord!"—this situation is not permissible. With respect to lordship, you must [protect] only My Sun and the descendants of My Sun. ... You must approach no other person.[112]

That Tudhaliya was under siege seems certain from the numerous favors he bestowed on members of the royal family, a sign that the king found himself increasingly dependent on the loyalty of his vassals and his court in the face of mounting pressures both external and internal. Recent archaeological discoveries have provided some clues as to just how heavy those pressures were.

Bullae with the seal impression of Kurunta bearing the title "Great King, Labarna, My Sun," have been found in Temple 3 of the Upper City at Boghazköy in the same context with later bullae of Tudhaliya IV's son and second successor, Suppiluliuma II. Kurunta also bears the title "Great King" in a recently discovered relief from Hatip in the territory of Tarhuntassa. The adoption of these titles by a vassal king was unheard of, and historians have been challenged to explain the presence of Kurunta's seals in the Hittite capital. Did Kurunta assume for himself the title Great King as a form of political propaganda?[113] Or did Tudhaliya IV confer the title upon him in an effort to stabilize his own position?[114] After all, in the Bronze Treaty he had already established Kurunta's status as a king equal in status to the viceroys

---

111. Nicoletta Tani, "More about the 'Hešni Conspiracy,'" 154–64; see also Bryce, *Kingdom of the Hittites*, 299–300. The conspiracy is revealed in a record of a court proceeding; see *KUB* 31.68 (*CTH* 297.8).

112. *KUB* 26.1 (*CTH* 255.2) i 9–29; ed. Einar von Schuler, *Hethitische Dienstanweisungen für höhere Hof- und Staatsbeamte* (Osnabrück: Biblio-Verlag, 1967), 9.

113. Itamar Singer, "Great Kings of Tarḫuntašša," *SMEA* 38 (1996): 63–71.

114. As argued by Clelia Mora, "On Some Clauses in the Kurunta Treaty and the Political Scenery at the End of the Hittite Empire," in Beckman, Beal, and McMahon, *Hittite Studies in Honor of Harry A. Hoffner Jr.*, 289–96.

of Karkamis.[115] Another theory suggests that Kurunta proclaimed himself Great King as an assertion of his right to his father's throne, which had been based at Tarhuntassa.[116] Whatever the situation, the growing weakness of the Hittite power base at Hattusa made it possible for a second "Great" King to assert himself. Tudhaliya had to resign himself to sharing the domination of Anatolia with Kurunta, and the two childhood friends, now rivals, would continue to cooperate in matters of common interest, such as the shipment of grain along the supply route that ran through Tarhuntassa from the port city of Ura.[117] This trade alliance at least would explain how Kurunta's seal would have come to be found at the Hittite capital.[118]

At some time either prior to the fulfillment of Kurunta's political aspirations or following them, Tudhaliya IV sent a desperate request to Ramesses II for help in treating an ailing Kurunta. Ramesses II's reply to Tudhaliya IV is preserved and displays a reassuring tone of concern, as the pharoah was able to report that the requested physician and medicines had been dispatched.[119] Whether Kurunta survived this illness we do not know, but if he did, his fate remains a mystery, as we do not hear from him again.

Despite the challenges of his reign, or rather because of them, Tudhaliya devoted considerable attention to cultic matters at home. A king's military success depended on fulfilling his religious obligations and thereby securing the continued goodwill of the gods. In a prayer to the Sun-Goddess of Arinna, Tudhaliya vowed to restore the cult of the goddess if she would support him against his enemy. This involved correcting persistent mistakes in the celebration of the spring and autumn festivals and replacing divine images that

---

115. Bronze Tablet §18.

116. Bryce, "The Secession of Tarhuntassa," 124–26.

117. So Singer, "New Evidence on the End of the Hittite Empire," 26. Hawkins ("Tarkasnawa King of Mira," 20–21) proposes that Parhuitta, king of a western vassal, perhaps Mira, and contemporary of Tudhaliya's heir Suppiluliuma II, may also have held near-equal status with the Hittite king at the very end of the empire. This theory is based on the nature of the opening address in the letter *KBo* 18.18 (*CTH* 186.4), edited by Hagenbuchner, *Die Korrespondenz der Hethiter*, 316–18 (no. 215). For a dissenting viewpoint, see Theo P. J. van den Hout, "Zur Geschichte des jüngeren hethitischen Reiches," in Wilhelm, *Akten des IV. Internationalen Kongresses*, 218–20; and see Bryce, *Kingdom of the Hittites*, 319–21.

118. It may be no coincidence that Tudhaliya's Yalburt inscription (northwest of Konya) lies just across the border from Kurunta's Hatip inscription, which is situated south of Konya in the territory controlled by Tarhuntassa (Singer, "Great Kings of Tarḫuntašša," 65). The Yalburt inscription was not found near the events that it describes and may have been positioned to make a statement.

119. *KUB* 3.67; see also *KUB* 3.66; Edel, *ÄHK*, 170–73 (nos. 71, 72).

had fallen into disrepair.[120] Tudhaliya's program of reorganizing the cult along these lines throughout the kingdom had the goal not only of restoring the favor of the Sun-Goddess but also of reasserting royal authority by making his presence felt throughout the kingdom.[121]

The fact that Tudhaliya was able to rebound from setbacks as serious as an assassination plot and a major military defeat is testimony to his resilience. He left his kingdom to his son Arnuwanda III, whose reign was too short to leave an heir or, for that matter, any archival or monumental records. Arnuwanda's premature death meant that his brother Suppiluliuma II would follow him on the throne, but the succession cannot have been unproblematic.

HATTUSA'S LAST DAYS

Like his father, Suppiluliuma II was preoccupied with the loyalty of his circle of peers. In this respect, the civil war between Mursili III and Hattusili III had taken a serious toll on the political stability of the kingdom. The large extended royal family must have felt that the kingship was effectively up for grabs by the strongest contender. At the end of the day, the kingdom had not learned the lessons of Hattusili I and Telipinu. The result was the undermining of royal authority, which, when combined with losses such as that suffered by Tudhaliya at Nihriya, caused the royal hold on the vassals to loosen as their confidence in their Anatolian overlord ebbed. The documents dating to Suppiluliuma's reign reflect these concerns, as they comprise mostly protocols and instructions regarding matters of internal security.[122]

Although the kingdom that Suppiluliuma II inherited was already in irreversible decline, all was not bleak. Tukulti-ninurta had resumed diplomatic and economic relations with the Hittites. Middle Assyrian tablets from Tell Chuera and Tell Šeih Hamad attest to Hittite diplomats and merchants operating in Assyrian-controlled areas east of the Euphrates,[123] an indication that relations with Assyria were on the mend following the fateful battle of Nihriya.

---

120. *KBo* 12.58 + 13.162 (*CTH* 385.9) obv. 2–11; see Joost Hazenbos, *The Organization of the Anatolian Local Cults during the Thirteenth Century B.C.* (CM 21; Leiden: Brill, 2003), 12.

121. So Franca Pecchioli-Daddi, "The System of Government at the Time of Tuthaliya IV," in *The Life and Times of Ḫattušili III and Tutḫaliya IV* (ed. Theo P. J. van den Hout; PIHANS 103; Leiden: NINO, 2006), 117–30.

122. Singer, "The Battle of Niḫriya," 120.

123. Singer, review of Klengel, *Geschichte des hethitischen Reiches*, 642, with bibliography.

Such indications of normalcy, however, are rare in what was other-wise a reign doomed to disaster. Sometime after Tudhaliya IV's conquest of Alasiya, the island was lost to Hittite control. Suppiluliuma II was forced to mount a new sea campaign involving three naval engagements.[124] These cannot have been entirely successful, as the enemy followed Suppiluliuma onto Anatolian soil for a final land engagement, where the Hittites ultimately prevailed. The need to protect the increasingly fragile supply routes must have been acute. Already in the reign of Hattusili III, the country's growing dependence on shipments of grain from abroad is evident. A letter from the period refers to grain that Ramesses II shipped from Egypt to help alleviate a famine in Hatti.[125] Another shipment was sent in the fifth year of Pharaoh Merneptah to "keep alive the land of Hatti."[126] By the time Niqmaddu III (or Ammurapi?) of Ugarit received a letter from the Hittite king (perhaps Suppi-luliuma II) demanding that he furnish a ship and crew to transport 2,000 kor (ca. 450 metric tons) of grain from Mukish (Alalakh) to Ura on the southern coast of Hatti, the matter had literally become one of life and death.[127] The elaborate grain silos constructed on Büyükkaya in the northwest part of the capital may be a sign of this growing dependence on foreign grain.[128]

Suppiluliuma recorded his Alasiya campaign on the Eternal Peak, the mortuary shrine at Nişantaş that he dedicated to his father in Hattusa. That Suppiluliuma II appears to have directed much of his energy to the construc-tion of such religious monuments has been taken as an indication of his growing desperation, as he appealed to the gods and the manes of the ances-tors for assistance. One of these monuments, a vaulted stone chamber about four meters deep, was decorated with reliefs of the Sun-God and the king (fig.

---

124. *KBo* 12.38 (*CTH* 121) contains the narratives both of Suppiluliuma's conquest of Cyprus and that of his father. The first narrative, recording Tudhaliya's conquest, is a cuneiform copy of a hieroglyphic inscription that originally was inscribed on a statue of Tudhaliya IV and includes a postscript added by Suppiluliuma II. The second text is by Suppiluliuma II himself and was also copied from a monumental hieroglyphic inscrip-tion—the nearly illegible Nişantaş inscription.

125. *KUB* 3.34 (*CTH* 165) rev. 15–17; Edel, *ÄHK*, 182–85 (no. 78); Klengel, " 'Hun-gerjahre' in Hatti," *AoF* 1 (1974): 167 with n. 13.

126. Karnak Inscription; James Henry Breasted, *Ancient Records of Egypt* (5 vols.; repr. of 1906 Chicago edition; London: Histories and Mysteries of Man, 1988), 3:244, §580.

127. RS 20.212; see Jean Nougayrol, *Ugaritica V* (Paris: Guethner, 1968): 105–7, no. 33. For further evidence of attempts to procure grain to alleviate food shortages, see Itamar Singer, "A Political History of Ugarit," in *Handbook of Ugaritic Studies* (ed. Wil-fred G. E. Watson and Nicolas Wyatt; HdO 1/39; Leiden: Brill, 1999), 715–19.

128. Klengel, *Geschichte des hethitischen Reiches*, 311.

Fig. 2.8. The "Südburg" monument formed one corner of a sacred pool complex and served as an entrance to the under-word. Here a relief of the Sun-God receives offerings at the back of the chamber. On the left is a relief of Suppiluliuma II, on the right the inscription recording the events of his last campaign. Photo by the author.

2.8). The structure itself was an entrance to the underworld, by which the royal petitioner could appeal to the gods of that realm for mercy. The chamber also contained a rather problematic hieroglyphic inscription that seems to record Suppiluliuma II's victorious campaigns against rebellious vassals in southwestern Anatolia.[129] If our understanding of the inscription is cor-

---

129. On the dating of the events recounted on the Südburg inscription after those of the Nişantaş inscription, see Singer, "Great Kings of Tarḫuntašša," 67. H. Craig Melchert questions the interpretation of the inscription as narrating the conquest of Tarhuntassa

rect, his campaign covered localities in and around the Lukka lands, some of which Tudhaliya IV had previously engaged, according to the Yalburt inscription. Following this campaign, the inscription reports that he undertook the conquest of Tarhuntassa.[130]

Why were the Lukka lands once again wreaking havoc? More curiously, why was Suppiluliuma II compelled to attack Tarhuntassa, which, so far as we know, had remained at peace with Hattusa even as the territories surrounding it seemed to spiral out of control? Indeed, an Akkadian letter from Ugarit in which an unnamed king of Tarhuntassa requests small ropes, presumably for use on ships or in building activities, from Ammurapi, the last king of Ugarit, indicates that Tarhuntassa retained its status as a kingdom until the last days of the empire.[131] Its ruler now was probably Hartapu, the son of Mursili III (Urhi-Teshub) and nephew and successor of Kurunta, whose recently discovered inscriptions at Karadağ, Kızıldağ, and Burunkaya declare his Great Kingship.[132] One plausible theory maintains that Hartapu sought to expand his holdings and eliminate Hittite control in the south by taking the lands named in the inscription,[133] perhaps with an invasion of Hittite core territory as the eventual goal.[134] Thus, Suppiluliuma's campaigns had the objectives first of recapturing the lost territories and then of conquering the rival kingdom of Tarhuntassa. These events may have occurred not long before the empire's final collapse, as Suppiluliuma himself barely had time to return to Hattusa to complete his victory inscrip-

---

("Tarḫuntašša in the SÜDBURG Hieroglyphic Inscription," in Yener and Hoffner, *Recent Developments in Hittite Archaeology and History*, 137–43).

130. Singer, "New Evidence on the End of the Hittite Empire," 27.

131. RS 34.139; F. Malbran-Labat, "Lettres," in Pierre Bordreuil et al., *Une bibliothèque au sud de la ville* (RSO 7; Paris: Éditions Recherche sur les Civilisations, 1991): 41–42, no. 14; Singer, "Great Kings of Tarḫuntašša," 66, 68.

132. On dating Hartapu to the Late Bronze Age, see Singer, "Great Kings of Tarḫuntašša," 68–71. The events surrounding Tudhaliya's conquest of Tarhuntassa and the survival of that dynasty are vigorously debated. I present here the scenario that in my view is the most plausible based on the present data.

133. Anna Margherita Jasink, "Šuppiluliuma and Hartapu: Two 'Great Kings' in Conflict?" in *Akten des IV. Internationalen Kongresses für Hethitologie Würzburg, 4.–8. Oktober 1999* (ed. Gernot Wilhelm; StBoT 45; Wiesbaden: Harrassowitz, 2001), 235–40; cf. H. Craig Melchert, "Tarḫuntašša in the SÜDBURG Hieroglyphic Inscription," 137–43, who does not believe that the inscription refers to conquest at all but to the dissolution of the city of Tarhuntassa and the removal of its citizens in punishment for crimes against the ancestors.

134. Bryce, "The Secession of Tarhuntassa," 127.

tion on the Südburg monument when he was forced to leave it again—and for the last time.[135]

What exactly caused the empire's collapse? Undoubtedly, internal dissension was a significant contributing factor, as was the secession of Tarhuntassa from the empire. At the same time, the population, especially in the west, was becoming increasingly restive as years of famine brought on by unfavorable climatic conditions in the dry farming regions of Anatolia took their toll. The effects were far-reaching. For example, Emar, a Hittite vassal in Syria, was forced to endure a drastic increase in the tribute it paid to Hatti. The resulting inflation, combined with food shortages, meant that its people were forced to sell their children.[136] For the starving populations of subject territories, however, flight was not an option, since vassal treaties stipulated the return of fugitives.[137] Bound by fear of capture or reprisal, the population stayed the course. Only with the disintegration of the bonds of vassalage and the breakdown of the system that enforced their terms could the inhabitants of Anatolia have risked running away. Local administrations, themselves heavily burdened, could no longer provide a measure of protection. It probably took years, but the dam finally broke, and starving peasants abandoned their villages in droves to seek more favorable conditions by land or sea. These forces, exacerbated by the interference of Tarhuntassa, may already have been at work when Suppiluliuma II came to reassert his authority over the region as recorded in the Südburg Inscription.

Egyptian records from the reigns of Merneptah and Ramesses III describe battles with ship-borne enemies whose unholy alliance included at various times the Sherden, Ekwesh, Lukka, Teresh, Peleset, Tjeker, Shekelesh, Denyen, and Weshesh. Modern scholarship has coined the term "Sea Peoples" to describe these marauders. The origin of these enemies remains one of the most stubborn mysteries of antiquity, but several are now believed to have secure connections to western and south-coastal Anatolia. Besides the equation of the Lukka with the Lycians, the Ekwesh have been connected with the Ahhiyawans,[138] the Teresh (Tyrsenoi) with Lydia, the Tjeker allegedly with the Troad (via the Homeric figure Teucer, who gave his name to the Teucri living in the Troad), and the Denyen (cf. Adana) with Cilicia.

---

135. For the suggestion that "Kammer 1" remained unfinished, see Singer, "Great Kings of Tarḫuntašša," 67.

136. Singer, review of Klengel, *Geschichte des hethitischen Reiches*, 642.

137. Carlo Zaccagnini, "War and Famine at Emar," *Or* 64 (1995): 93 with n. 2.

138. On the possibility that Cilicia was settled at this time by Ahhiyawans/Mycenaean Greeks (=> Hiyawa), see Jak Yakar, "Anatolian Civilization Following the Disintegration of the Hittite Empire: An Archaeological Appraisal," *Tel Aviv* 20 (1993):3–28.

An Aegean or Anatolian point of origin has been proposed as well for the Sherden, Peleset (Philistines), and Shekelesh (Sikila), some of whom, in the diaspora following the crisis, settled along the coast of Palestine (at Acco, in Philistia, and at Dor, respectively).[139] Western Anatolia is the logical genesis for the disturbance, since this is where the political structures first began to disintegrate in the struggle between Hatti and Ahhiyawa for control.[140] The growing ferment in the region was fed by food shortages resulting from a combination of crop failure and disrupted supply routes.

Moreover, the south-coastal regions of Anatolia—Caria, Lycia, and Cilicia—were notorious for their piratical activities as early as the fifteenth century, with Cyprus and Egypt frequent targets. Ramesses II had also complained of Sherden piratical attacks on his coastal towns. The famine that ravaged Anatolia probably turned these scattered raids into vast population movements involving not disenfranchised militants on a pillaging rampage but entire families turned to a marauding lifestyle in the search for new places to settle.[141] For the most part a disorganized and heterogeneous collection of peoples, they were as much victims of as they were contributors to the circumstances that brought the Bronze Age in the Near East to an end.[142]

Suppiluliuma II knew his empire was under serious threat. In a letter that he wrote to a Ugaritic official, he sought to interview someone who had been kidnapped by the Sikila (Shekelesh), "who live on boats," in an effort to gather intelligence.[143] His sea battles with the unnamed enemies off the coast of Cyprus probably had to do with the movements of these dislocated populations. Unfortunately, in appropriating the ships and troops of the king of Ugarit to help in this fight, he left one of his most important subject states vulnerable to attack. Ammurapi complained vociferously in a letter to the king of Alasiya about the damage that seven ships of the enemy had inflicted

---

139. See Itamar Singer, "The Origin of the Sea Peoples and Their Settlement on the Coast of Canaan," in *Society and Economy in the Eastern Mediterranean, ca. 1500–1200 BC* (ed. Michael Heltzer and Edward Lipiński; OLA 23; Leuven: Peeters, 1988), 239–50. Populations of Sherden and Shekelesh also made their way west to settle in Sardinia and Sicily, respectively.

140. Bryce, *Kingdom of the Hittites*, 338–39; Singer, "Origin of the Sea Peoples," 243–44.

141. Itamar Singer, "Western Anatolia in the Thirteenth Century B.C. according to the Hittite Sources," *AnSt* 33 (1983): 217.

142. Bryce, *Kingdom of the Hittites*, 335.

143. RS 34.129, Malbran-Labat "Lettres," 38–39, no. 12.

while his own ships were in the Lukka lands and his army in Hatti.[144] With his depleted resources, the Ugaritic king had no hope of repelling the invaders and was advised by the Hittite viceroy in Karkamis to fortify his capital as best he could and to await the enemy there.

How long the end stages of this crisis took to unfold is unclear. Of the sites from the Aegean as far east as Norşuntepe whose destructions are attributed to this catastrope, the so-called Sea Peoples were most likely responsible only for those that occurred on Cyprus and along the eastern Mediterranean seaboard. These coastal areas, including Ugarit and Tarhuntassa, probably fell very close to 1200 B.C.E.[145] More inland regions were destroyed by other elements a decade or two later.[146] Emar fell in 1185 B.C.E., the second year of Melishipak, probably to Arameans or other local groups.[147] By Ramesses III's eighth year (1175 B.C.E.), as recorded in his inscription at Medinet Habu, the devastation was complete: "All at once the lands were removed and scattered in the fray. No land could stand before their arms, from Hatti, Qode (Cilicia), Karkamis, Arzawa, and Alasiya (Cyprus) on, being cut off at one time."[148]

What about Hattusa? By the time it was put to the torch, the city already lay derelict, its inhabitants having long since evacuated it. The site was devoid of any personal items, furniture, and any but the most basic cultic equipment, a sign that the population had packed up and moved out well before enemies arrived at the gates of the city. The residents and the palace and temple bureaucracy systematically cleared the buildings of their valuables, including the kingdom's most important official records, which explains why so few documents dating to Suppiluliuma II's reign have been recovered. Not for the first time, the royal court apparently fled its capital to find refuge in a safe haven. Their age-old enemy, the Kaska, ever ready to take advantage of

144. RS 20.238 ll. 19–25; Nougayrol, *Ugaritica V*, 87–90, no. 24; however, see Singer, "A Political History of Ugarit," 721, on the possibility that the Ugaritic king's complaint was disingenuous.

145. The *terminus post quem* for the fall of Ugarit is provided by a letter (RS 86.2230) sent to Ammurapi by an official in the reign of Pharaoh Siptah, who ruled from 1197 to 1192 B.C.E. (Singer, "New Evidence on the End of the Hittite Empire," 24).

146. Singer, "Dating the End of the Hittite Empire," *Hethitica* 8 (1987): 413–21; idem, "Origin of the Sea-Peoples," 240.

147. For the suggestion that Emar fell to Arameans, see Singer, "New Evidence on the End of the Hittite Empire," 25; idem, "Dating the End of the Hittite Empire," 418–19.

148. Translation by John A. Wilson, *ANET*, 262; cf. William F. Edgerton and John A. Wilson, *Historical Records of Ramses III: The Texts in Medinet Habu* (SAOC 12; 2 vols; Chicago: University of Chicago Press, 1936), pl. 46.

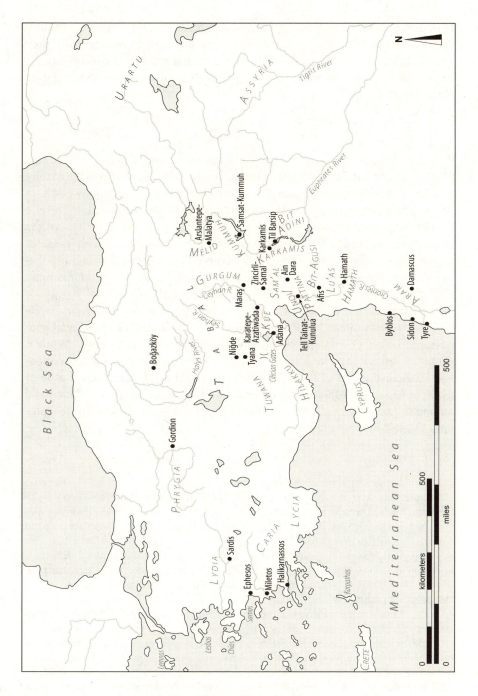

Fig. 2.9. The Neo-Hittite kingdoms.

Hittite weakness, were probably responsible for the final torching of Hattusa, but if so, by the time they arrived, there was little left to pillage. Still, they spared little: the citadel, many of the temples, and areas of the fortifications, including the sacred Sphinx Gate, were consumed by fire. The devastation of Hatti was complete.[149]

THE NEO-HITTITE KINGDOMS

A small segment of the Hittite population of Anatolia, weary of famine, plague, and political upheaval, probably fled the highlands of Anatolia for the relatively peaceful and still somewhat affluent regions of northern Syria, where some measure of Hittite culture could still be found.[150] Despite Ramesses's pronouncement that Karkamis was among the casualties of the catastrophe that ended the Bronze Age, the city itself survived with its architecture and its royal house intact.[151] It is more than a passing possibility that members of the Hittite court found refuge here after evacuating their capital. Karkamis, still in control of much of the eastern half of the empire, was for the moment the strongest power in the region.[152] In such circumstances, its king Kuzi-Teshub can hardly have failed to see himself as the logical successor to Hittite power, and he quickly adopted the title Great King. While it probably did not take long for Karkamis's territories to diminish, nevertheless in the early part of the Iron Age its political influence reached at least as far as Emar and Malatya along the Euphrates, and it would continue to be among the most important and influential of the so-called Neo-Hittite states until the end of the eighth century.

---

149. The Kaska are probably also to be blamed for the destruction of other sites within the Halys basin: Alaca, Alişar, Maşat, and Kuşaklı, as well as Karaoğlan west of the Halys basin. Other local groups are probably to be attributed with the destruction of sites such as Lidar Höyük, Tille Höyük, and Norşuntepe in eastern Anatolia; according to Yakar, to pastoralist groups from the Caucasus/Van region (1993:23).

150. With Yakar, "Anatolian Civilization Following the Disintegration," 3, there is no reason to suppose that the surge of emigres included the majority of the Anatolian population. Most peasants probably returned to their villages soon after the dust had settled and adapted to the new political reality.

151. Ramesses II may have been referring, broadly, to the loss of Karkamis's territories; see, e.g., Bryce, "History," 88.

152. Aleppo, too, had been the seat of a viceroy and perhaps also continued to be ruled by descendants of the Hittites, at least for a time (Sanna Aro, "Art and Architecture," in Melchert, The Luwians, 298); however, the ancient city is inaccessible to archaeologists, since it lies beneath the modern city, so confirmation of this will not be forthcoming.

The eleventh and tenth centuries, the period immediately after the collapse of Hittite power, are poorly represented both archaeologically and textually. By the time we once again have a steady supply of written records to illuminate the history of the region, the ethnic makeup of eastern Anatolia and Syria had changed considerably (fig. 2.9). The political vacuum created by the collapse of Hittite power in Anatolia and Syria allowed for considerable mobility on the part of peripheral groups. In Anatolia, Phrygians (Muski) had settled in the highlands from the west, while the Kasku, to be identified with the Kaska tribes of the Late Bronze Age, had entered the interior of Anatolia as far as the southern bend of the Marassantiya River; the Assyrians later encountered them as far east as the upper Euphrates. The south-coastal areas of Anatolia, on the other hand, enjoyed continuous settlement into the early Iron Age. The relatively isolated regions of Cilicia and Lycia may have retained a portion of their precatastrophe populations while also experiencing an influx of immigrants from inland areas, although there is as yet no archaeological support for this.[153] In Syria, in addition to Luwian-speakers, we find Arameans and Phoenicians, both descendants of the Late Bronze Age populations of Syria.

With the merging of disparate and dynamic populations and in the absence of a strong central authority, the former Hittite provinces rapidly fragmented. We refer to the small kingdoms or city-states that arose at this time collectively as Neo-Hittite. In Anatolia, these included the small kingdoms known to the Assyrians collectively as Tabal,[154] in the area between the upper Halys and the Seyhan Rivers and including parts of the former kingdom of Tarhuntassa, Hilakku (Rough Cilicia), and Kue (the Cilician Plain).[155] In the east, from north to south were Melid, Kummuh, Gurgum, and Karkamis. Just north of the Orontes River lay Unqi/Pattina (Late Bronze Age Mukish) and Samal, and to their east toward the Euphrates was Bit-Agusi. Southward on the Orontes were Lu'as and Hamath. Damascus was the center of the country of Aram. East of the Euphrates opposite Karkamis was Bit-Adini, with its capital at Til Barsip. These states were for the most part strategically located along major trade routes, accounting for their reputation as centers of affluence and sophistication.

---

153. The retention of Luwian place names and the appearance of Luwian onomastic elements in southern Anatolia into the classical period is one indication of this; see Bryce, "History," 101–2.

154. The various states that made up Tabal were ruled from capitals some of which were likely situated at modern Kululu, Kemerhisar, and possibly Niğde.

155. Corresponding to Kizzuwatna in the Late Bronze Age but not as extensive.

The competition between these states often erupted into military conflict, and they were never unified politically. Neo-Assyrian inscriptions nevertheless refer to them individually and together as "Hatti," and it is becoming increasingly clear that they shared a cultural identity (see below). However, it was only in the face of Assyrian aggression that any kind of cooperation was achieved between them.

ASSYRIAN MIGHT

Indigenous monumental inscriptions in stone, while plentiful, are not helpful for reconstructing a history of the period, since they are commemorative and contain few historical references.[156] They do, however, provide names of rulers who also appear in the Assyrian sources, thus providing synchronisms that have contributed to the beginnings of a relative chronology for the region. For the most part, however, we are dependent on Assyrian sources, which, focused as they are on conquest, give a one-sided and one-dimensional view of life in these city-states.

Even the Assyrian sources, however, are limited for the eleventh and tenth centuries. Tiglath-pileser I (1115–1077 B.C.E.) records imposing tribute on a "king of Hatti" named Ini-Teshub (probably a descendant of Kuzi-Teshub, the last Hittite viceroy at Karkamis), as well as on Allumari of Melid, king of "the Great Land of Hatti." In the tenth century, a dynastic struggle seems to have erupted at Karkamis between the line of Great Kings and the members of the house of Suhi, possibly also descendants of Kuzi-Teshub, who bore the title Country Lord. The latter line succeeded in wresting control of the city from the ruling dynasty. Directly after the fall of the Hittite state, Karkamis had continued to control the territories north up to Melid. Melid, too, had been ruled from the twelfth century by a line of Country Lords who claimed descent from Kuzi-Teshub. At some point, perhaps already by the time of Tiglath-pileser I recorded his tribute, this state seceded from Karkamis. These Country Lords of Melid may be responsible for the numerous reliefs excavated from Malatya-Arslantepe, which are among the oldest Iron Age reliefs, dating to the twelfth–eleventh centuries B.C.E.

Ashurnasirpal II (r. 883–859 B.C.E.) was the first Assyrian king to cross the Euphrates since Tiglath-pileser I, and the states closest to the Euphrates were among the first targets of this new wave of Assyrian expansion. He invaded Karkamis (ruled by Sangara), Unqi (ruled by Lubarna), and Luʿas,

---

156. J. David Hawkins, "Karkamish and Karatepe: Neo-Hittite City-States in North Syria," in *CANE*, 1299.

who submitted easily. Shalmaneser III (r. 858–824 B.C.E.) conducted a series of campaigns between 858 and 831 B.C.E., returning to northern Syria, where he conquered Bit-Adini, giving Assyria a bridgehead on the Euphrates. In the 830s he conducted a series of campaigns farther north, in Gurgum and Kummuh, meeting resistance throughout the region. In an inscription from this period, Kulamuwa of Sam'al admits to inviting the interference of the Assyrian king in order to end Kate of Kue's oppression of Samal.[157] Such shifting alliances would become rather commonplace, as we will see.

With his northern flank secured, Shalmaneser turned south to Hamath and Damascus. Toward the end of his reign he returned to Kue and even ventured into Tabal, whose local kings submitted to him. After Shalmaneser, Assyria went into a period of retrenchment, and the Neo-Hittite states were able to reassert some independence.

In the meantime, the kingdom of Urartu around Lake Van had become a major power in the region, and Melid and Kummuh in particular came under its influence. But in a major campaign, Tiglath-pileser III (r. 744–727 B.C.E.) decisively defeated the Urartian-led coalition that included Arpad, Melid, Kummuh, and Gurgum. The list of tributary kingdoms of 738 B.C.E. thus included Kue (ruled by Awariki), Tabal (ruled by Wasusarma), Tuwana (under Warpalawa; fig. 2.10), Samal, Melid, Kummuh, Gurgum, Karkamis (under Pisiri), Hamath, and Damascus. Even the Kaska (under Dadilu) were included in the list.

With Tiglath-pileser III, a concerted program of aggression began. When Unqi and Hamath rebelled in Syria, this Assyrian king raided the states, pillaged their cities, deported their populations, and added them to the list of tributary kingdoms. This policy of destruction and deportation spelled the end for the Neo-Hittite states.

On Sargon's accession (r. 721–705 B.C.E.), a major rebellion broke out under the leadership of Yaubidi of Hamath and supported by Arpad to its north and Damascus and the newly subjected Samaria, capital of the kingdom of Israel in the south. Sargon defeated the coalition, and Yaubidi was flayed, an image that was preserved in relief at the Assyrian capital. In the meantime, a new player had entered the stage in Anatolia. Mita of Mushku, who later entered Greek legend as Midas of Phrygia, ruling from his capital at Gordion, persuaded his neighbor, the Tabalian king Kiakki, to defect from Assyria.[158] Although Sargon retaliated and replaced Kiakki with a more

---

157. J. David Hawkins, *CHLI* I, 1:41.

158. See Maya Vasileva, "King Midas in Southeastern Anatolia," in Collins, Bachvarova, and Rutherford, *Anatolian Interfaces*.

Fig. 2.10. Warpalawa king of Tuwana is depicted in this relief from İvriz with his personal deity, the Storm-God of the vineyard. From Kurt Bittel, *Les Hittites* (Paris: Gallimard, 1976), pl. 328.

loyal ruler, Midas continued to interfere, this time with Pisiri of Karkamis. As a result, in 717 B.C.E. the population of Karkamis and its royal house were deported, and the city was raided and made into a provincial capital. A similar fate befell Tabal (718 and 715), Melid (712), Gurgum (711), and Kummuh (708).

Midas now suddenly adopted a new policy with Assyria, helping Sargon against the former king of Kue, Awarikku, who, now in exile, had been seeking an alliance with Urartu against Assyria. Urartu, however, was threatened by the arrival of a new threat in the region, namely, Cimmerian marauders from the north, to whom they succumbed in about 714 B.C.E. Indeed, it was probably this new threat that motivated Midas's *volte face*. In 705, at Midas's invitation, Sargon II intervened in Tabal against the Cimmerians, only to fall in battle. Midas would suffer the same fate only ten years later.

The sudden death of Sargon forced Assyria to give up much of the control of the northern provinces of Tabal, Melid, and Kue. Sennacherib (r. 704–681 B.C.E.) campaigned in Cilicia in 696 against a revolt centered in Hilakku (Rough Cilicia). Ruling from his fortress at Karatepe, Azatiwada may have taken the side of Assyria at this time. Esarhaddon (r. 680–669 B.C.E.) returned to Tabal in 679 to face the Cimmerians, this time successfully; however, Tabal and Melid retained their independence and may have united into a single state. Not long after, Sanduarri, ruler of the cities Kundu and Sissu, probably to be located in Kue, joined Abdi-Milkutti of Sidon in an unsuccessful revolt against Esarhaddon, who captured and beheaded him in 676 B.C.E. With this, Kue was returned to Assyrian control and probably remained so during the reign of Ashurbanipal (r. 668–627 B.C.E.). If Sanduarri is to be identified with Azatiwada, as has been proposed, then the Karatepe bilingual is the latest known example of the Luwian hieroglyphs, ending a script tradition that began in the sixteenth century.

The Question of Continuity

It had not taken long for the Syrian cities to reinvent themselves after the collapse of the empire of the Hittites. Already in the second half of the twelfth century, the region entered a period of reurbanization that would continue through the ninth century.[159] Many of the cities belonging to the Neo-Hittite polities of the tenth to eighth centuries were either new foundations or refoundations of older cities.[160] Such building activities were frequently the object of boasting in the hieroglyphic inscriptions of the Neo-Hittite rulers. Like their Anatolian and Syrian predecessors, the Neo-Hittite kings ruled

---

159. Stefania Mazzoni, "Syria and the Periodization of the Iron Age: A Cross-Cultural Perspective," in *Essays on Syria in the Iron Age* (ed. Guy Bunnens; ANES 7; Leuven: Peeters, 2000), 32. The significant exceptions are Ugarit, Alalakh, and Emar, which were never resettled.

160. Foundations: Samal, Azitawantiya, Guzana (Tell Halaf), Hadatu (Arslan Taş); refoundations: Hama, Til Barsip, Aleppo (?), Damascus (?); cities with new importance: Arpad, Tainat, Hatarikka (Tell Afis), Sakçagözü; see Horst Klengel, "The 'Crisis Years' and the New Political System in Early Iron Age Syria: Some Introductory Remarks," in Bunnens, *Essays on Syria in the Iron Age*, 28.

from atop a citadel overlooking a lower town, although the palace-centered economy of the previous era now gave way to the smaller economies of family households.[161] The royal inscriptions of this period also reflect a new emphasis on familial descent from the founder of the dynasty.[162]

This new urbanization was part of an emergent regionalism that is also apparent in the adoption of a new ideology of kingship.[163] That the rulers of southeastern Anatolia and northern Syria wanted to be perceived as the successors of Hittite authority is most obvious in their use of royal names from the empire: note, in particular, Qatazili at Gurgum, Uspilulume and Mutallu at Kummuh,[164] Arnuwantis at Malatya, and Lubarna and Sapalulme at Unqi. Also like their Hittite predecessors, these kings were responsible for the security and prosperity of the country and its inhabitants. As late as the end of the eighth century, Azatiwada boasted:

> In my days I extended the Adanawean frontiers on the one hand toward the west and on the other hand toward the east, and even in those places that were formerly feared, where a man fears to walk the road, so in my days even women walk with spindles. In my days there was plenty and luxury and good living, and peacefully dwelt Adanawa and the Adanawean plain. I built this fortress, and to it I put the name Azatiwataya … for it to be a protection for the plain of Adana and for the house of Mopsos.[165]

Another key element in this new ideology and the reurbanization that accompanied it was an artistic revival. Because they had been so closely connected to royal ideology, Hittite artistic and architectural styles became the trademark of the Neo-Hittite kingdoms, which sought to incorporate a visual form of propaganda into their urban planning. The wholesale adoption of gate lions as well as sphinxes, some of them inscribed, and the use of carved orthostat blocks on temples, palaces, and gate entrances were part of the systematic formation of a common urban ideology, most likely following the model established at Karkamis, whose kings Suhi II and Katuwa (see fig.

---

161. Ibid., 26.

162. On this as an Aramean influence, see ibid., 28.

163. On the emergence of Luwian city-states in North Syria in the Iron Age as a cultural choice, see Guy Bunnens, "Syria in the Iron Age: Problems of Definition," in Bunnens, *Essays on Syria in the Iron Age*, 17.

164. Trevor Bryce has speculated that the Iron Age Mutallu could even have been a direct descendent of Muwatalli II ("The Secession of Tarhuntassa," 127–28).

165. KARATEPE 1 §§XXXII–XLIII; adapted from translation by J. David Hawkins, *CHLI* I, 1:52–54.

1.2) were responsible for building that city's famed Processional Entry and Long Wall of Sculpture in the tenth century.[166]

Equally important to the creation of a new cultural identity was the adoption of the hieroglyphic script. Why the Neo-Hittite rulers chose to ignore the cuneiform script and the Hittite language in favor of hieroglyphs and Luwian for their inscriptions is unclear. That Luwian had to compete with Phoenician and Aramaic, among others, in the mixed culture of the Neo-Hittite cities is evident in the boast of Yariri, a ruler of Karkamis:

> [...] in the City's writing (Luwian hieroglyphs), in the Suraean writing (Urartean?), in the Assyrian writing and in the Taimani writing (Aramaic?), and I knew twelve languages. My lord *gathered* every country's son to me by wayfaring concerning language, and he caused me to know every skill.[167]

The success of hieroglyphic Luwian may have been due in part to the fact that it was especially well suited to a program of visual propaganda, even becoming a part of the monumental architectural decoration, and so was easily integrated into the new urban ideology. However, the adoption of Luwian hieroglyphs was not merely a trapping of kingship,[168] as the script and language would not have been used had no one been able to understand it.[169] The hieroglyphs were employed not only for monumental stelae but also for letters, contracts, and legal documents, which were written on perishable materials that have not survived, such as waxed writing boards[170] and leather. Fortunately, the chance discovery of administrative documents in the form of strips of lead inscribed with hieroglyphic writing confirms that the script could be applied to everyday uses.[171] It is thus possible that the Neo-

---

166. On the emulation of Karkamis artistic styles, see Mazzoni, "Syria and the Periodization of the Iron Age," 38. On the attribution of the architecture to these kings, see Hawkins, "Karkamish and Karatepe," 1302; Aro, "Art and Architecture," 299.

167. KARKAMIS A15b §§18–22; translated by J. David Hawkins, *CHLI* I, 1:131; see also 133 on the identification of the scripts.

168. Bryce ("History," 125) notes that in Lycia and Rough Cilicia, where we have continuity of population, no hieroglyphic inscriptions have been found, which could be taken as a sign that the adoption of the hieroglyphs was a deliberate effort at creating an identity for those who used them.

169. Hawkins, "Karkamish and Karatepe," 1297.

170. As we know from the stela of Bar-rakib of Samal that depicts a scribe holding a hinged diptych, i.e., a wooden writing board, although we do not know in which language he was writing.

171. The examples of this small corpus from modern Kululu, once a part of the kingdom of Tabal, are supplemented by six letters excavated at Assur, all dating perhaps to

Hittite rulers simply opted for the language and script most familiar to them. By the end of the Bronze Age, and through a process that is not yet fully understood, Luwian had become the vernacular in Anatolia.[172] Moreover, the cities of northern Syria in the Late Bronze Age were already home to a small number of Luwian-speakers, a fact that no doubt facilitated the adoption of the hieroglyphs as the new official script.[173]

Even the erection of funerary monuments to memorialize the dead, royal and nonroyal alike, can be understood in the context of the dynamic process of renewal and the search for a new identity.[174] While the custom of honoring the dead with mortuary rites was known in both Anatolia and Syria well before the first millennium, the widespread use of funerary monuments was an innovation introduced in the Neo-Hittite cities in the ninth and eighth centuries.[175] Funerary monuments with depictions of the deceased as objects of worship became, along with dynastic genealogies, a vehicle for the assertion and maintenance of identity and played an important role in the process of planning and proclaiming new cities and states.[176] The practice was symptomatic of a society that placed emphasis on a personal afterlife and is consistent with a new focus on the family as a symbol of social order.[177]

It is in the area of funerary beliefs, among the most conservative of human activities, where the strongest arguments for religious continuity with the Anatolian past have been made, but the evidence has proved equivocal.

---

the eighth century; see Hawkins, "Scripts and Texts," in Melchert, *The Luwians*, 151 and pl. III.c.

172. Theo P. J. van den Hout ("Institutions, Vernaculars, Publics: The Case of Second-Millennium Anatolia," in *Margins of Writing, Origins of Cultures* [ed. Seth L. Sanders; Chicago: The Oriental Institute of the University of Chicago, 2006], 237) has suggested that the plague that decimated the population hit especially hard in the Hittite heartland, thus stimulating a linguistic imbalance that favored Luwian-speakers.

173. On the presence of Luwian elements in northern Syria (at Emar, Ugarit, Tell Afis, and Hama), see Mazzoni, "Syria and the Periodization of the Iron Age," 34 n. 13; cf. Bryce, "History," 127.

174. Singer sees continuity with the funerary monuments in the tendency in the early Iron Age to inscribe or decorate stone shafts marking the burial ground; see Singer, "The Hittites and the Bible Revisited," in *"I Will Speak the Riddle of Ancient Times": Archaelogical and Historical Studies in Honor of Amihai Mazar on the Occasion of His Sixtieth Birthday* (ed. Aren M. Maeir and Pierre de Miroschedji; Winona Lake, Ind.: Eisenbrauns, 2006), 742.

175. Dominik Bonatz, "Syro-Hittite Funerary Monuments: A Phenomenon of Tradition or Innovation?" in Bunnens, *Essays on Syria in the Iron Age*, 193–202.

176. Ibid., 207, 210.

177. Ibid., 193.

The seemingly sudden appearance of cemeteries with cremation burials (the burial of urns containing the cremated ashes of the dead) in areas of Syria-Palestine where cremation had previously been unknown has been viewed as evidence of new populations arriving from Hittite lands. However, cremation had already been introduced to northern Syria in the Late Bronze Age, as indicated particularly by the finds at Alalakh.[178] (No Late Bronze Age cemetery has been found at Karkamis to attest to continuity or discontinuity with its Iron Age cemetery at Yunus, where cremation was the norm.) Thus, the notion that cremation was introduced by Anatolian refugees in the Iron Age becomes less likely, particularly when one considers that this form of disposal could be adapted independently of religious beliefs; economic, sociological, and cultural factors can also play an important role in the choice of burial practices.[179] In a socially mobile environment like that of Iron Age Syria, perhaps under certain social pressures, individuals or communities chose to practice cremation over inhumation. The choice was not ethnically driven, and the presence of cremation burials alone cannot be used to assume the presence of a large population of Luwians or other Anatolians in Syria.

In other areas of religious belief, Karkamis and other Hittite centers in the region probably never really conformed with the Hittite state religion but rather favored local forms of worship, so religious continuity with Late Bronze Anatolia is unlikely to have been an issue from the very beginning. Rather than the Storm-God and the Sun-Goddess of the Hittite pantheon, in Iron Age Karkamis we find a divine triad comprising the Storm-God, the city-goddess Kubaba, and the protective deity Karhuha. In the Hamathite inscriptions, on the other hand, the Storm-God is identified with Syrian Baal, whose consort is Baalat (or Pahalatis). The Storm-God, who was important in both Anatolia and Syria in the Bronze Age, continued to be important throughout these areas in the Iron Age, although his character may have been modified to reflect a growing emphasis on plenty and abundance (fig. 2.10).[180] The reference to the gods of grain and wine beside the Storm-God Tarhunza in Azatiwada's inscription at Karatepe is a conscious advertisement for the prosperity of the polity:

---

178. Piotr A. Bienkowski, "Some Remarks on the Practice of Cremation," *Levant* 14 (1982) 80–89; Mazzoni, "Syria and the Periodization of the Iron Age," 35.

179. See Bienkowski, "Some Remarks on the Practice of Cremation," 83–84, 87, who points out that the Iron Age cremations are not all uniform but show different practices, which belies a common origin among the Hittites.

180. Manfred Hutter, "Aspects of Luwian Religion," in Melchert, *The Luwians*, 276–77.

And may Tarhunza the highly blessed and this fortress's gods give to him, Azatiwada, long days and many years and good abundance, and let them give him all victory over all kings. And so let this fortress become (one) of the Grain-god and the Wine-god.[181]

The religion of the various centers reflected local customs that underwent regional developments consonant with changing political and cultural influences. Among these developments was the introduction of the goddess Kubaba in both Tabal and Kue (at Karatepe) and of Ea in Kue, no doubt a consequence of the dominance of Karkamis.[182] Similarly, the worship of the sun and moon, who are depicted in the reliefs at Karkamis, also now appear among the pantheon in Tabal and Kue.

The presence of Luwian/Hittite dynasts at Karkamis and Malatya provided a measure of stability in a period of dynamic change and formed the basis for the generation of a new cultural identity. Cultural and political interaction between Syria and Anatolia continued, as attested by substantial imports of Anatolian pottery into Syria.[183] The characteristics of the Neo-Hittite states that have been used to diagnose an Anatolian presence in the region—cremation, Luwian hieroglyphs, and artistic and architectural styles—confirm that these royal lines continued to wield considerable cultural influence in northern Syria but do not support the idea of a major migration of Anatolians or Luwians into Syria following the collapse of the Hittite Empire.[184]

---

181. KARATEPE 1, §§LI–LIII; translated by J. David Hawkins, *CHLI* I, 1:55.

182. On the religion of Tabal, see Hutter, "Aspects of Luwian Religion," 270–75. For more on the shifting pantheons of these cities under Phoenician and Aramean influence, see Herbert Niehr, "Religiöse Wechselbeziehungen zwischen Syrien und Anatolien," in *Brückenland Anatolien?* (ed. Hartmut Blum, Betina Faist, Peter Pfälzner, and Anne-Maria Wittke; Tübingen: Attempto, 2002), 339–62.

183. Mazzoni, "Syria and the Periodization of the Iron Age," 36.

184. See, e.g., Paul Zimansky, "The 'Hittites' at 'Ain Dara," in Yener and Hoffner, *Recent Developments in Hittite Archaeology and History*, 179. The temple at Ain Dara, which has been dated to the final two centuries of the second millennium, was a fusion of Syrian sacred architecture (the tripartite plan) and Anatolian decoration (gate lions), but Zimansky argues that there is no evidence that Anatolian tastes permeated the rest of the society. Although we do not know who was worshiped in the temple, it is unlikely that it was a Hittite deity, and we cannot assume based on artistic echoes that Luwians or Hittites formed a significant part of the population of this, or indeed any, Neo-Hittite city.

3

SOCIETY

ANATOLIA DID NOT LACK FOR ARABLE LAND that farmers could cultivate without having to rely on irrigation or for pasturage on which shepherds could graze their herds. Each man, woman, and child at every level of society was dependent directly on the productivity of the land. For this reason, the Hittite worldview was deeply rooted in agrarian concerns of fertility and the maintenance of balance and order in an unpredictable world. Any disruption of the natural balance could be devastating, as became painfully obvious when famine wracked key parts of the empire in its last decades. For these reasons, a ritual that was performed when a new town was established lists qualities such as well-being and opulence among the blessings it seeks to secure for the land.[1] This list of blessings also includes two abstract concepts, rightness (^{d}*āraš*) and providence, or divine justice (*handandatar*). The latter may be understood as the divine promise of an ordered, just, and balanced world. Where *handandatar* made possible the correct functioning of the world, *āra* "right, acceptable, permitted" circumscribed human behavior. The term *āra* and its inverse *natta āra* "wrong, unacceptable, not permitted" identified what was considered appropriate and civilized, that is, normative, behavior in Hittite society.[2] Like *handandatar*, *āra* was bestowed by the gods; thus it had to do with divine law as distinguished from human law and, in religious contexts, with the sacred as opposed to the profane. As we will see, these norms were formalized in the laws, treaties, diplomatic and historiographic texts, and cultic procedures that originated in the royal chancelleries.

---

1. *KUB* 17.20 (*CTH* 492) ii 1–16; see Volkert Haas, *Geschichte der hethitischen Religion* (HdO 1/15; Leiden: Brill, 1994), 258.

2. See Yoram Cohen, "The Image of the 'Other' and Hittite Historiography," in *Historiography in the Cuneiform World* (ed. Tzvi Abusch et al.; Bethesda, Md.: CDL), 113–29; idem, *Taboos and Prohibitions in Hittite Society: A Study of the Hittite Expression* natta āra *("Not Permitted")* (THeth 24; Heidelberg: Universitätsverlag, Winter, 2002).

GOVERNANCE

THE KINGSHIP

The ideology of kingship prior to the thirteenth century found its clearest expression in the reign of Hattusili I, the first historical king of the Hittites. From the moment that this ambitious ruler crossed the Euphrates River for the first time, intent on expanding Hittite interests in Syria, the expectation that Hittite kings should engage actively in military campaigning became a fundamental principle of kingship. His military successes determined a king's fitness to rule, and only when age, illness, or other obligations prevented his direct participation in war did the Hittite king delegate military responsibility to his direct heir (the Tuhkanti) and trusted generals. Hattusili I went to particularly great lengths to portray himself as a ferocious and deadly enemy. Possessing superhuman qualities, he fell upon his enemy like a lion pouncing on its prey: "In a matter of days I crossed the Ceyhan River and overthrew (?) Hassuwa like a lion with its paws."[3] His heir was expected to follow in his awe-inspiring footsteps, since "the god [will install only] a lion in the place of the lion."[4]

Such was Hattusili I's legacy that he became to later generations a paradigmatic figure for all that kingship should be. This reputation may not have been unduly earned, as the documents from his reign suggest. His Edict cautions a young Mursili (I) with the words, "Let [no] one think, 'In secret the king [does] what he pleases (saying), "I can justify it, whether it is (right), or whether it is not (right)." ' "[5] Still, the king had to exercise independent judgment, acting according to his own instincts and not depending on the advice of others: "My Son, always do what is in your heart."[6] And, as fierce and merciless as he was in battle, in his rule he was to exercise justice and mercy. Hattusili I's annalistic account of his own reign was as quick to boast of his compassion as of his conquests:

> I, the Great King Tabarna,[7] took the hands of (the enemy's) slave girls from the handmills, and I took the hands of his (male) slaves from the sicles, and I freed them from the taxes and the corvée. I unloosed their belts (fetters?), and I gave them over to My Lady, the Sun-Goddess of Arinna.[8]

---

3. *KBo* 10.2 (*CTH* 4) ii 17–19 (Hittite); *KBo* 10.1 obv. 34–36 (Akkadian).
4. *KUB* 1.16 (*CTH* 6) ii 39.
5. "Bilingual Edict of Ḫattušili," translated by Gary Beckman (*COS* 2.15:234, §10).
6. Ibid., §22.
7. An alternative spelling of Labarna, a standard part of the royal titulary (see below).
8. *KBo* 10.2 (*CTH* 4) iii 15–20.

This ideology is carried over to a text authored by a high-ranking official named Pimpira, believed to be the guardian of Mursili I during his minority, which provides a model for ideal princely behavior that is reminiscent of Egyptian wisdom texts:

> To the one who is hungry give bread, [to the one who is weary (?)] give oil, to the one who is naked [give] clothing. If he suffers the heat, [place him where it is cool.] If he suffers the cold, [place] him [where it is warm].[9]

The kingship was a sacred appointment, but, although the king's rule was divinely mandated, it was the gods, not he, who owned the land over which he served as steward:

> May the Tabarna, the king, be dear to the gods! The land belongs to the storm-god alone. Heaven, earth, and the people belong to the storm-god alone. He has made the Labarna, the king, his administrator and given him the entire Land of Hatti. The Labarna shall continue to administer with his hand the entire land. May the storm-god destroy whoever should approach the person of the Labarna, [the king], and the borders (of Hatti)![10]

As the protegé of the national deity, the Storm-God or, later, the Sun-Goddess of Arinna, the king acted as his or her chief priest. The Sun-Goddess was said to run before the king in battle, thus ensuring his victory. From the earliest records, the throne-deity Halmasuitt was a divine patron of the office she symbolized. In a ritual for the foundation of the king's palace, she delivered the insignias of power to the king.[11] The kings of the empire period also enjoyed the protection of a personal deity. In monumental reliefs as well as on seals, the personal deity is sometimes shown protectively embracing the king, as Sharruma embraces Tudhaliya IV at Yazılıkaya. Muwatalli II's prayer to his personal deity, the Storm-God of Lightning, credits the deity with giving him refuge. Similarly, Hattusili III credits Shaushga of Samuha with taking him by the hand and giving him kingship over the land. Mursili II sought the blessing of his god, Telipinu, through prayer:

> Grant to the king, the queen, the princes and the land of Hatti life, health, vigor, longevity, and brightness of spirit forever! Grant forever growth of

---

9. *KBo* 3.23 (*CTH* 24) iv 7'–10'; see Alfonso Archi, "L'humanité des Hittites," in *Florilegium Anatolicum: Mélanges offerts à Emmanuel Laroche* (Paris: de Boccard, 1979), 41–42.

10. *IBoT* 1.30 (*CTH* 821) 2–8; translated by Gary Beckman, "Royal Ideology and State Administration in Hittite Anatolia," *CANE*, 530.

11. *KUB* 29.1 (*CTH* 414) i 23–24.

grain, vines, fruit-trees (?), cattle, sheep, goats, pigs, mules, asses, together
with the beasts of the field, and mankind.[12]

As this petition suggests, a blessing on the king and his family was synony-
mous with a blessing on the land. As the personification of the Hittite state,
the king was directly accountable for any divine disfavor that brought adver-
sity to Hatti. The state administration effectively functioned in large part
to maintain the balance between the human and divine worlds, and prayers
composed in the royal chancellery often served as a kind of legal defense
or justification before the gods. In this way Arnuwanda I and Asmunikal
appealed to the Sun-Goddess to spare Hatti from the ravages of the Kaska:

> Only Hatti is a true, pure land for you gods, and only in the land of Hatti do
> we repeatedly give you pure, great, fine sacrifices. Only in the land of Hatti
> do we establish respect for you gods. § Only you gods know by your divine
> spirit that no one had ever taken care of your temples as we have. § No [one]
> had ever shown more reverence to your [rites (?)]; no one had ever taken care
> of your divine goods—silver and gold rhyta, and garments—as we have.[13]

Surely the goddess could see that the king and queen had done nothing to
warrant her sending the Kaska as an instrument of divine punishment! In
return for their divine favor, the gods received sustenance and care from the
king and his subjects. The dependence of the divine sphere on human toil is
manifest in the fact that temples received a share of the booty of war and a
percentage of the agricultural production.

As the symbolic representative of the land of Hatti and its chief priest, the
king was required to put in an appearance at the most important state festivals. For the most part, however, he remained a passive observer of the ritual
entertainments taking place before him. Some kings, such as Mursili II, were
so devout that major campaigns were postponed while important festivals
were carried out. Others, like Suppiluliuma I, sometimes neglected their religious duties in favor of their martial activities. Such delinquincy invariably
caught up with the king, or his successor, who would have to make restitution
of one kind or another. It fell to Mursili II, for example, to make amends for
past neglect of a religious cult, as he notes in his prayer to the Storm-God
regarding the plague that ravaged the land during his reign,

> [The matter of the plague] continued to trouble [me, and I inquired about
> it] to the god [through an oracle]. [I found] two old tablets: one tablet dealt

---

12. Translated by Singer, *Hittite Prayers*, 56 (no. 9).
13. Ibid., 41 (no. 5).

with [the ritual of the Mala River]. Earlier kings performed the ritual of the Mala River, but because [people have been dying] in Hatti since the days of my father, we never performed [the ritual] of the Mala River.... As for the [ritual] of the Mala River, which was established for me as a cause for the plague, since I am herewith on my way [to] the Mala River, forgive me, O Storm-god of Hatti, my lord, and O gods, my lords, for (neglecting) the ritual of the Mala River. I am going to perform the ritual of the Mala River, and I will carry it out.[14]

Upon his enthronement, the Hittite king was anointed with fine oil and received the "name of kingship," that is, his throne name. Thus, Tashmi-Sharri became Tudhaliya III, Urhi-Teshub became Mursili III, and so on. He was also provided with the royal vestments, the robe and cap in which the kings were regularly depicted in Hittite relief art (see fig. 3.1). Although priests presumably administered this important rite of passage, the king's anointment was an act of the gods.[15] A Palaic passage invokes the Sun-God: "to *tabarna* the king you are indeed the father (and) the mother. Anoint him, and exalt him now! You will both see/build him high (and) see/build him strong."[16] As this passage suggests, the divine anointing of the kings had two goals: ritual cleansing in preparation for the king's role as priest ("build him high"); and empowerment in preparation for the king's role as military leader ("build him strong").[17]

The king was also the highest judicial body in the land, and in theory all subjects of the realm had recourse to his court. He personally sat in judgment on the most serious cases, even when the circumstances of the crime prevented him from coming into contact with the accused, and heard appeals on cases that had been adjudicated without resolution in the lower courts.

---

14. Ibid., 58–59 (no. 11).

15. An incantation in the Palaic language suggests that the anointing of the king was the responsibility of the gods. For a list of Hurrian and Hittite passages that also refer to anointing, see Ilya Yakubovich, "Were Hittite Kings Divinely Anointed? A Palaic Invocation to the Sun-God and Its Significance for Hittite Religion," *JANER* 5 (2005): 122–37.

16. *KUB* 35.165 obv. 21–23 and *KUB* 32.17 : 7'–9' (*CTH* 751); translated by Yakubovich, "Were Hittite Kings Divinely Anointed," 121.

17. Among the civilizations of the ancient Near East, only the Hittites and the Israelites anointed their kings. Although they borrowed the idea of kingship, and presumably its trappings, from their neighbors in Mesopotamia and Egypt (1 Sam 8:19–20), the possibility that the Israelites imported the idea of anointing from the Hittite world, either via the Hurrians in the second millennium or the Neo-Hittites states in the first, must be considered; see Yakubovich, "Were Hittite Kings Divinely Anointed," 135.

Fig. 3.1. In this relief of Tudhaliya IV in the main chamber of the rock sanctuary at Yazılıkaya, the king is dressed in the attire of the Sun-God. Photo by the author.

Even officials in the remotest outposts of the kingdom could hope to defend themselves against slander and abuse directly before their imperial overlord. Challenging the judgment of the king or of his appointee was itself a capital offense: "If anyone rejects a judgment of the king, his house will become a heap of ruins. If anyone rejects a judgment of a magistrate, they shall cut off his head."[18]

18. Law 173a; translated by Harry A. Hoffner Jr. in Martha T. Roth, *Law Collections from Mesopotamia and Asia Minor* (2nd ed.; SBLWAW 6; Atlanta: Scholars Press,

When he was not campaigning, attending to his religious duties, or dispensing judicial decisions, the king was heavily engaged in matters of diplomacy. Composing letters, negotiating treaties, and settling disputes among his vassals were all unavoidable parts of his routine. Although the Hittite kings did not boast of it in their official records to the extent that Mesopotamian and Egyptian kings did, building was also an important element of kingship. Some kings stand out in this respect. Hantili II claimed to have fortified Hattusa; Mursili II completed the foundation of the new city of Emar just upstream from the old one, establishing a new vassal kingdom in the process; Hattusili took considerable pride in restoring the sacred city of Nerik; and Tudhaliya IV and Suppiluliuma II significantly embellished the religious establishments at Hattusa.

The royal titulary always began with the title "Labarna" (sometimes spelled "Tabarna") and the king's name, followed by a series of epithets. He was proclaimed "Great King," indicating his high status among the kings of the ancient Near East. This was followed by the titles "King of the Land of Hatti," reflecting his administrative role, and "Hero," reflecting his military role. Occasionally a king was also identified as the "beloved of the god(dess) such-and-such," indicating his special relationship to his personal deity. Finally, the kings, beginning even before Suppiluliuma I the Great, referred to themselves as "My Sun" (i.e., "My Majesty"), a reminder of their intimate connection with the Sun-God of Heaven, the divine dispenser of justice.[19]

With the reign of Muwatalli II, kings were represented for the first time in the iconography, both glyptic and reliefs. They are represented either in ceremonial attire that mirrored the dress of the Sun-God (fig. 3.1) or, beginning with Mursili III (Urhi-Teshub), battle-ready, in the short kilt worn by warrior-gods, including even the peaked cap usually reserved for the gods. The king's ceremonial dress also included an axe and a shepherd's crook that was a symbol of his office. When the king appeared in warrior guise, bow and spear replaced the crook. The winged sun-disk typically accompanied images of the king and was placed above his hieroglyphic name, which was flanked by his titles "Great King" and "Labarna" in the hieroglyphic script. The sacralization of the person of the king that is reflected in the royal images escalated in inverse proportion to the security of the institution itself,

---

1997), 234.

19. On the possibility that the connection between the king and the Sun-God goes back to the Early Bronze Age, as evidenced by the Alaca Höyük tombs, see Beckman, " 'My Sun-God': Reflections of Mesopotamian Conceptions of Kingship among the Hittites," in *Ideologies as Intercultural Phenomena* (ed. Antonio C. D. Panaino and Giovanni Pettinato; Melammu Symposia 3; Milan: Associazione Culturale Mimesis, 2002), 38.

culminating with Tudhaliya IV, who adopted the Mesopotamian title "King of the World" and added the "horns of divinity" to his royal portraits, indicating his elevation during his lifetime to the status of a god.[20]

Aside from the apparent apotheosis of Tudhaliya IV and his successor Suppiluliuma II, Hittite kings did not enjoy divine status during their lifetimes, as in Egypt, but only "became gods," as the Hittite phrase goes, upon their deaths. This concept did not imply that the former kings could operate on a divine level like other gods but rather was an extension of the Hittite belief that unhappy ghosts had the power to trouble the living. Superhuman in life, a royal ghost had considerably more power than that of an ordinary person and so logically belonged among the gods. Offering lists for deceased royalty were dedicated to ensuring that the former kings and their immediate family received the appropriate offerings in order to forestall any potential harm a royal ghost might inflict upon the land.

In contrast to the intimacy that the Hittite king enjoyed with the divine sphere, his connection to his subjects was guarded. This relationship is expressed officially in the imagery of the shepherd protecting his flock: "May the land of Hatti graze abundantly (?) in the hand of the *labarna* (i.e., the king) and *tawananna* (i.e., the queen), and may it expand!"[21] In reality, however, outside of his family and principal advisors, the king probably had almost no contact with the people he ruled, living instead an isolated existence designed in part to preserve his life and in part to protect him from pollution. As priest of the gods, the king's purity was a matter of considerable concern, and the lives of those whose carelessness jeopardized his higher state were forfeit. One cannot help but wonder what the average farmer or coppersmith privately thought of this remote figure.

THE QUEENSHIP

The woman who bore the title Great Queen was the first-rank wife of the king, and her primary role was to provide first-rank children. For the most

---

20. Theo van den Hout, "Tuthalija IV. und die Ikonographie hethitischer Großkönige des 13. Jhs.," *BiOr* 52 (1995): 545–73; Beckman, "My Sun-God," 37–43. Tudhaliya IV's building projects in the Upper City, even if not as extensive as previously thought, may have been in imitation of Tukulti-ninurta's own such program, perhaps even with the similar goal of winning over the nobility to a new ideological program; see Singer, "A City of Many Temples," 42; for Tukulti-ninurta, see Peter Machinist, "Literature as Politics: The Tukulti-Ninurta Epic and the Bible," *CBQ* 28 (1976): 455–82.

21. *KUB* 57.63 (*CTH* 385.10) ii 12–15 with duplicate *KUB* 57.60; translated by Singer, *Hittite Prayers*, 26 (no. 3, §7').

Fig. 3.2. A reconstruction of the citadel at Hattusa, which included the royal residence, several shrines, the palace archives, a reception hall, and several courtyards and cisterns. Courtesy of the Bogazköy-Archive, Deutsches Archäologisches Institut.

part, queens were selected from among the prominent families within the empire, although a few were foreign-born. The reigning queen bore the title "Tawananna," a position she retained until her death. If she outlived her husband, she continued as ruling queen into the reign of his successor. The queen operated primarily within the harem on the royal citadel (Büyükkaya; fig. 3.2), overseeing the royal household, which included the royal concubines and their children. As chief priestess of the gods, she also figured prominently in the cults of the state pantheon, presiding over ceremonies and performing other functions, which included managing the assets of certain temples or religious endowments. Her cultic duties sometimes took her to religious centers outside the capital. Like their husbands, the queens were entitled to a funerary cult upon their deaths, and, just as the kings were identified with the Sun-God of Heaven, the queen was identified with the Sun-Goddess of Arinna and was represented in death by an image of this goddess in a temple.[22]

With the kings' frequent absences from the capital, the drama and intrigue at court could, and frequently did, reach a crescendo. Hattusili I had ostracized both his sister, "the snake," who had aggressively pursued

22. Beckman, "My Sun-God," 40–41 with n. 45.

her son's interests,[23] and his daughter, who may have had aspirations to the throne for her own sons, for their treasonous acts against him. Mursili I's sister Harapsili, having conspired in his assassination, met with divine retribution when she, together with her sons, was killed, probably at the hands of the Hurrians. Tudhaliya II had been the target of his sister Ziplantawi's sorcerous activities.[24] Henti, the mother of Suppiluliuma's five known sons, was banished, perhaps to Ahhiyawa.[25] Suppiluliuma subsequently married a Babylonian princess who bore the title Tawananna as a name, and it may be that Henti's only offense was that she stood in the way of the king making a politically advantageous marriage. Tawananna was also responsible, according to Mursili II, of killing his beloved wife Gassulawiya, among other serious offenses. Muwatalli's wife Danuhepa also fell out of favor and was banished, although Mursili III (Urhi-Teshub) later ended her exile and reinstated her as Tawananna. Notably, no matter how badly they are alleged to have behaved, no Great Queen of Hatti is on record as having been put to death.

What we know of the activities of the queens comes to us primarily through the often-unflattering lenses of their male counterparts. Asmunikal, the daughter of Tudhaliya II, whose voice is preserved in the prayer she co-authored with her husband, Arnuwanda I, provides a rare exception to this rule. Individual queens probably wielded considerable power within the court, and their influence may have been circumscribed only by the limits of their kings' forbearance and their own ambition. But although more than simply royal consorts, the Hittite queens were not co-rulers.

Only with Puduhepa, the wife of Hattusili III (1290–1265 B.C.E.), do we encounter a queen who wielded real political power. She sealed treaties alongside her husband, carried on diplomatic correspondence with Egypt, and even adjudicated legal cases. She likely owed her power to her own extraordinary personality coupled with Hattusili's chronic ill health, which left him increasingly dependent on her leadership skills. She is shown alongside her husband on reliefs depicting the royal pair presenting offerings to the gods and had her own private seals with which she conducted official business independently of her husband. Even the copy of the Egyptian-Hittite treaty that was sent to Egypt was co-signed by Puduhepa. As was the custom, Puduhepa continued in her role as Tawananna following the death

---

23. On the possibility that his sister was the Tawananna whose ostracism, pronounced in his Edict (*CTH* 5), included her descendants, see Bryce, *Kingdom of the Hittites*, 93–94.

24. *KBo* 15.10 + *KBo* 20.42 (*CTH* 443); see Klengel, *Geschichte des hethitischen Reiches*, 111 n. 118.

25. On Henti's possible fate, see Bryce, *Kingdom of the Hittites*, 159–60.

of Hattusili III. Her son, Tudhaliya IV, had wedded a Babylonian princess, a prestigious marriage probably arranged by his mother before his accession and no doubt designed to strengthen his position as heir. But Puduhepa's strong personality eventually led to clashes with her son and his Babylonian bride, who must have felt frustrated by the limitations of her own position as the king's first-rank wife but not Great Queen. The outcome of this domestic civil war is unknown beyond its apparent negative affect on Tudhaliya's health, which became the subject of an oracular investigation.[26]

THE ROYAL COURT

The royal court included all the members of the king's family and those in his direct service. When Telipinu made his Proclamation concerning the royal succession, he addressed it to the *pankus*, a body composed of the palace servants, royal bodyguard, "men of the golden spear," cup-bearers, table-men, cooks, heralds, stableboys, and captains of the thousand, that is, the offices of the royal court. Over time, these positions evolved, and new ones were created. Tudhaliya IV would later encapsulate this class in the phrase "lords and princes," referring to the aristocracy and the royal family, both bound to the king.[27] Although the kings ruled by divine mandate and so in theory wielded unlimited power, in reality their power was circumscribed by a need to maintain some consensus among this elite class. A king who lost this base of support could find himself in a precarious position indeed.

Among the lords and princes were the "king's men" (LÚ SAG), who comprised the king's innermost circle. This elite group included individuals occupying various positions, such as Anuwanza, scribe and "Lord of Nerik"; Pala, the "Lord of Hurma"; and Zuzu, the *kartappu* (secretary of foreign affairs).[28] High-ranking scribes working on behalf of the palace, such as Anuwanza and Mittannamuwa, naturally belonged among the most trusted officials by virtue of their work on the king's most sensitive business. Also operating in close proximity to the king were the royal guards (*MEŠEDI*), whose task it was to protect the king's person, whether on festival occasions or in battle. After the king and his designated heir, the chief of the royal guard was the highest-ranking official in the land. His responsibilities some-

---

26. *KUB* 22.70 (*CTH* 566); for which see "Excerpt from an Oracle Report," translated by Gary Beckman (*COS* 1.78:204–6). The assignment of this text to the reign of Tudhaliya IV is not certain.

27. Pecchioli-Daddi, "System of Government," 122.

28. Itamar Singer, "Takuḫlinu and Ḫaya: Two Governors in the Ugarit Letter from Tel Aphek," *TA* 10 (1983): 10–11.

times involved leading military contingents into battle, and the position often went to a prince not in line to inherit his father's throne. Zida, Suppiluli-uma's brother, as well as Hattusili III and Tudhaliya IV, neither of whom was originally intended to ascend the throne, each held the post for a time. Sharing the responsibility of protecting the king were the "men of the golden spear," who guarded the palace courtyard and the gates leading to and from the palace precinct.

The kingship, like property, was inherited through the male line. There were no restraints, not even divine ones, on the king's power to determine his successor, although rival claims to the throne almost always threatened to undermine a peaceful succession. All male descendants of kings, regardless of age, would have been considered princes of the Hittite Great Family, not just the sons of the current king, but, as stipulated in Telipinu's Proclamation, only the sons of the first-rank wife were in direct line for the kingship. The "crown prince," that is, the son officially chosen to succeed to the throne, bore the Hattian title Tuhkanti, meaning "crown prince." Secondary wives, or concubines, produced secondary sons, who were eligible for kingship only if no sons of the first rank were available. If sons were lacking altogether, then a daughter's husband could be chosen as heir. Telipinu himself was the son-in-law of his predecessor, and his Proclamation may have been little more than a justification of his own usurpation. In any case, the rules he set out in this document were upheld until the end of the empire.

Sons and daughters alike of the royal house might find themselves in ser-vice as priest or priestess to one deity or another, although, because priestly titles are not generally accompanied in the texts by the holders' names, we know precious little about the circumstances in which such roles were filled. Sons of the royal house who did not have careers in either the military or religious administration had the option of entering the diplomatic corps. A letter from Ramesses II tells of a Hittite expedition to Egypt led by prince Hishmi-Sharruma, another son of Hattusili and Puduhepa, whose mission was to organize and expedite a consignment of grain to be shipped by sea.[29]

The title "Great Princess" was borne by daughters of Great Kings of Hatti and of other great powers.[30] Princesses of the royal house were the principal instrument in foreign policy, serving as pawns in the lively trade in diplo-matic brides. They were commodities to the extent that we often do not know their names. In Hattusili III's reign alone, with Puduhepa responsible for

---

29. *KUB* 3.34 (*CTH* 165); see Singer, "Takuhlinu and Haya," 5.
30. Itamar Singer, "The Title 'Great Princess' in the Hittite Empire," *UF* 23 (1992): 335.

all the arrangements, Hittite princesses were married to the kings of Egypt, Babylon, Isuwa, Amurru, and the Seha River Land. The bride prices alone must have helped to boost considerably the depleted palace coffers. Kilush-epa, wife of Ari-Sharruma, king of Isuwa, and her half-sister Gassulawiya, wife of Benteshina of Amurru, were both Great Princesses who entered into advantageous marriages on behalf of the Hittite state. The princesses would have been accompanied by large entourages, evidence of which has recently been uncovered in the Egyptian city of Pi-Ramesses, the new home of Ramesses II's bride. Molds for the production of Hittite "figure eight"-style shields may have accompanied her guard to Egypt.[31] Such entourages would perhaps have included companions (ladies in waiting) who would have helped alleviate the princess's homesickness. Fairytale endings were no doubt rare in these circumstances. Ramesses II's bride was eventually exiled to the oasis at Fayum, where she lived out her life in obscurity. The marriage of Ehli-Nikkal, a daughter of Benteshina and Gassulawiya and sister to the current king of Amurru, Shaushgamuwa, to Ammistamru II of Ugarit had an even darker outcome. The princess committed an offense whose nature is unknown, but it was serious enough for Ammistamru to demand a divorce. The princess's return to Amurru in disgrace did not satisfy Ammistamru, however, who demanded her extradition to Ugarit to face punishment for her offense. After a protacted negotiation that required the intervention of both the viceroy in Karkamis and Tudhaliya IV, Shaushgamuwa was compelled to give up his sister to her fate, almost certainly ending in her death.

ROYAL ADMINISTRATION

The Marassantiya River (classical Halys, modern Kızıl Irmak) cradled the Hittite heartland, in the bend of which, beside the Hittite capital itself, other important cities such as Sapinuwa (modern Ortaköy), Ankuwa (modern Alişar), Tawiniya (Taouion), Zippalanda (modern Alaca Höyük?), and Samuha (modern Sivas) were nestled. This area remained under the direct rule of the Hittite king from the beginning of the Hittite kingdom until its collapse at the end of the Bronze Age.

In the empire period, districts that lay outside the core territory included Pala-Tumanna, Kassiya, Hurma, Tegarama, Pahhuwa, the Upper Land, the Lower Land (which encompassed the region around the Salt Lake), and

---

31. Thilo Rehren, Edgar B. Pusch, and Anja Herold, "Qantir-Piramesses and the Organisation of the Egyptian Glass Industry," in *The Social Context of Technological Change: Egypt and the Near East, 1650–1550 BC* (ed. Andrew J. Shortland; Oxford: Oxbow, 2001), 227.

Kizzuwatna, with its capital at Kummanni. Those provinces that abutted potentially hostile lands were given to the oversight of a district governor. To Hattusa's immediate north and east, Hakpis and Tapikka (modern Maşat) were on the frontlines of the Kaska frontier and required such governors to protect and administer their territories. Some of these individuals we know by name. At Tapikka, he was Himuili, perhaps appointed by Tudhaliya II. Approximately a century later, Muwatalli II appointed his brother Hattusili governer at Hakpis.

Beyond the Hittite provinces were the vassal kingdoms whose rulers were members of local dynasties and whose own ambitions were kept in check by treaties that bound them in loyalty to the person of the Hittite king. At the empire's height, these vassals included, from west to east, Wilusa, the Arzawa lands of Seha, Hapalla, Mira, the Lukka lands, Tarhuntassa, Kizzuwatna, Isuwa, and Azzi-Hayasa. The empire's Syrian holdings—Ugarit, Amurru, Nuhasse, Halpa, and Ashtata (Emar)—fell under the purview of the viceroy of Karkamis, who also ruled a substantial kingdom himself. The form that the administration of a region took depended on the "zone" to which it belonged.

The details of Hittite royal administration come to us from a variety of texts recovered from the royal and provincial libraries. Royal edicts such as those composed by Hattusili I and Telipinu laid down the future direction of the kingdom. Royal decrees documented decisions regarding certain noble persons, towns, or institutions. Land grants, which are among the earliest archival documents, record the gift of lands with their accompanying towns and occupants bestowed by the king upon his most loyal servants or noblemen. Oaths bound everyone from the "king's men" to the lowliest soldier to protect the king and the first family. Inventories of local cultic installations asserted the king's religious authority throughout the heartland. Professional diviners performed and recorded oracular inquiries to ascertain the will of the gods on a variety of matters. Letters served the purposes of diplomacy with foreign powers as well as being the primary form of communication with vassals and administrators operating in the countryside.

As the state administration grew more complex, particularly during the reigns of Tudhaliya II and Arnuwanda I, the kings began to impose detailed sets of intructions for their officials. These documents were a formal means of describing duties and responsibilities of particular offices and of binding the bearers of those offices to carry them out as instructed. Such sets of instructions exist for priests and temple personnel, city mayors, military officers, district governors, border officials, the royal bodyguard, palace personnel, and even the aristocracy as a whole.

At Hattusa, a town mayor (*HAZANNU*) oversaw civic matters, including fire protection, public sanitation, securing the water supply, posting of the guard, and ensuring that the city gates were properly secured each night. We recall that Muwatalli II had appointed Mittannamuwa, Mursili's chief scribe, to this position when the former vacated the capital. The mayor headed a local bureacracy that included two city superintendents (MAŠKIM), one for the Upper City (the royal residence) and one for the Lower City, as well as a herald (NIMGIR) and the sentries responsible for guarding the city's fortifications.

The more remote or peripheral the town, the more important politically were the councils of elders, whose members functioned as local politicians. In the heartland of the kingdom itself, their role was limited to assisting state-appointed officials with judicial and cultic matters. At Maşat-Tapikka, for example, the only elders listed in the texts belong to the Kaska. Aside from the elders, locals did not participate in their own governance; rather, administrators were selected from among the few families that made up the ruling elite.

As noted above, the provinces were under the oversight of district governors, identified in the texts by the Akkadian title *BEL MADGALTI*, which means literally "lord of the watchtower." These governors were royal appointees, often a close relation of the king, who supervised sizeable territories along Hatti's frontiers, bearing the responsibility for any number of towns at a time. Their responsibilities, as detailed in their instructions and borne out by the correspondence from Maşat-Tapikka, included the surveillance of enemy forces in the border area, the organization of agriculture on state lands, the upkeep of royal buildings and temples, and the administration of justice in their district. In fulfilling these responsibilibites, the district governors worked closely with local elders and city superintendents.

Despite their considerable responsibilities, the district governors were given little leeway for individual initiative. Their duty was to provide the king with the information he needed in order to issue orders, which the governors then carried out unquestioningly.[32] They were based at Hattusa and returned there frequently to report in person. This is the picture from Maşat-Tapikka, in any case, where the situation may have been sensitive enough to warrant such a short leash.[33]

---

32. Gary Beckman, "Hittite Provincial Administration in Anatolia and Syria: The View from Maşat and Emar," in *Atti del II Congresso Internazionale di Hittitologia* (ed. Onofrio Carruba, Mauro Giorgieri, and Clelia Mora; Studia Mediterranea 9; Pavia: Gianni Iuculano Editore, 1995), 23.

33. Trevor R. Bryce, *Life and Society in the Hittite World* (Oxford: Oxford University Press, 2002), 17.

Overseeing Hittite interests in Syria was the viceroy of Karkamis, who served on behalf of his king. At no time in the two hundred years of this arrangement, so far as we know, did the viceroy fail in his absolute and unwavering loyalty to his king. Perhaps this can be atributed in part to the exceptional latitude he was allowed in the region. Ini-Teshub, cousin of Tudhaliya IV and grandson of Sharri-Kushuh, is the best-attested viceroy of Karkamis. During his periodic visits to the towns in his jurisdiction, he interceded in various local legal and economic matters. His involvement in real-estate sales, wills, and legal cases is attested in the texts from Emar and Ugarit. He also adjudicated disputes between vassals. The viceroy handled all but the most important matters of state; the conclusion of treaties, for example, would have required the involvement of the Great King in Hattusa.

Hittite bureaucrats and diplomats were stationed in and around the vassal kingdoms. "Princes" (Sumerian DUMU.LUGAL; the title was in many cases purely honorific) seem to have worked closely with the local kings, interceding in matters directly concerning the state administration, although at Emar they are attested only as witnesses to transactions. The "overseers of the land" (Sumerian UGULA.KALAM.MA), like the district governors of Anatolia, were responsible for a large portion of territory and traveled about from town to town in the performance of their duties, which included military intelligence, overseeing administrative matters, and witnessing various legal transactions, as well as participation in the local cult. At Emar, a *hazannu* "mayor" and elders shared administrative responsibility with the ruler.

In binding the vassal by treaty, the Hittite king generally respected the right of the local dynasts to retain their positions. The vassal states remained administratively and economically independent of Hatti, but the vassal treaties guaranteed their loyalty to the king, the payment of tribute, military assistance, the refraining from all independent foreign diplomatic relations, the extradition of fugitives, and the protection of the designated successor to the Hittite throne. Thus Mursili II bound Tuppi-Teshub of Amurru by oath:

> And as I took care of you according to the request of your father, and installed you in place of your father, I have now made you swear an oath to the King of Hatti and the land of Hatti, and to my sons and grandsons. Observe the oath and the authority of the King. I, My Majesty, will protect you, Tuppi-Teshub. And when you take a wife and produce a son, he shall later be king in the land of Amurru. As you protect My Majesty, I will likewise protect your son. You, Tuppi-Teshub, in the future protect the King of Hatti, the land of Hatti, my sons, and my grandsons. The tribute which was imposed upon your grandfather and upon your father shall be imposed upon you: They paid 300 shekels of refined gold by the weights of Hatti,

first-class and good. You shall pay it likewise. You shall not turn your eyes to another.[34]

Controlling this unruly empire required constant vigilance on all fronts simultaneously, a feat that necessitated a substantial standing army. Apart from the king, the Tuhkanti, and the chief of the royal guard, the highest ranking military position in the kingdom was that of the "chief of the wine" (GAL GEŠTIN), a title of humble origin that evolved into one of highest military posts in the empire and that frequently involved independent military command on behalf of the king. Not surprisingly, the command was often held by a royal prince. The officers following him in rank included the chiefs of the chariot warriors, the standing-army troops, the "shepherds," and so on down the line.[35] In addition, an overseer of the military heralds (UGULA NIMGIR. ÉRIN.MEŠ), named Kassu, is attested at Maşat-Tapikka, where he enjoyed similar rank with Himuili, the district governor.

The king was kept informed of every military engagement, however small, particularly on the precarious frontier with the Kaska lands. Archaeology has confirmed the presence of a number of fortified Hittite sites (the garrisons mentioned in the instructions for the district governers) strategically located at prominent points across the landscape along the northern frontier. These settlements would have been connected by tracks that facilitated the movement of armies and supplies as they patrolled the dangerous border zones. Also dotting this terrain as a key element in this network of control were lookouts posts situated on high ridges that would have afforded expansive views over the approaches to the garrisons from all directions, providing an early warning system against enemy attack.[36]

The most important and elite branch of the Hittite military was the chariotry. Each chariot was pulled by a pair of horses and carried a driver and an archer. A third rider, whose job it was to protect the archer with his shield, was added later. One unusual text authored by a man named Kikkuli is a manual describing in great detail the rigorous training regimen through which chariot horses were put.

Representing some 90 percent of the king's forces, the infantry formed the backbone of the army. Each troop was equipped with a bronze sword and a spear. The troops were recruited from among the population of Hatti and supplemented with auxiliary corps from vassal kingdoms and with mercenar-

---

34. Translated by Beckman, *Hittite Diplomatic Texts*, 60 (no. 8).

35. Richard H. Beal, "Hittite Military Organization," *CANE*, 546–47.

36. Roger Matthews, "Landscapes of Terror and Control: Imperial Impacts in Paphlagonia," *NEA* 67 (2005): 200–211.

ies. Each soldier was bound by oath to serve the king loyally in battle. The formidable gods of the oath could be counted on to punish those who broke this bond:

> He (the ritual practioner) places malt and beer seasoning in their hands and they lick it. He says to them as follows: "Just as they mill this beer seasoning with a millstone and mix it with water and cook it and mash it, who transgresses these oaths and takes part in evil against the king, the queen or against the princes or against the land of Hatti, may these oath deities seize him and in the same way may they mill his bones and in the same way may they heat him up and in the same way may they mash him. May he experience a horrible death." They (the soldiers) say, "So be it."[37]

A small cavalry probably performed scouting and messenger duties. The landlocked Hittites did not employ a navy to speak of, preferring to commandeer the navy of its Syrian vassal Ugarit and perhaps also merchant ships, when needed. Here again, the role of the viceroy of Karkamis in monitoring the movements of the Ugaritic fleet was crucial to protecting Hittite interests.

Seasonal campaigns were costly in time, money, and human resources and thus were undertaken only when necessary, which is to say, virtually all the time. The 47,500 troops that made up Muwatalli II's forces at Qadesh—if Ramesses' account can be believed—included 3,500 chariotry and 37,000 infantry. The use of war captives as a supplemental work force back home meant that loyal (if not always willing) subjects were freed up to serve at least part of the year on campaign with their king.

Despite its large army, the Hittite Empire was not won by brutal tactics. In contrast to the Assyrians, the Hittite ethos did not include control by terror. Instead, the Hittites developed a series of strategies designed to bind conquered territories inexorably to them. Fully half of such treaties recovered from the ancient Near East were composed in Hatti. In these treaties, in addition to the stipulations discussed above, borders were redefined to reward loyalists and punish rebels. This form of control was such an integral part of the Hittite system that it carried over into the Neo-Hittite period, when the kingdoms of northern Syria effectively encouraged the Assyrians to apply this same tactic in their competition among themselves.[38] Another mechanism of control was the practice of deportation, which the Hittites engaged in extensively beginning at least with the reign of Tudhaliya II. Transporting a significant portion

---

37. "The First Soldiers' Oath," translated by Billie Jean Collins (*COS* 1.66:166, §7).

38. Nili Wazana, "Border Descriptions and Cultural Barriers," in Wilhelm, *Akten des IV. Internationalen Kongresses*, 700–706. The boundary stelae in the Neo-Hittite period are even locally made! And note that Neo-Assyrians did not use this tactic on other fronts.

of the enemy population following military campaigns served to diminish the threat of future anti-Hittite activities in the region, while at the same time providing a supplemental work force in the homeland.[39]

Treaties, and a strong military to enforce them, provided a workable model for empire. Ultimately, it was not the imperial structure that failed so much as the internal structure of the kingdom. Tudhaliya IV's reign offers us a glimpse into the mechanisms by which Hittite kings asserted control over the core cities of the kingdom and just how tenuous they were. Because the legitimacy of his reign was seriously in question, he had a particular interest in developing a policy of control that would increase consensus among his ruling class. To achieve this, he employed two primary strategies.[40] The first was to administer, on his accession to the throne, an oath to the entire Hittite aristocracy, the "lords and princes." Such oaths were not unusual, but to include the entire ruling class in the ceremony was a significant break with tradition. The second strategy was the taking of inventories of the cults in towns throughout the countryside. This process, which had been carried out by kings before him, afforded him an opportunity to make his presence felt among the royal appointees governing the countryside while strengthening the religious legitimacy of the royalty through a very public show of piety.

EXCURSUS
WHAT DO HITTITE TREATIES HAVE TO DO WITH THE SINAI COVENANT?[41]

In the ancient Near East, the earthly realm mirrored the heavenly, particularly where the exercise of power was concerned. The sovereignty of kings was modeled on the sovereignty of the gods. In this way, royal authority was

---

39. Bryce, *Kingdom of the Hittites*, 217–18.

40. See Pecchioli-Daddi, "System of Government," 117–28.

41. This excursus draws on the work of Joshua A. Berman, "God's Alliance with Man," *Azure* 25 (2006): 79–113, including references to all the standard treatments of this topic. Online: http://www.azure.org.il/magazine/magazine.asp?id=309; to appear in idem, *Biblical Revolutions: The Transformation of Social and Political Thought in the Ancient Near East*. I have adopted Berman's terminology of "sovereign" and "subordinate" here. Where I differ from Berman is in the notion that the Hittite treaties should be understood as a cross-cultural phenomenon. To say that the Hittites were not contiguous to Israel and therefore cannot have impacted it is to ignore the role of imperial Hatti in Syria at the end of the Bronze Age and the continuity of certain elements of their civilization among the Neo-Hittite kingdoms. Given that Egypt did not have treaties but one-sided oaths, and neither Assyria nor Egypt recognized the sovereignty of other nations, it is not correct to say that the form of the Hittite treaties is representative of a form of political discourse that was *de rigeuer* throughout the Near East.

assured as the king became the focal point between the world of the gods and of humans, a "symbolic representation of the community" before the gods and conversely of the gods before his subjects. In the account of Yahweh establishing his covenant with Moses on Mount Sinai, the biblical authors did not follow this model, although they could have. Psalm 2 tells us that the king is legitimate because he has been *chosen* by God, but the close identification of God and king is simply absent in the Bible. In the place of a king as mediator between God and the people, the biblical authors articulated "the relationship between God and Israel through the political concept of a covenant,"[42] that is, as a contract agreement between a sovereign and his subordinate.

In the middle of the last century, scholars noticed for the first time the similarity between the covenant formed at Sinai between Yahweh and Israel as attested in Exodus, Leviticus, Deuteronomy, and Josh 24 and the preserved treaties that the Hittites concluded with their vassal states in the Late Bronze Age. The basic elements identified as characteristic of both Hittite treaties and the biblical covenant as a genre include, in order: (1) the historical prologue, in which the relationship between the two parties prior to their entering into the present agreement is reviewed; (2) the stipulations of the obligations imposed upon and accepted by the vassal as well as the responsibilities of the sovereign toward the subordinate; (3) the deposition of the treaty within the temple along with a provision for the periodic public reading of the treaty; (4) the calling of witnesses to the treaty; and (5) the issuance of blessings and curses on those who keep or break the terms of the agreement, respectively.[43] Indeed, the overall structure of the Pentateuch, it has been argued, is that of a political treaty between God and Israel that is patterned after the Hittite political treaty.[44]

Conceptual similarities also link the Sinai covenant to Hittite treaties. In both the treaties and the covenant, the subordinate partner must enter into the agreement willingly. The historical prologue provides a narrative foundation for the sense of gratitude and moral obligation borne by the subordinate party in response to the favor bestowed upon him by the sovereign.

---

42. Berman, "God's Alliance with Man," 85.

43. The relevant biblical passages are: historical prologue: Exod 20:1–2; Deut 1:6–3:29; Josh 24:2–13; stipulations: Exod 20:2–17; Lev 1–25; Deut 12–26; Josh 24:14–25; deposition: Exod 24:3–4, 7–8; Deut 10:1–5; 27:2–3; 31:10–13, 24–26; Josh 8:30–32; 24:26; witnesses: Deut 4:26; 31:19–22, 26–28; 32:39–43, 46; Josh 24:22, 26–28; blessings and curses: Lev 26:1–13 (blessings), 14–33 (curses); Deut 28:1–68; Josh 24:20.

44. Edward L. Greenstein, "On the Genesis of Biblical Prose Narrative," *Prooftexts* 8 (1988): 350.

In other words, these are "self-subjugation" treaties.[45] Thus Israel declares, "All the things that the Lord has spoken, we will do and obey."[46] In addition, the agreements are reciprocal; that is, the sovereign also has obligations to fulfill. Just as the Hittite king promises to protect the vassal, support the claim of the rightful heir to the throne, and so on, so Yahweh promises to protect Israel. Further, just as the vassal king in the Hittite treaties retains his royal status and with it his honor, so too the people of Israel enjoy an elevated status as God's chosen people. Finally, like the Hittite vassal treaties, the Sinai covenant is an agreement between two individuals, God and the people of Israel, with each Israelite taking the position of the subordinate king.

The reciprocal, multicentered worldview reflected in the Hittite treaties is unique in the ancient Near East,[47] and it is further demonstrated in the Hittites' use of borders as a means of reward and punishment. The Hittite kings used the treaties to define the boundaries of the vassal state, entrusting territory to the faithful and taking it away from the rebellious. In the same way, in Num 34:2–12 Yahweh allotted the promised land to the people of Israel and defined its borders in precise geographical terms that mirror the level of detail known from Hittite treaties. Further, God's admonition to the people to "take possession" of the land he has given them (Deut 1:8, 21) echoes Mursili II's exhortation to the king of Arzawa regarding his allotment: "you must protect it!"[48] Even the respect we see in Hittite treaties for the borders of others is carried over into the Bible when, in Deut 2:5, 19, God warns the Israelites not to provoke war with Edom, Amon, or Moab.[49] The suzerain alone is responsible for defining boundaries, and only he has the right to make territorial changes. Therefore, God functions in a way similar to the Hittite king.

LAW AND SOCIETY

Life in Anatolia under Hittite rule was highly regulated. In this world, every farmer, craftsman, and soldier labored to benefit the state. Every festival

---

45. Berman, "God's Alliance with Man," 88.

46. Exod 24:7; see also Exod 19:8; 24:3; Deut 5:24; Josh 24:16–18.

47. Nili Wazana, "Border Descriptions and Cultural Barriers," 697.

48. Moshe Weinfeld, *Deuteronomy and the Deuteronomistic School* (Oxford: Clarendon, 1972), 72.

49. This concept could have entered Israel via the Neo-Hittites, who inherited from their Late Bronze Age predecessors in Anatolia the idea of using borders as a tool for political maneuvering; see Wazana, "Border Descriptions and Cultural Barriers," 710.

that was performed, piece of sculpture that was fashioned, or tablet that was inscribed ultimately served the interests of the king. The palace economy of the Late Bronze Age effectively centralized control of Anatolia's resources even as it inexorably bound the inhabitants of the land who were dependent on those resources to the ruling house.

THE SOCIOECONOMIC STRUCTURE OF THE KINGDOM

Small-scale farming and animal husbandry formed the backbone of the Hittite economy. Hunting and fishing, although practiced, were not a significant factor in the economy. Farmers cultivated a wide variety of grains, legumes, fruits, and vegetables. Livestock included cattle, sheep, goats, pigs, donkeys, asses, horses, and poultry. The revenues collected from agricultural surpluses in the form of the *sahhan* tax, a tithe determined as a percentage of one's produce, formed the chief source of revenue for the state.

Almost as important to the economy was the tribute collected from vassal states and the booty taken in military campaigns, which consisted not only of precious objects looted from palaces and temples but also of livestock and prisoners, both civil and military. What of the booty taken on campaign did not end up in the king's treasury was divided up among his officers and troops. The captives who were resettled in underpopulated areas of the kingdom helped to alleviate Hatti's perpetual manpower shortage and so formed a crucial component of the Hittite economy. Some of these people were distributed as property among the king's military officers. The remainder were sent to work as laborers on state land or to serve as militia and workers at the border garrisons or were given in service to a temple.

The tax on trade is not well attested in the texts, although we may assume it also formed a small part of the state revenues. Trade was not the economic boom in Hittite Anatolia that it had been in the Assyrian Colony period, having been replaced by a large palace economy in which desirable commodities were obtained through diplomatic gift exchanges and tribute. Industrial production of textiles and raw metals such as gold, silver, tin, and lead probably constituted the limit of the Hittites' commercial offerings to the Near Eastern global economy.

In Syria, the royal house at Karkamis managed a lively trade in slaves and horses with cities such as Ugarit, which reciprocated with linen garments, dyed wool, oil, *alun*-stone, and lead, copper, and bronze objects.[50] Most of the merchants plying their wares in Hatti proper were probably for-

---

50. Singer, "A Political History of Ugarit," 656–57.

eign entrepreneurs operating under royal protection. Whether conducted by land or sea, trade was a particularly dangerous enterprise, since merchants were an obvious target for brigands and pirates. Turkey's southern coast was particularly notorious for piracy throughout antiquity. Merchant ships carrying luxury goods and grain destined for Hittite lands would have found safe harbor at ports such as Ura on the Cilician coast and Minet el-Beida on the Levantine coast. In Syria in particular many judicial cases presided over by the viceroy related to the settlement of cases where merchants had been robbed, hijacked, or murdered.[51] The penalty in the Hittite laws for murdering a merchant was four thousand shekels of silver, a fine intended to cover the stolen property as well as provide restitution to the family of the murdered man.[52] The territories and towns through which the merchants traveled were responsible for their safe passage and were liable for the fine if the culprit had made a clean getaway.

As the seat of a king, Hattusa was not a production center but owed its importance entirely to its political function.[53] Wealth was funneled both to the central government at Hattusa and redistributed locally via provincial redistributive centers called "palaces" under the oversight of stewards (Sumerian AGRIG), who were accountable directly to the king. In the course of the KI. LAM festival, which was performed in the capital, the AGRIGs of a number of towns were introduced to the king before their respective storehouses in a symbolic expression of royal control over the redistributive system.[54] Other institutions with similar roles were the "stone houses," or mausoleums of deceased kings, and seal houses, so-called because of the bullae (lumps of stamped clay) that were used to seal the vessels stored in them. These institutions were situated in towns that together formed a network for the collection and redistribution of agricultural produce.

Recent excavations at Hattusa reveal only the proverbial tip of the iceberg in this complex system. Behind the "postern wall" on the southwest of the lower city that forms a part of the city's earliest fortification (fig. 2.2), an underground storage complex consisting of two parallel rows of sixteen chambers each and dating to the Old Kingdom is estimated to have had a

51. Bryce, *Life and Society*, 89.

52. See the translation of the Hittite laws by Hoffner in Roth, *Law Collections*, 217.

53. Gary Beckman, "The City and the Country in Ḫatti," in *Landwirtschaft im Alten Orient: Ausgewählte Vorträge der XLI. Rencontre Assyriologique Internationale, Berlin, 4.–8.7.1994* (ed. Horst Klengel and Johannes Renger; Berliner Beiträge zum Vorderen Orient 18; Berlin: Reimer, 1999), 165–69.

54. Ibid., 168; Itamar Singer, *The Hittite KI.LAM Festival* (StBoT 27; Wiesbaden: Harrassowitz, 1983), 62–63.

total capacity of nine thousand cubic meters of grain (mostly barley), an amount sufficient to feed up to thirty thousand people for a year![55] The chambers were airtight and could have stored grain safely for years. Extensive underground grain silos on the ridge north of the citadel called Büyükkaya belonging to the thirteenth century have also been uncovered, the largest of which alone had the capacity to hold 260 tons of grain.

To what extent the temples participated in the state economy is unclear. The massive storerooms within the precinct of the Great Temple at Hattusa are witness to the redistributive role that temples played with the agricultural products harvested from temple-owned lands (fig. 3.3). Beyond this, evidence of an independent economic role for the temples is lacking. In Hatti, the Great Temple and its priests never attained the kind of autonomous power that we see at times in Mesopotamia and Egypt. As the cult inventories suggest, individual temples, although administered by priests, were ultimately under the control of the king, and the extent of their resources depended on the degree of royal patronage that they enjoyed.

In all likelihood, only the personnel required for the running of state and temple business, as well as security forces, lived within the walls of Hattusa, which presumably also provided lodging for visiting merchants, diplomats, and anyone else having business to conduct with the royal court. Similarly, fortified towns such as Kuşaklı-Sarissa and Ortaköy-Sapinuwa probably housed administrative and temple staff, merchants, and others whose occupations suited an urban lifestyle. The remainder of the population lived in small villages either as free, independent farmers or as dependents of the king or a wealthy landowner or state institution (e.g., a royal mausoleum or temple).

The instructions for the district governors indicate that farmers left the garrisons in the morning to tend their fields and returned at night. However, the situation along the Kaska frontier may have been atypical and designed to keep the population (probably mostly resettled deportees) safe from raids. In more secure regions, peasant farmers and their families probably lived in relative security in their unfortified villages.

Villages consisted of a number of households, which included the immediate and extended members of the family as well as the livestock and land holdings of that family. Pulliyanni's household, for example, included three

---

55. Jürgen Seeher, "Getriedelagerung in unterirdischen Großspeichern: Zur Methode und ihrer Anwendung im 2. Jahrtausend v.Chr. am Beispiel der Befunde in Ḫattuša," *SMEA* 42 (2000): 261–301; idem, "Die Ausgrabungen in Boğazköy-Ḫattuša 1999," *AA* (2000): 356–67.

Fig. 3.3. The extensive storerooms attached to the Great Temple once occupied two or three stories and served as a collection center for agricultural produce from the countryside surrounding the capital. Photo by the author.

boys and three girls, one man besides Pulliyanni, and six adult women, two of them elderly—a total of fourteen souls. In addition, he owned six cattle, two asses, and seventeen goats, and his crops included a vineyard, an olive tree, and fig trees.[56] On average, seven to ten personnel were needed to oper- ate a small farm, and families with the means to do so could hire extra hands on a contract basis. To facilitate this need, the Hittite laws covered wages for hire. Pulliyanni's family probably lived in a house built of mudbrick rein- forced with wood on a stone foundation. Its lower level would have had at least two rooms facing a forecourt. A ladder from the courtyard would have provided access to the upper story. The roof would have been flat and sup- ported by wooden beams packed with mud and twigs. Furnishings would have been simple and made of wood.

Free persons (*arawanni*) could buy and sell property, enter into contracts, change their place of residence, and enter and leave marriage without need-

56. See Beckman, "Royal Ideology and State Administration," 538.

ing to secure the approval of a superior. As land owners, they were required to render the *sahhan* tax and corvée labor (*luzzi*) to the state. Exemptions to these obligations could be granted only by the king. For some people, such as scribes,[57] the exemption was a part of the job; for others, the king would grant exemptions as a form of reward. The exemption that Hattusili III granted to Kurunta is one extreme example (see ch. 2).

In the case of dependent villages, that is, those in which the peasants worked land belonging to the king or to a state institution, such as a local "palace," temple, or mausoleum of a deceased ruler, royal bureaucrats would have been responsible for gathering the taxes and organizing the corvée. The estates granted to wealthy landowners as the result of royal gifts drawn from the confiscated property of conquered enemies were also worked by dependent peasants, but in this case, the landowner was responsible for organing the tax and service due to the state. Usually, this land was granted in nonadjacent plots, presumably to prevent a member of the aristocracy from establishing a base of power or, it has been suggested, to encourage maximum cultivation.[58]

In many cases the peasants who populated dependent villages were captured civilians and prisoners of war (Sumerian NAM.RA, Hittite *arnuwalla-*) who were dispersed among the temple and public lands to work them as tenant farmers. As we have seen, they were often used to resettle abandoned or sparsely populated areas and were probably sent to populate border garrisons along the Kaskean front. The local governor was then responsible for providing them with the necessities of life and with the equipment to do their work:

> A deportee who (has been) settled on the land you must supply with winter food stores, seed, cattle, (and) sheep. Provide him also with cheese, rennet (and) wool. Sow seed for whoever stays in the place of a deportee who leaves your province and let him have sufficient fields. Let them promptly assign him a plot.[59]

As a rule, the rights of these relocated individuals were limited; for example, they could not buy or sell land, and their movements were monitored. Whether their status as *arnuwala*-people passed to the next generation or their descendants were integrated into Hittite society as slaves, we do not

---

57. According to *HKM* 52:10–18; see Beckman, Provincial Administration, 26.

58. Bryce, *Life and Society*, 75.

59. "Instructions to Commanders of Border Garrisons," translated by Gregory McMahon (*COS* 1.84:224, §39').

know, but their lives in Hatti cannot have been easy, since many sought to escape to foreign lands.[60] Their importance to the Hittite economy, however, was such that the treaties with vassal states always included a stipulation that required the extradition of deportees on the run from Hatti. At the same time, the Hittite administration reserved the right to retain any fugitives from its vassal kingdoms, such was the pressing need for manpower in Hatti.

The kings frequently recorded the number of these captives taken in their campaigns: "The transplantees whom I, My Majesty, brought back for the royal estates, because I overcame all of Arzawa, numbered all together 66,000. Those whom the Hittite lords, infantry and horse-troops brought back were innumerable."[61] Such resettlements could sometimes backfire, as when Tudhaliya II took Kukkuli, a member of the anti-Hittite confederacy in the west, into vassalage and resettled him along with his ten thousand infantry and six hundred charioteers somewhere in the kingdom. Kukkuli used his forces to rebel against the king. Although he was killed and order restored, it must have been a lesson in royal management hard learned.

At the lowest level of society (ignoring the thieves, pirates, nomads, and gypsies who also certainly made a living in Anatolia but operated at the fringes of society) were the slaves. A person could become a slave through debt, through indentured servitude, as punishment for a crime, or through warfare. What percentage of the population was enslaved is impossible to say, but it seems unlikely that they outnumbered the deportees, at least in the last two centuries of the empire. The Hittite laws give a great deal of attention to the rights and obligations of slaves, and the district governors were admonished not to give less attention to judicial cases involving slaves and widows. It seems that some slaves had the means to accumulate wealth and land.[62] A slave who had the means to pay the bride price (*kusata*) could marry a free woman and thereby ensure that his offspring were free, although he remained a slave. In mixed marriages that did not involve the paying of a bride price, the woman could expect to enter into indentured servitude for a limited period.[63] Alternatively, a slave of means might be able to secure a free son-in-law, thus ensuring that his grandchildren would be free. Such

---

60. Jörg Klinger, "Fremde und Außenseiter in Ḫatti," in *Aussenseiter und Randgruppen: Beiträge zu einer Sozialgeschichte des Alten Orients* (ed. Volkert Haas; Konstanz: Universitätsverlag, 1992), 196–97.

61. "The Ten Year Annals of Great King Muršili II of Ḫatti," translated by Richard H. Beal (*COS* 2.16:86, Year 4).

62. See Harry A. Hoffner Jr., "Legal and Social Institutions of Hittite Anatolia," *CANE*, 565.

63. See Bryce, *Life and Society*, 121–23, for a discussion.

opportunities may have been limited to those slaves fortunate enough to have lenient masters. A slave owner held the right of life or death over his slaves and could inflict physical punishment (usually blinding or cutting off the ears or nose) as he chose. Law §173 leaves no doubt about the fate of an untrustworthy slave: "a slave who rebels against his owner will be stuffed in a jug." As valuable pieces of property (they cost 20 to 30 shekels, according to laws §§176b–177), however, slaves were unlikely to have been subjected to such punishment lightly.

Law

The two hundred cases collected in the so-called Hittite Law Code do not represent a systematic code of law so much as a compilation of precedents for unusual cases where no obvious solution presented itself. They were accumulated, perhaps over a period of years, as a reference manual to be distributed to those responsible for passing judgment on cases in the courts throughout the land. The Hittite laws cover both civil and criminal matters and are loosely organized by legal category. These include homicide; assault; stolen and runaway slaves; marriage; land tenure; lost property; theft or injury to animals; unlawful entry; arson; theft of or damage to plants; theft of or damage to implements; wages, hire, and fees; prices; and sexual offenses. Obviously, a collection of two hundred laws cannot represent all possible crimes and civil matters. The processes for handling disputes arising from civil matters were no doubt outlined in legally binding contracts, while most criminal offences probably fell under the ambit of customary law or, in some circumstances, left to the discretion of the victim or his family, as in the case of premeditated murder: "Whoever commits murder, whatever the heir himself of the murdered man says (will be done). If he says: 'Let him die,' he shall die; but if he says: 'Let him make compensation,' he shall make compensation. The king shall have no role in the decision."[64]

   The content of the Hittite Code as it has come down to us was originally drawn up early in the Old Kingdom, probably in the reign of Hattusili I, although the earliest surviving copies may date to the reign of Mursili I, Hattusili I's heir. It was preserved and recopied continuously from the sixteenth century through the thirteenth, a sure sign of its continuing importance as a legal resource. Because the earliest surviving version in many cases reduced penalties that had been applied in the past using the formula, "formerly they

---

   64. As pronounced by King Telipinu in his Proclamation (*CTH* 19, §49); translated by Hoffner in Roth, *Law Collections*, 237.

did such-and-such, but now they do such-and-such," the laws may represent a legal reform, probably initiated by Hattusili I.[65] In many cases, this reform involved a change from physical punishment to monetary restitution. For example, where previously the punishment for the theft of active beehives was a bee sting, it was now six shekels of silver (§92). The principal of *lex talionis* (an eye for an eye) did not apply in Hittite Anatolia.

The Hittite Law Code was an entirely secular document; unlike the Code of Hammurabi and the Covenant Code, it was not given to humanity by the gods. Nor apparently was it intended as a form of royal propaganda, as the copies that have survived lack any prolegomenon announcing its purpose, much less an extensive prologue aggrandizing the king, as with Hammurabi's Code. If the reforms instituted in its earliest version were designed to advertise the king's beneficence, there is no evidence of it—no sign that they were publicly displayed or carved on monumental stelae or read out loud before an audience.

As with the Code of Hammurabi and the Covenant Code, the cases are casuistic in form; that is, they begin with a conditional clause ("If someone kills a merchant...") followed by the ruling ("he shall pay 4,000 shekels of silver"). For example, the first case deals with unpremeditated homicide: "[If] anyone kills [a man] or a woman in a [quarr]el, he shall [bring him] (for burial) and shall give 4 persons, male or female respectively, and he shall look [to his house for it]."[66] The phrase "He shall look to his house for it" appears frequently and probably means that the claimant is entitled to recover damages from the estate of the perpetrator if the latter is unable or unwilling to pay by other means.

Several Hittite laws share some similarities with laws in the Hebrew Bible. For example, §IV, a case of murder by an unknown assailant in the countryside, shares with Deut 21:1–2 the procedure of measuring the distance to the nearest town to determine where responsibility for the dead man lies, on the principle that towns were responsible for criminal activity within their territories. Like Exod 21:18–19, §10 of the Hittite laws requires someone who has incapacitated another person to cover his medical costs and to compensate him for time lost, in the case of the Hittite law, also providing someone to work his estate while he is out of commission. Section 197 of

---

65. It is not clear whether an earlier version of the laws actually existed or whether the earlier judgments that are referred to were preserved orally; see, e.g., Itamar Singer, review of Harry A. Hoffner Jr., *The Laws of the Hittites*, *JNES* 60 (2001): 289.

66. Translated by Harry A. Hoffner Jr., *The Laws of the Hittites: A Critical Edition* (DMOA 23; Leiden: Brill, 1997), 17.

the Hittite laws deals with rape: "If a man seizes a woman in the mountain (and rapes her), it is the man's offence, and he shall be put to death, but if he seizes her in (her) house, it is the woman's offence: the woman shall be put to death. If the (woman's) husband finds them (in the act) and kills them, he has committed no offence."[67] The assumption here is that, had the woman cried for help in the mountains, her cries would not have been heard, but had she cried out in her own home, she would have been rescued, and no rape could have occurred. The Deuteronomistic laws make this same distinction (Deut 22:23–27).

The large number of laws relating to sexual behavior suggest a concern in Hatti's pluralistic society with defining precisely what pairings were socially acceptable and what were not. Having sexual relations with one's mother, daughter, or son, with two sisters, a living brother's wife, a wife's daughter by another man, or a wife's mother or sister were considered incestuous. Other sexual liaisons, however, were condoned, including sexual relations with one's stepmother or unwittingly having sexual relations with two sisters who did not live in the same country, marriage to the sister of one's deceased wife, having sexual relations with sisters or mother and daughter who were slaves, a father and son having sexual relations with the same slave or prostitute, and two brothers in a consensual liaison with a free woman.

These laws were put to the test when, as part of a treaty agreement with the ruler of the tributary state of Hayasa, Suppiluliuma I, who had just concluded a political marriage between his sister and its ruler, Huqqana, went to considerable trouble to explain to his new brother-in-law how he was expected to behave toward his bride:

> Furthermore, this sister whom I, My Majesty, have given to you as your wife has many sisters from her own family as well as from her extended family. They belong to your extended family because you have taken their sister. But for Hatti it is an important custom that a brother does not take his sister or femail cousin (sexually). It is not permitted. In Hatti whoever commits such an act does not remain alive but is put to death here.[68]

Suppiluliuma continues in this vein at some length, noting in particular the case of a man named Mariya who was put to death for admiring a palace woman from afar. Although recognizing that his sister had been married into a culture alien in its practices, in this matter in particular Suppiluliuma was adamant that the vassal should conform to Hittite custom. Such a stipulation

---

67. Translated by Hoffner, *The Laws of the Hittites*, 156.
68. Beckman, *Hittite Diplomatic Texts*, 31 (no. 3, §25).

in a treaty agreement is unique. Suppiluliuma's detailed demands regarding Huqqana's sexual conduct conclude with the command that he take no more women from Azzi as wife, although his current wife may become his concubine. Suppiluliuma's concern goes beyond a desire to ensure that his sister's status as first wife is secure, although this is part of it. He must take measures to ensure that there is no threat of contamination to himself or any member of the royal family through forbidden sexual pairings.[69]

Sexual pairings between humans were not the only concern. The laws stipulate that a man attacked sexually by an ox (or a pig) was not considered culpable, but the ox was killed. While willingly coupling with a cow (§187; cf. Exod 22:18; Lev 20:15–16), sheep (§188), dog, or pig (§199; cf. Exod 22:18; Lev 18:23), meant an appearance at the king's court and a likely death sentence, sexual relations with a horse or mule (§200a) were not forbidden. Such acts must have been occurring, or else there would have been no need for laws regulating them; on the other hand, the laws are a collection of atypical cases, so just how frequently these issues came up is open to speculation. The indemnification of the equids probably has less to do with a perverse fondness on the part of the Hittites for their horses than with the distinct status of the equids among the domesticates. Whereas sheep and cows might end up as food served both to gods and humans and thus spread the pollution to them, and while pigs and dogs lived in close proximity to humans and might spread pollution through contact, horses and donkeys were not eaten and lived outside the immediate environment of humans and thus were less likely to spread contamination. Still, the offender did not get off scott free; the pollution that attached itself to him would remain with him throughout his life.

As we have seen, the king presided over the highest court in the land, to which the most difficult or important cases were referred—even those that occurred in the farthest reaches of the empire. The nature of some cases meant that they went automatically to the king's court, such as petitions for relief from the state-imposed tax and corvée and capital cases. The *pankus*, although a judicial body and composed of the members of the upper echelon of the state bureaucracy, had a role that was limited to witnessing agreements and royal proclamations of great importance. In the empire period, even these functions were diminished. Instead, in the Old Kingdom, judicial authority

---

69. The Hittite expression *natta āra* "not permitted" used in the treaty with Huqqana and its sister term in the Hittite laws, *hurkel* "forbidden act," are comparable to biblical *tôʿēbâ* "abomination," used in reference to sexual prohibitions similar to those outlined in the Huqqana treaty (Lev 18:11, 18; 20:17; Ezek 22:11); see the discussion in Cohen, *Taboos and Prohibitions in Hittite Society*, 93–94.

was given to royal appointees called magistrates (Sumerian DUGUD, Hittite *nakkes*), who were assigned to specific districts to serve as judges in local courts. Unfortunately, these officials were easily corrupted in favor of the rich. A royal instruction thought to have been issued by Mursili I sharply admonishes them for falling short of the ideal in carrying out their duties:

> Has my father not engraved a tablet for you magistrates, which says, "When you go to your territory, will you then not investigate the murder of the poor?" But now you are in fact not questioning the provision bearers. Rather, you are doing the will of the rich. You go to their houses, eat and drink and receive gifts from them. But you pay no attention to the plight of the poor man nor investigate his complaints. Is this the way you hold the command of my father as a limit on your behavior?[70]

From at least the Middle Hittite period, the district governors oversaw legal proceedings in their territories in cooperation with royal administrators and local councils of elders during their tours of inspection. They too were ordered to administer justice fairly and equitably, even for slaves and widows, the most helpless members of society:

> In whatever city you enter, call of the people of the city. Judge a case for anyone who has one and make things right. If a man's slave, or a man's female slave or a widow has a case, judge it for them and make things right.[71]

In the penalty phase, the governors were instructed to give precedence to local tradition: "In a city in which they are accustomed to execute, let them continue to execute. In a city, however, in which they are accustomed to exile, let them continue to exile."[72]

Minutes of court procedure resemble transcripts of testimony or deposition of witnesses or the accused given at a legal inquest. Each testimony is introduced with the words: "So-and-so took an oath and gave the following testimony." The deposition is then given, but no cross-examination or verdict follows, suggesting that these inquests may have been part of a preliminary investigation. In cases where sufficient evidence in either direction was lacking and a decision was not possible, the judge could make the defendant

---

70. *KBo* 22.1 (*CTH* 272) rev. 21'–31'; translated by Hoffner, "Legal and Social Institutions," 561.

71. "Instructions to Commanders of Border Garrisons," translated by McMahon, *COS* 1.84:224, §38'.

72. Ibid., *COS* 1.84:224, §35'.

swear an oath to the effect that, if he was lying, the gods were to strike him dead, or, in more serious cases, he could prove his innocence by undergoing a river ordeal. A river ordeal confirmed the guilt of Zuliya, an official responsible for the king's water supply, of failing to protect the water (the king found a hair in it), and the punishment was death.[73] Hattusili submitted to "the wheel," another form of ordeal, when accused of sorcery by his political enemy, Arma-Tarhunda. The case was judged in the king's court, that is, by Hattusili's brother Muwatalli II, in his favor.

Only the king could sentence a free person to death. Beheading was the usual method of putting criminals to death. Exile was an alternative to death in capital cases. Blinding was reserved for rebel leaders and for those failing to keep an oath. Individuals so punished were put to work in millhouses (compare the biblical story of Samson).[74] Penalties were adjusted according to the offender's social status, whether he was free or a slave. Slaves (or probably their owners) typically paid compensation at half the rate expected of free persons. For example, "[If] anyone sets fire to [a field], and (the fire) catches a fruit-bearing vineyard, if a vine, an apple tree, a pear (?) tree or a plum tree burns, he shall pay 6 shekels of silver for each tree. He shall replant [the planting]. And he shall look to his house for it. If it is a slave, he shall pay 3 shekels of silver (for each tree)" (§105).[75] On the other hand, slaves were more likely to suffer mutilation, in the form of blinding or cutting off the ears or nose, or death as punishment for a crime.

DAILY LIFE

A century has passed since excavations began at Hattusa, yet we still know remarkably little about the daily lives of the subjects of the Hittite king. The single document among the surviving Hittite records whose focus is entirely on the common people is the Hittite Law Code. It informs us about family life through laws regulating situations that might arise concerning marriage and divorce, adultery, rape, adoption, and inheritance. The laws standardizing wages and prices also provide information about how the common people made their livings and filled their days.

Marriages typically were arranged by the parents of the bride and groom. The prospective groom paid to the bride's family a bride price (*kusata*), at

---

73. *KUB* 13.3 (*CTH* 265) §§8–9.

74. Harry A. Hoffner Jr., "The Treatment and Long-Term Use of Persons Captured in Battle according to the Masat Texts," in Yener and Hoffner, *Recent Developments in Hittite Archaeology and History*, 68–69.

75. Translated by Hoffner, *The Laws of the Hittites*, 101–2.

which point the couple was betrothed. Upon marriage, the bride's family provided her with a dowry (*iwaru*). Custom dictated that the woman then went to live in the household of her husband. In some cases (e.g., if they were otherwise without a male heir), the family of the bride might choose to adopt the groom as a son. In these cases, called *antiyant*-marriages, the groom joined the household of the bride's family. Although marriages were arranged, laws dealing with attempted elopements suggest that concessions might be made when love entered the equation (§§28a, 35, 37). Two relief vases from Inandik and Bitik, sites within the Hittite heartland, provide visual narrations of what are probably marriage celebrations. The Bitik vase shows the bride and groom seated in a bridal chamber (fig. 3.4), a scene frozen at the moment when the man's hand reaches out to lift the hood covering the woman's hair.

Monogamy was the rule for common people, if only because it was the most practical arrangement economically. However, the possibility of levirate marriage (§§192–193), that is, when a male relative of a deceased husband takes the widow as wife, means that in some cases polygamy was practiced. In the case of the Hittites, such arrangements were probably intended to ensure that widows were provided for rather than to perpetuate the name and family of the dead man and to keep the estate in the family, as in Israelite law (Deut 25:5–6).[76]

No marriage contracts have survived, but there is little doubt that such contracts were recorded in some form. They would have spelled out the terms of the union and probably provided for its dissolution as well. The laws themselves cover only cases of divorce between a free person and a slave (§§31–34). Extrapolating from these examples, it seems that in a divorce between persons of equal status, the couple's assets were generally divided equally and all the children but one remained with the mother; if the wife was of lesser social status, the husband retained custody of all but one of the couple's children.

Adultery committed by the wife was potentially punishable by death, at the discretion of her husband, but whatever his decision, it had to apply equally to the wife and her lover (§198). The Hittite laws do not cover adultery on the part of the husband, and we might infer from this that a husband's infidelty was not considered an offense.

Among the general population, men found employment either as farmers, herdsmen, merchants, artisans, soldiers, low-level priests, physicians, augurs, cooks and other kitchen staff, or entertainers. Artisans were often slaves and fetched a high price on the market: "If anyone buys a trained arti-

---

76. Bryce, *Life and Society*, 131–32.

Fig. 3.4. A fragment of the Bitik vase showing newlyweds in a bridal chamber. Photo from Bittel, *Les Hittites*, pl. 140. Anatolian Civilizations Museum, Ankara.

san: either a potter, a smith, a carpenter, a leather-worker, a fuller, a weaver, or a maker of leggings, he shall pay 30 shekels of silver" (§176b; see also §200b).[77] Skilled craftsmen were usually attached either to the palace or to a temple. Herdsmen were of low social standing, and the job of tending the flocks probably often fell to deportees and slaves.[78] Upward mobility was possible for those fortunate enough to enter the king's service, but the opportunities for such advancement among the poorest members of society would have been extremely limited. A large portion of the free male population would have spent many of its summers on campaign with the king as a

---

77. Hoffner, *The Laws of the Hittites*, 140–41, but with the emendation of the figure "10" to "30." See ibid., 220.

78. Gary Beckman, "Herding and Herdsmen in Hittite Culture," in *Documentum Asiae Minoris Antiquae: Festschrift für Heinrich Otten zum 75. Geburtstag* (ed. Erich Neu and Christel Rüster; Wiesbaden: Harrassowitz, 1988), 38–39.

kind of army reserve, leaving the women, deportees, and slaves to care for the crops and livestock. The spring and fall, when the male members of the community would have been at home, were a time for celebration, and agricultural and religious festivals filled the calendar, providing welcome relief from the harshness of life on the plateau. Such festivals would have involved feasting, dancing, singing, and athletic games.

A woman's most important responsibility was to produce children. Male children especially were economically vital to a household and were responsible for caring for their parents both in old age and, after their deaths, in their mortuary cults. Women did not necessarily operate entirely within the domestic sphere, however, as they could occupy positions as millers, cooks, weavers, fullers, doctors, ritual practitioners, musicians, and dancers, attached to the palace or to a temple. Women no doubt found their best outlet for independent expression in the religious sphere, whether through ritual performance or by providing magico-medical assistance to those in need.

ARTS

It is not difficult to understand why Hittite art and architecture has not captured the interest of the modern public in the way that Mesopotamian and Egyptian art have. The Hittites left behind no royal tombs rich in luxurious grave goods, and their monumental structures—what few of them remain—appear modest beside the pyramids of Egypt and the ziggurats of Mesopotamia. Moreover, the reliefs depict humans and gods who, by modern standards, are simply odd in appearance. No idealized images surrounded by decorative detail meet the casual observer, and what may once have been colorfully painted reliefs now appear gray and stark. Nevertheless, Hittite art is both original, recognizable, and deserving of our interest because it tells us a great deal about the people who created it.

Although Hittite artists imported some commonly used motifs, most notably the sphinx (from Egypt) and winged sun-disk (via northern Syria), and seal engravers and ivory carvers found their inspiration in Syro-Mesopotamian traditions, Hittite art has its roots firmly in Anatolia, where artists superimposed their unique style over an existing indigenous artistic tradition. Animal-shaped ceremonial vessels and pottery decorated with molded relief continued forms that had been popular in the Assyrian Colony period, although they seem to become less popular in the last century of the empire.[79]

---

79. R. M. Boehmer, *Die Reliefkeramik von Boğazköy* (Berlin: Mann, 1983), *passim*; Jeanny Vorys Canby, "Jewelry and Personal Arts in Anatolia," *CANE*, 1679.

Although stamp seals continued to be preferred over cylinder seals, the popular motifs and crowded scenes of the Assyrian Colony period were replaced on Hittite-period seals with royal motifs such as the double-headed eagle, as well as geometric patterns and, of course, hieroglyphs.[80] The recent discovery of wall paintings in Temple 9 in the Upper City are the only known example of such and may be an indication that a Hittite king was patronizing foreign (Mycenaean?) artists.

Our understanding of the development of the art has been hampered by the fact that most examples have been found outside of stratigraphic contexts and therefore cannot be dated with any precision. The stereotypical composition of human forms, particularly in the later period, only confounds efforts further. Even the magnificent gates that afforded entry to the capital are difficult to place within a diachronic sequence, since they cannot be connected to any stratigraphy or datable structure and no Hittite king has claimed credit in his official records for the fortification in the Upper City. Many would put them in the last fifty years of the empire, but new evidence suggests that they may belong to the beginning of the thirteenth century rather than to its end.[81] The existence of early examples of monumental sculpture and relief carving do indicate that the Hittite sculptural tradition had a long indigenous development and was not a foreign influence, as some have suggested.[82] The promise of new finds from excavations at Hittite regional centers such as Ortaköy-Sapinuwa offers hope of fresh insights.[83]

The Hittites' love of stone is apparent both in the architectural use of monumental blocks of cut stone and in the use of living rock in its natural

---

80. On Hittite glyptic, see, most recently, Ali Dinçol and Belkis Dinçol, "Große, Prinzen, Herren: Die Spitzen der Reichsadministration im Spiegel ihrer Siegel," in *Die Hethiter und ihr Reich: Das Volk der 1000 Götter* (Stuttgart: Theiss, 2002), 82–87; and Ali Dinçol, "'Tabarna-' und 'Ädikula'-Siegel: Die Siegel hethitischer Großkönige und Großköniginnen," in *Die Hethiter und ihr Reich*, 88–93.

81. Jürgen Seeher, "Chronology in Ḫattuša: New Approaches to an Old Problem," in *Structuring and Dating in Hittite Archaeology* (ed. Dirk Paul Mielke, Ulf-Dietrich Schoop, Jürgen Seeher; BYZAS 4; Istanbul: Deutsches Archaeologisches Institut, 2006), 207.

82. On these early examples, see Jeanny Vorys Canby, "The Sculptors of the Hittite Capital," *OrAnt* 15 (1976): 39; Kutlu Emre, "Felsreliefs, Stelen, Orthostaten: Großplastik als monumentale Form staatlicher und rleigiöser Repräsentation," in *Die Hethiter und ihr Reich*, 219; Kay Kohlmeyer, "Anatolian Architectural Decorations, Statuary, and Stelae," *CANE*, 2643.

83. Seeher ("Chronology in Ḫattuša," 210) notes the relief at the entrance to Building D at Ortaköy of a male figure with a lance and a bow, which he dates to the pre-empire period (i.e., pre-Alaca reliefs; Aygül Süel and Mustafa Süel, "Ortaköy-Šapinuva," *Arkeo-Atlas* 3 [2004]: 60).

setting as the canvas for large relief carvings. In both contexts, the surface of the rock was cut back to expose figures in low relief. On some reliefs, such as at Firaktin, the figures are flat with little interior modeling, while on others, such as the so-called King's Gate at Hattusa, the reliefs show rounded, plastic forms, and great attention is given to interior details such as musculature and clothing.

Located either on ancient roads or mountain passes, the numerous examples of Hittite rock reliefs would have required scaffolding to create and illustrate how in Hittite art the physical setting becomes a part of the work. These reliefs, either of a single figure or of groups of figures in religious scenes, might be of royal personages or deities or both. A few of the reliefs are accompanied by inscriptions that allow us to date them. Muwatalli II's (1295–1272 B.C.E.) relief at Sirkeli is the earliest that is datable, and it depicts the single figure of the king dressed in ceremonial garb.[84] Similar lone figures, but dressed in warrior fashion, are those of a prince at Hamide in Cilicia and Karabel in the west, the latter representing Tarkasnawa, king of the vassal state of Mira during the reign of Tudhaliya IV (fig. 2.7). Hattusili III and his queen Puduhepa offer libations to a god and a goddess, respectively, in adjacent scenes on a rock face at Firaktin (fig. 2.6). Attributable to the same king are the three figures in procession on a relief in the Taşçi River valley. Nearby at Imamkulu, another warrior figure, identified as Prince Kuwalamuwa, who has yet to turn up in the Hittite texts, stands at the back of a tableau of divine figures. Teshub on his chariot rides above three mountain deities who stand on griffin demons. A winged and naked goddess stands ready to receive him. A relief at Hanyeri near Imamkulu depicts the same Prince Kuwalamuwa facing a bull representing the god Sharruma. The seated deity high on Mount Sipylos (Manisa Dağ) at Akpınar, whom Pausanias identified as a weeping Niobe, is poorly preserved (she could be a he) and is unique among Hittite reliefs in presenting a deity fully frontal and in high relief. It likewise appears to be signed by the ubiquitous Prince Kuwalamuwa.[85] At Gavurkalesi, west of Ankara, two large male figures (a king and his personal deity?) approach a seated goddess from the right in a rare example of an unsigned relief. The tradition of Hittite rock reliefs culminates at Yazılıkaya, the official open-air sanctuary of the Hittite capital, with its procession of gods and its large relief of Tudhaliya IV (see further below).

---

84. Adjacent to Muwatalli's figure, another relief, defaced in antiquity, may have repesented his son Mursili III (Urhi-Teshub).

85. Hans G. Güterbock, "Gedanken über ein Hethitisches Königssiegel aus Boğazköy," *IstMitt* 43 (1993): 113–14. A Kuwalamuwa is attested in Mursili II's annals; see J. David Hawkins, "Kuwatnamuwa," *RlA* 6 (1983): 398.

Outwardly religious in focus, Hittite relief art served the purposes of the state. Scenes in relief of divine processions, sacred hunts, and festival celebrations reveal the calculated piety of the Hittite kings, who from Muwatalli on also had themselves represented in the protective embrace of their patron deities or presenting offerings to the gods. The double-headed eagle, found both at Yazılıkaya (fig. 3.13) and Alaca as well as on seals, was an emblem of the royal family and was distinctive enough to survive antiquity and resurface in Byzantine iconography.

The rock reliefs also served the state. Both Sirkeli and Firaktin had associated Hittite settlements and might have served as mortuary shrines for Muwatalli II and Hattusili III, respectively, as well as redistributive centers (the "stone houses" or mausolea mentioned in the texts; see ch. 4). The rock reliefs are scattered but fall well within the range of the Hittites' greatest influence, that is, in territories where they could be "read" and serve as a symbol of royal control within the kingdom. The exceptions are, of course, Tarkasnawa's relief at Karabel and that of Kurunta at Hatip in Tarhuntassa, which obviously ran counter to the interests of the Hittite state and are an additional sign of Tudhaliya IV's loosening grip on his empire.

With cut stone, the art became an integral part of the architectural scheme. Monumental examples in the round include the unfinished monument of a storm-god standing on a bull found at Fasillar, which was located not far from the sacred spring of Eflatun Pinar. This sacred precinct consists of a sacred stone-lined pool complex from which emerges large blocks of cut stone, each with an individually carved relief that fit together to form a composite monument in which the Storm-God and Sun-Goddess are seated over a series of five mountain gods. Flanking them are ten genii who support three winged sun-disks, the uppermost of which, carved on a single piece of stone, caps the series of stone blocks. Both of these monuments marked sacred precincts of some importance.

Popular subjects such as lions and sphinxes offer the best opportunity for understanding artistic developments over time. The gate structure at Alaca Höyük, with its decorated orthostat blocks and monumental sphinx guardians, was probably cut sometime before 1400 B.C.E. and thus provides a chronological basis for stylistic comparison. Probably also belonging to the early (or pre-)empire period are the sphinxes that once flanked the ediface on Nişantaş. Lions and sphinxes protected the entrances to several temples in the Upper City.[86] Although the idea of gate lions as guardians is not origi-

---

86. See Peter Neve, Ḫattuša: Stadt der Götter und Tempel (Mainz: von Zabern, 1992), Abb. 112–119.

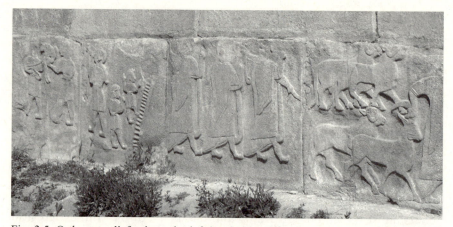

Fig. 3.5. Orthostat reliefs along the left-hand side of the gate entrance at Alaca Höyük showing a festival procession, including musicians and acrobats, moving toward a scene of worship before the Storm-God in the form of a bull (not shown). Photo by the author.

nal with the Hittites, making the animal an integral part of the gate structure itself was a Hittite invention.[87]

Of the elaborate sculptures that formed the gate entrance to Alaca Höyük, only two sphinxes, greeting visitors entering the city, remain intact. They emerge from cyclopean blocks of stone that are 13 feet high and 6.5 feet thick. Unlike the reliefs on living rock, which are self-contained, the two tiers of orthostat blocks that form part of the wall of the gate structure at Alaca Höyük are decorated with independent compositions that form a continuous narrative intended to be "read" (fig. 3.5). On the right, a procession of figures proceeds toward a seated goddess, perhaps the Sun-Goddess. On the bottom left register, a procession of acrobats, musicians, cultic officials, and royal children, led by the king and queen, end at an image of the Storm-God in the form of a bull standing on a pedestal. The only inscription is to identify the Storm-God. Two more registers placed above this composition show hunting scenes in which deer, boar, and lion fall prey to hunters armed with bows and arrows or spears and accompanied by their dogs.

At the capital, three monumental gates offered access from the south. The sculpture of all three shows meticulous attention to interior detail. The lions that greet the visitor entering the city on the southwest emerge from single cyclopean blocks and must be viewed from the front for the full effect to be felt. They are carved with such detail that the tufts of the manes are

87. Canby, "The Sculptors of the Hittite Capital," 40.

visible. The divine figure who, with a gesture, ushers visitors from the city on its southeastern side is carved, unusually, in high relief, so that a passerby can look directly into his eyes, and even his chest hairs are delineated.

Four sculpted sphinxes once adorned the gate on the artificial promontory called Yerkapı on the southern end of the capital. Only one of the exterior sphinxes remains, the other having been carried off for reuse in the Roman or Byzantine period. The two interior sphinxes were badly damaged in the fire that destroyed the city and have long since been removed to museums. The heads, fore-, and hindquarters of these eight-feet-tall sculptures were carved in the round, with the rest of their bodies in high relief on the sides of the door jambs. Wearing caps with horns, the slightly smiling sphinxes on the gate's city side once looked down benignly upon the Upper City. The Sphinx Gate is narrow, off-center, inconvenient to traffic, and its entrance on the city side was open. For these reasons, it probably never served as a city entrance; rather, its role may have been to provide ceremonial entry to the sacred temple quarter.[88]

Hittite relief art was not limited to monumental stone. Vessels of metal, clay, and ivory also characteristically bore scenes in relief or animal figures. The human figures in such scenes tend to follow the conventions established for the rock reliefs. The ceramic vases from Bitik and Inandik discussed above are thought to be Old Hittite (ca. 1650–1400 B.C.E.) on stylistic grounds. The better-preserved Inandik vase (fig. 3.6) depicts fifty human figures altogether, including musicians, acrobats, and revellers, over four tiers of relief. A relief vase of similar execution that came to light recently in the vicinity of Hüseyindede in north-central Anatolia bears a relief decoration that points to an Anatolian origin for the "sport" of bull-leaping better known from Minoan Crete.

Vessels in silver are among the most celebrated objects of Hittite manufacture today. A silver rhyton in the shape of a fist is inscribed "Tudhaliya, Great King," and may belong to the reign of Tudhaliya II, or perhaps to Tudhaliya III (fig. 3.7).[89] The relief around the wrist of the vessel depicts a

---

88. Jeanny Vorys Canby, "The Walters Gallery Cappadocian Tablet and the Sphinx in Anatolia in the Second Millennium B.C." *JNES* 34 (1975): 244.

89. For a dating to Tudhaliya II, see Singer, review of Klengel, *Geschichte des hethitischen Reiches*, 639; for Tudhaliya III, see Hans G. Güterbock and T. Kendall, "A Hittite Silver Vessel in the Form of a Fist," in *The Ages of Homer* (ed. Jane B. Carter and Sarah P. Morris; Austin: University of Texas Press, 1995), 57. Another object possibly from this era is a silver bowl in the Ankara Museum that bears a hieroglyphic inscription identifying the object as a gift from Asmaya, a Hittite, to King Mazakarhuha (of Karkamis?) and noting that it was made in the year Tudhaliya Labarna smote the land

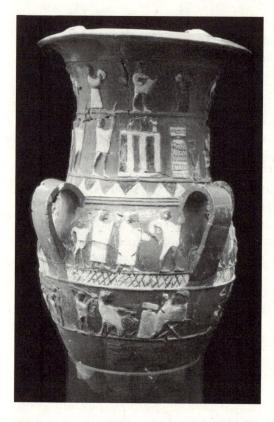

Fig. 3.6. Vase from the vicinity of Inandik depicting a festival celebration. From Tashin Özgüç, *İnandıktepe: An Important Cult Center in the Old Hittite Period* (TTKY 5/43; Ankara: Türk Tarih Kurumu Basımevi, 1988), pl. F/1.

ceremonial procession the focal point of which is a king pouring a libation to a storm-god holding a bull's reins. The deity stands before a masonry structure that may represent Hattusa itself. Another silver rhyton, in the shape of a stag's forequarters and probably belonging to the reign of Tudhaliya IV, bears a ceremonial scene connected with a deity of the hunt, who is shown twice in the relief, once standing on a stag and once seated behind an altar (fig. 4.2). A priest or king offers a libation from a vase of the sort that have been excavated from temples in Hattusa's temple quarter. Behind the deity, the tools of the hunter's trade—spears, a quiver, and a hunting bag—are shown alongside a fresh "kill," a dead stag. In both cases the vessel would have been used in the cult of the deity its relief depicts.

Tarwiza (= Taruisa/Troy?; see J. David Hawkins, "A Hieroglyphic Luwian Inscription on a Silver Bowl in the Museum of Anatolian Civilizations, Ankara," *Studia Troica* 15 [2005]: 193–204). If the inscription refers to Tudhaliya I/II's Assuwa campaign, it is the earliest existing example of a Luwian hieroglyphic inscription outside of the seals.

Fig. 3.7. Ceremonial silver vessel in the form of a fist dating to Tudhaliya II or III. Photo courtesy of the Museum of Fine Arts, Boston.

The minor arts are also represented in Hittite Anatolia, particularly in the form of objects in precious materials manufactured for the wealthier members of society. Figural representations are miniature versions of those on monumental relief sculpture. For example, two-dimensional lapis figures surrounded by gold frames from Karkamis are almost exact copies of the figures in procession at Yazılıkaya. A lapis figure from Alalakh of a Hittite goddess with her cloak pulled back is comparable to the goddess at Imamkulu,[90] while the Storm-God in the Imamkulu relief may be identified with the chariot-riding Storm-God on a seal of Mursili III, believed to be the

---

90. Canby, "Jewelry and Personal Arts in Anatolia," 1679.

Fig. 3.8. The "dagger-god" in the small chamber at Yazılıkaya is an underworld deity, and his presence in the room (among other clues) suggests that it was used as a royal funerary chamber. From Bittel, *Les Hittites*, pl. 254.

Storm-God of Aleppo.[91] An elaborately carved ceremonial axe head from Sarkişla in eastern Cappadocia is another example of small sculpture that imitates relief sculpture (compare the "dagger-god" on the wall of the small chamber at Yazılıkaya, for which see below and fig. 3.8). The minor arts are also represented by figures in the round, as, for example, the tiny pendants of the gods in precious materials. The seated Sun-Goddess pendants call to mind the deity enshrined on Mount Sipylos (fig. 3.9). The rarity of finds of objects of personal adornment, such as the earrings, bracelets, necklaces, and rings worn by figures (both male and female) in the reliefs, can be attributed

---

91. For this identification, see J. David Hawkins, "The Storm-God Seal of Mursili III," in Beckman, Beal, and McMahon, *Hittite Studies in Honor of Harry A. Hoffner Jr.*, 169–75.

Fig. 3.9. Pendants of women or goddesses wearing solar headdress-
es such as this have been found in cultic contexts. Norbert Schimmel Collection, Metropolitan Museum of Art, New York.

to the absence of identifiably royal tombs of the Hittite period and to the fact
that the residents of Hattusa took their personal belongings with them when
they abandoned the capital.

A handful of objects of Hittite art found in Palestine attest to contacts
between the two regions. A silver scrap hoard found in a late-seventeenth to
early-sixteenth century context at Shiloh included a crescent-shaped pendant
and a large pendant decorated with the "Cappadocian" symbol, a variation of
the sun-disk motif peculiar to Anatolia.[92] Moon crescents and sun-disks were

---

92. Israel Finkelstein and Baruch Brandl, "A Group of Metal Objects from Shiloh,"

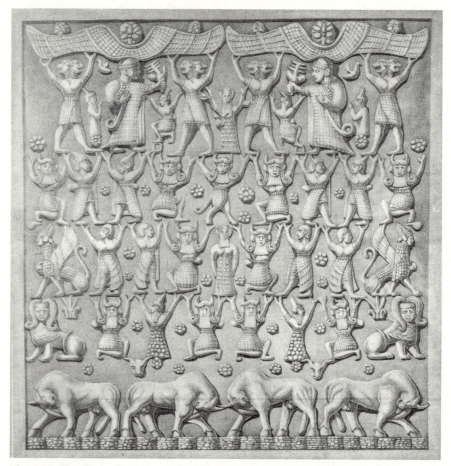

Fig. 3.10. The Hittite ivory from Megiddo bears a distinctively Hittite composition with cosmic scenes. Courtesy of the Oriental Institute of the University of Chicago.

popular motfis in Anatolia from the Assyrian Colony period on.[93] An ivory panel from a Late Bronze Age level at Megiddo was found in a hoard of ivories from the "Treasury" of the palace (fig. 3.10). The panel depicts two Hittite deities (or kings) in an antithetic position supported by several tiers of divine symbols and was certainly of Hittite manufacture. An ivory box

Israel Museum Journal 4 (1985): 17–26; Israel Finkelstein, Shelomoh Bunimovitz, and Zvi Lederman, *Shiloh: The Archaeology of a Biblical Site* (Tel Aviv: Tel Aviv University Institute of Archaeology, 1993), 243–45.

93. Singer, "The Hittites and the Bible Revisited," 739.

decorated with lions and sphinxes found in the same hoard is probably also from Anatolia. Ivories are one of the few classes of Hittite art found outside of the Hittite Empire.[94]

Equally interesting are the objects of local Levantine manufacture that show undeniable Hittite influence.[95] Among these, the lions that once flanked the entrance to the temple at Late Bronze Age Hazor have received the most attention, as they are the only lion-gate sculptures to be found in Palestine. The question of who carved the lions, Hittite artisans or Canaanites borrowing a Hittite form, remains open. Notably, a sherd incised with a one-inch-long smiting god—a type common to Syria and Anatolia in the Late Bronze Age—was found on the surface of the mound at Hazor. The upturned shoes, pointed hat, and short skirt indicate its Hittite inspiration. A krater of local manufacture from early Iron Age Raddana decorated with a tubular pipe and bull-head spouts attached to its interior wall is similar to libation vessels from the Hittite Old Kingdom. Two well-publicized cult stands from eleventh–tenth century Taanach are of the type bearing relief and incised decoration. One has five superimposed pairs of winged sphinxes and lions. The other has four tiers. The bottom tier depicts a naked female flanked by lions. Two winged sphinxes (cherubim) flank a vacant space in the third tier. The second tier shows two lions flanking two ibexes that in turn flank a sacred tree. In the top tier, containing the most complex scene, two voluted columns flank the central scene. Behind these, on the sides of the stand in side view are the figures of two griffins. The central scene is of a quadruped, above which is a winged sun-disk.[96] The motif of alternating, superimposed sphinxes and lions is quintessentially Anatolian and is already apparent in glyptic art from Middle Bronze Age Kültepe-Kanes and Acemhöyük-Purushanda.[97] Two clay towers from Hattusa with protruding

94. Canby, "Jewelry and Personal Arts in Anatolia," 1679.

95. The alleged stylistic similarity of courtyard structures in the sanctuary architecture at MB IIB Tell Balatah-Shechem to temples in Hattusa (G. Ernest Wright, *Shechem: The Biography of a Biblical City* [New York: McGraw-Hill, 1965], 107) and the proposed parallels at Boghazköy to the Tell es-Saidiyeh waterworks (Jonathan Tubb, "Sea Peoples in the Jordan Valley," in *The Sea Peoples and Their World: A Reassessment* [ed. Eliezer D. Oren; University Museum Monograph 108; Philadelphia: University Museum, University of Pennsylvania, 2000], 182) are not compelling.

96. Pirhiya Beck, "The Cult-Stands from Taanach: Aspects of the Iconographic Tradition of Early Iron Age Cult Objects in Palestine," in *From Nomadism to Monarchy: Archaeological and Historical Aspects of Early Israel* (ed. Israel Finkelstein and Nadav Na'aman; Jerusalem, Israel Exploration Society, 1994), 352–81, figs. 1, 2, and 8.

97. Beck, "The Cult-Stands from Taanach," 357, figs. 3 and 4.

Fig. 3.11. Hittite clay towers upon which certain Israelite cult stands may
have been modeled. They are characterized by the use of fenestration and
carved figures. From Bittel, *Les Hittites*, pl. 50. Anatolian Civilizations Museum, Ankara.

superimposed animal protomes are also rendered two-dimensionally on seals
(fig. 3.11), suggesting that the superimposed lions and sphinxes on the Anatolian seals were intended to represent three-dimensional cult objects of a
kind similar to the Taanach stands.[98]

---

98. Beck, "The Cult-Stands from Taanach," 357–59 and figs. 5, 6, 7. For the references to the tower-shaped models from Late Bronze Age Meskene-Emar, Tell Frey, and
other Middle Euphrates sites that provide the closest comparisons, see Singer, "The Hittites and the Bible Revisited," 740 with n. 96.

Fig. 3.12. General view of Yazılıkaya's main chamber with the procession of gods on the left and goddesses on the right. From Bittel, *Les Hittites*, pl. 232.

EXCURSUS
Yazılıkaya, a Royal Sanctuary

The most ambitious sculpture project in living rock was Yazılıkaya, a natural outcropping situated a little more than a kilometer northeast of Hattusa. The natural structure contained two main chambers that were open to the sky and enclosed by twelve-meter-high walls. The structure was in use as a religious sanctuary—perhaps as the location of the New Year's festival—from at least the fifteenth century, but only in the thirteenth, with the addition of elaborate scenes in relief, was a manmade temple constructed across the front of the outcropping to block access. Visitors passed through a stepped gateway that led to an enclosed courtyard with an altar. Turning left, they passed through another stepped gate before finding themselves in the main chamber of the sanctuary (fig. 3.12).

Here one is greeted on either side by reliefs of gods and goddesses in procession. Cartouches beside many of the figures identify them as belonging to the Hurrian pantheon, which became especially important in the state

Fig. 3.13. The central scene of the reliefs at Yazılıkaya, depicting Teshub and Hebat with their entourage. Photo by the author.

religion of the mid-thirteenth century. A narrow ledge for the placement of votive offerings lines the rock face below the figures. Among the deities in procession on the male side are several mountain gods, the Sun-God of Heaven, a moon-god, the war-gods Ashtabi and ZABABA, and even a winged Shaushga in her masculine form, attended by Ninatta and Kulitta. On the female side, among other, lesser-known goddesses, Allatu, queen of the underworld, is identified.

The processions meet at the back of the chamber, where the divine couple Teshub and Hebat face one another in greeting (fig. 3.13). Hebat stands on a feline, as does her son Sharruma, who is positioned behind her. He is followed by two goddesses, Alanzu, the daughter of Teshub and Hebat, and a granddaughter of Teshub, who stand on a double-headed eagle. Teshub stands on a pair of mountain deities and carries a short sword in his belt and a mace in his hand. Behind him are two more gods standing on mountains, one of them probably Kumarbi. The two bulls that peek out from behind the god and goddess provide a rare example of overlapping figures in Hittite art.

Across an open space on a third rock wall, as if he were observing the procession from a distance, is a well-preserved relief of Tudhaliya IV, shown in the dress the Hittite king wore when presiding over religious ceremonies, with skull cap and holding the crook/lituus (fig. 3.1). He stands on mountains. The figure of Tudhaliya IV constitutes a self-contained element, twice the size of the figures in the procession. Did he place his image here to announce his ownership of the sanctuary, or was it put there by his son Suppiluliuma II after his death?

Entrance to the smaller, eighteen-meter-long chamber was protected by two winged lion-demons in relief, their arms raised in threat to the unauthorized visitor. Here, at the top of the narrow chamber, a life-sized statue once stood, we assume of Tudhaliya IV. His image appears here in relief as well, this time in the embrace of his protective deity, Sharruma. Across the aisle from Tudhaliya, a group of twelve gods with scimitar-shaped swords (also depicted at the end of the procession in the large chamber) run toward an unknown goal. The room may have served as a mortuary chamber honoring Tudhaliya IV, a theory supported not only by this king's presence in the room but by the unusual image of a "dagger-god," a god of the underworld (Nergal?) represented in the form of an upright dagger (fig. 3.8). The pommel of the dagger is fashioned in the shape of a head in profile wearing the peaked cap of divinity. His shoulders are the foreparts of two lions facing outward. The hilt is formed by two crouching lions facing downward toward the dagger's point. Three niches cut deep into the sides of the chamber may have held the lamps needed for nocturnal rituals.

LETTERS

The Hittites adopted an Old Babylonian form of the cuneiform script for the writing of texts in the Hittite language possibly as early as the Assyrian Colony period.[99] To date, more than thirty thousand tablet fragments, representing roughly 3,000 to 3,500 separate tablets, have been recovered from the ruins of the Hittite capital at Boghazköy since excavations began there in 1906,[100] as well as from recent excavations at the provincial Hittite-period sites of Maşat-Tapikka, Kuşaklı-Sarissa, and Ortaköy-Sapinuwa. The Hittite libraries at Hattusa housed historical documents; treaties; edicts;

---

99. Hans Gustav Güterbock, "Hittite Historiography: A Survey," in *History, Historiography and Interpretation: Studies in Biblical and Cuneiform Literatures* (ed. Hayim Tadmor and Moshe Weinfeld; Jerusalem: Magnes, 1983), 24–25; Jörg Klinger, "Wer lehrte die Hethiter das Schreiben? Zur Paläographie früher Texte in akkadischer Sprache aus Boğazköy," in Alp and Süel, *Acts of the IIIrd International Congress of Hittitology*, 365–75.

100. van den Hout, "Another View of Hittite Literature," 864–65.

instructions; laws; myths and legends; medical, ritual, and festival prescriptions; oracle texts; lexical lists; and hymns and prayers. In addition, texts in Hattian, Palaic, Luwian, and Hurrian, as well as Sumerian and Akkadian compositions, have been recovered. The scribes also archived a wide variety of more ephemeral documents, including letters, vows, cult inventories, and administrative and economic texts such as deeds, court depositions, hippological texts, and shelf lists. Most of the tablets at Hattusa have been found on the citadel (especially in building A), in the storerooms surrounding the Great Temple, and in the so-called House on the Slope. The archives at Maşat-Tapikka and Ortaköy-Sapinuwa date to the Middle Hittite period, supplementing the limited information from the capital for this period with numerous letters but also, at Ortaköy, with religious and administrative documents, including many Hurrian religious texts. At Kuşaklı-Sarissa, Building A housed tablets of a religious nature belonging to the period of the Hittite Empire.

With the cuneiform script, the Hittites also imported an entire literary tradition from Mesopotamia.[101] Sumero-Akkadian lexical lists, hymns, omens, fragments of the epics of Gilgamesh and Atrahasis, and legends about Sargon and Naram-Sin, the great kings of Akkad, are among the documents recovered from the libraries at Hattusa. In fact, stories about Sargon and Naram-Sin were circulating in Anatolia already in the nineteenth century B.C.E.[102] A Hittite translation of the King of Battle legend celebrates Sargon's defeat of Nur-Dagan, king of Purushanda (modern Acemhöyük), an important city from the Old Assyrian Colony period.[103] A Hittite-language version of the the Great Revolt against Naram-Sin[104] shows that the Hittites freely adapted the stories to reflect their own interests, choosing to focus on events and places in Anatolia, such as by adding Pamba, king of Hattusa, to the Hittite version of

---

101. See Beckman, "Mesopotamians and Mesopotamian Learning at Ḥattuša," *JCS* 35 (1983): 97–114; Alfonso Archi, "Hittite and Hurrian Literatures: An Overview," *CANE*, 2367.

102. A recently published school text from Kültepe-Kanes deals with Sargon's suppression of a revolt; see Gary Beckman, "Sargon and Naram-Sin in Hatti: Reflections of Mesopotamian Antiquity among the Hittites," in Kuhn and Stahl, *Die Gegenwart des Altertums*, 88.

103. A similar version uncovered at El Amarna, the city of the fourteenth-century pharoah Akhenaton, may have come from a Hittite source.

104. *CTH* 311. For the Akkadian-language prism from Hattusa (*KBo* 19.98; *CTH* 819) with the same story, see Joan Goodnick Westenholz, *Legends of the Kings of Akkade* (Winona Lake, Ind.: Eisenbrauns, 1997), 280–93.

the story.[105] These texts demonstrate a reverence in the Hittite Old Kingdom for Mesopotamian literary and cultural traditions, but more than that, with their local interest, they tied Anatolian history to that of the wider world, even if it meant perpetuating and enhancing a tradition in which Anatolian kings were on the losing side.[106] These stories may in fact have been appropriated by the Old Kingdom rulers (perhaps Hattusili I) as a means of creating a cultural tradition and a history that the Hittite dynasty itself lacked.[107]

Their indebtedness to Mesopotamian culture and learning notwithstanding, the Hittites' own contribution to the development of ancient Near Eastern literature is considerable, particularly in the genres of historiography, myth, and prayer.

HISTORIOGRAPHY

Hittite historiographic texts include primarily royal annals and edicts, as well as a few narratives of a more literary character. As a rule, they share a single purpose: "the justification of kingship and its current occupant in the eyes of both gods and men."[108] The origin and development of Hittite historiography, as well as its relationship to the Mesopotamian historiographic tradition, is not yet fully understood.[109] The royal annals (or "manly deeds," as the Hittites referred to them) are first-person narrations of the military conquests of the king organized by regnal year. The Hittite royal annals take the form of a military itinerary in which military victories, the destruction of cities, and lists of booty and captives taken are recounted. Unlike the Luwian monumental inscriptions of the thirteenth century, they were apparently not composed for public consumption; that is, they were not propagandistic in purpose.[110] Since the annals are rarely comprehensive and do not utilize any means of marking time long-term (the passage of time is indicated simply

---

105. Sargon in Anatolia was already a known element of the story in Mesopotamia in the Old Babylonian period and thus was not a Hittite invention; see Amir Gilan, "Hittite Ethnicity? Constructions of Identity in Hittite Literature," in Collins, Bachvarova, and Rutherford, *Anatolian Interfaces*.

106. Gilan, "Hittite Ethnicity?"; Beckman, "Sargon and Naram-Sin in Hatti," 89.

107. Gilan, "Hittite Ethnicity?"

108. Gary Beckman, "The Siege of Uršu Text (CTH 7) and Old Hittite Historiography," *JCS* 47 (1995): 32.

109. See Jörg Klinger, "Historiographie als Paradigma: Die Quellen zur hethitischen Geschichte und ihre Deutung," in Wilhelm, *Akten des IV. Internationalen Kongresses*, 272–91.

110. See, e.g., van den Hout, "Institutions, Vernaculars, Publics," 221.

by the phrase "in the next year...") the chronological framework that they provide is minimal. The Anitta Chronicle, the earliest surviving example of this type of history writing, is a record of the conquests of Anitta, the pre-Hittite-era ruler who destroyed Hattus. The tradition of annalistic writing culminated in the extensive annals of Mursili II (r. ca. 1321–1295 B.C.E.), whose proclivity for history writing extended to recording the events of his father Suppiluliuma's reign as well.

Later annals are considerably more formulaic in their expression than earlier examples. Certainly Hattusili I's annals, in keeping with the style of the texts from his reign generally, were not stereotypical in their phrasing in the way that Mursili II's were. The reigns of Hattusili I and his successor Mursili I mark a high point in literary development, in which there was considerable experimentation in various text genres, including historiography. The Political Testament of Hattusili I illustrates the free expression typical of early historiographic texts:

> You are my foremost subjects. You [must keep] my words, those of the king. You may (only) eat bread and drink (only) water. Then [Ḫattuša] will stand tall, and my land will be [at peace]. But if you don't keep the king's word, you won't live [much longer (?)], but will perish. [Whoever] confounds the king's words, ... such a person should not be a high-ranking servant. [His throat (?)] shall be slit. Didn't his sons set aside these words of my grandfather [...]? In Sanahuitta my grandfather had proclaimed his son Labarna (as heir to the throne). [But afterwards] his subjects and high noblemen had confounded his words [and] set Papaḫdilmah (on the throne). How many years have now passed, and [how many (of them)] have escaped (their fate)? The household of the high noblemen—where are they? Haven't they perished?[111]

Appealing to the past to lend force to an argument and justfiy the present remained a characteristic of Hittite historiography until the end and later became an especially useful political tool in the historical prologues to the treaties (see above). The account of the Siege of Urshu, a text written in Akkadian and also attributed to Hattusili I, paints a picture of a long-suffering monarch and his incompetent subordinates. The unusual use of direct discourse in the Urshu text is reminiscent of speeches used to advance the plot in Greek historiography. As Gary Beckman notes, this device demonstrates that we are dealing in this text not with a primary historical source, "but rather with a conscious effort to understand and interpret the course of

---

111. "Bilingual Edict," translated by Beckman (*COS* 2.15:81, §20).

events, that is, with historiography."[112] The use of irony also sets this composition apart, as when Hattusili I asks of one of his inept generals: "Why have you not given battle? Do you stand [as] on chariots of water, or have you perhaps (yourself) turned to water?"[113]

The Palace Chronicle, attributed to Mursili I, is a collection of anecdotes, performed in the context of a festival banquet,[114] about disloyal and corrupt officials under the king's father (Hattusili I) and the punishment they received. This unusual text packages lessons about the importance of competence and obedience in an entertaining format directed at the participants in the banquet. The glorification of the old king by contrasting him with inferior humans in both the Palace Chronicle and the Siege of Urshu is unique to the Old Kingdom, as is their anecdotal (as opposed to chronological) format.

More linear narratives begin only with Telipinu's Proclamation, in which the past is presented not as a series of anecdotes but in a continuous chronological sequence. Here, too, however, the purpose of recounting the past is didactic. Telipinu's edict preaches harmony in unity and uses the mistakes of the past to justify the present edict, the ostensible purpose of which is to establish rules for dynastic succession but which also serves to justify his own usurpation of the throne and legitimate his rule. In this respect, Telipinu's Proclamation most closely resembles Hattusili III's so-called Apology.

"Let me proclaim the divine providence of Shaushga (of Samuha). Let humanity hear it!" are the words with which Hattusili III begins his Apology, the best-known, and certainly the most written about, composition in the Hittite textual corpus. Framed in the form of a decree establishing a religious endowment for the goddess Shaushga, who is attributed with a central role in Hattusili's rise to power, the document is unique among royal propagandistic literature of the Late Bronze Age. Although autobiographical, it is not an autobiography; nor is it a royal annal, although its dependence on the annalistic tradition is apparent. Despite its focus on the events surrounding Hattusili III's usurpation of the throne from his nephew, Mursili III, the Apology's most important goal may have been to designate his heir, Tudhaliya IV.[115]

---

112. Beckman, "The Siege of Uršu Text," 31.

113. *KBo* 1.11 (*CTH* 7) rev. 10–11; translated by Beckman, "The Siege of Uršu Text," 26.

114. Amir Gilan, "Bread, Wine and Partridges—A Note on the Palace Anecdotes (CTH 8)," in Groddek and Zorman, *Tabularia Hethaeorum*, 299–304.

115. Fiorella Imparati, "Apology of Ḫattušili III or Designation of his Successor?" in *Studio Historiae Ardens: Ancient Near Eastern Studies Presented to Philo H. J. Houwink*

The affinities of Hattusili's Apology to the story of King David's rise recounted in 1 Sam 16–2 Sam 6 have long been known.[116] The two accounts share several significant themes, among them the king's utter blamelessness in his dealings with his predecessor as his path to the kingship is ineluctably smoothed for him by popular support, the trust of the royal family, and the favor of the deity. His loyalty to his predecessor is irrefutable; the latter is ultimately brought down only by his own questionable decisions. Despite the thematic similarities between the two texts, scholars have been reluctant to suggest a direct dependence of the one upon the other, preferring instead to understand them as sharing a "loose literary form" common to political self-justifications. The distance in time and space between the two compositions dictates caution, and it may be that the Hittite text at best provides clues to understanding the apologetic nature of the biblical story. Still, given the interest that Hattusili III had in advertising his legitimacy and that of his line, and the close ties that his administration enjoyed with the Levantine coast during the peace with Egypt, we cannot, in my view, rule out the possibility that copies of his Apology were circulating in Palestine at the end of the thirteenth century, where they could have been absorbed into the local literary tradition.

Other folkloristic elements pervade Hattusili's text. His "exile" as governor of the Upper Land, his period of waiting as Mursili III sat on the throne, his restoration to a leadership position (the kingship of Hatti), and his establishment of a cult to honor his divine patron are elements that can be found in many Near Eastern (Egyptian Sinuhe, Idrimi of Alalakh) and biblical (Jacob, Joseph, Moses, David) stories. Hattusili also relates how, under the command of Muwatalli II, he was dispatched as commander of a force of 120 chariots to meet an invading force of eight hundred chariots and innumerable infantry. Hattusili scattered the enemy by single-handedly killing the "champion" sent by the enemy to face him.[117] Hoffner has noted the similarity of this episode to the biblical story of the David and Goliath contest of champions (1 Sam

---

ten Cate on the Occasion of His 65th Birthday (ed. Theo P. J. van den Hout and Johan de Roos; Leiden: NINO, 1995), 143–58.

116. See, e.g., Harry A. Hoffner Jr., "Propaganda and Political Justification in Hittite Historiography," in *Unity and Diversity: Essays in the History, Literature, and Religion of the Ancient Near East* (ed. Hans Goedicke and J. J. M. Roberts; Baltimore: Johns Hopkins University Press, 1975) 49–62; P. Kyle McCarter, "The Apology of David," *JBL* 99 (1980): 489–504.

117. "Apology of Ḫattušili III," translated by Theo van den Hout (*COS* 1.77:201, §7).

17).[118] Such folkloristic elements are significant but do not call into question the basic historicity of the events, as other documents more or less confirm Hattusili's account. In effect, Hattusili's Apology presents Mursili III's reign as a disruption of the perfect order, represented by the reign of Muwatalli II, that the hero, Hattusili III, restores when he returns triumphant to Hattusa.

The role of the gods in shaping historical events is an important issue in any discussion of ancient Near Eastern historiography, as it provides a background for understanding Yahweh's intervention in Israelite history. Already in Hattusili I's annals the Sun-Goddess was said to "run before" the king in battle, ensuring his victory, but in the Old Kingdom the notion of divine guidance—of the intervention of the divine in human affairs—is not pronounced. The Siege of Urshu text, for example, does not attribute any role to the gods. Humans were accountable for their own actions and their own successes or failures. In Telipinu's Proclamation, divine judgment of Hantili and other "failed" kings was implied but not stated. In the empire period, divine causality in historical events is much more in evidence. In addition to "running before" the king, the deity's intervention might take the form of a thunderbolt striking the enemy king to his knees or making the king and his men invisible to the enemy—both instances reported by Mursili II in his annals. In this period we also find the notion of divine vindication of the just cause of the victor; it was the goddess Shaushga through her divine providence (*handandatar*) who judged the outcome of the civil war between Hattusili III and his nephew. In all these cases, however, history was not shaped by the gods directly but by the actions of men and whether they were pleasing or displeasing to the gods. A deity might send a plague, but only if the king had drawn down divine wrath upon himself through his own actions.

MYTHOLOGY

For the most part, "Hittite" mythological narratives belong to either the Hattian or Hurrian traditions, but some compositions of Hittite origin are also identifiable. The Zalpa Legend serves as a mythological prologue to a semi-historical account of the relations between the early Hittite state and the city of Zalpa on the Black Sea, which had been prominent in the period of the Assyrian colonies.[119] The queen of Kanes gave birth to thirty sons whom she

118. Harry A. Hoffner Jr., "A Hittite Analogue to the David and Goliath Contest of Champions?" *CBQ* 30 (1968): 220–25.

119. The myth has political overtones, perhaps intended to explain the mythic origins of past hostilities between the two cities. Itamar Singer ("Some Thoughts on Translated

set adrift in baskets on the river. The infants floated to Zalpa on the coast where—in keeping with the best folkloristic traditions of the time—they were rescued and raised by the gods. When they were grown, the boys set out with donkey in tow to return to Kanes. On their journey, they learned that the queen of Kanes had given birth to thirty daughters and thus deduced that they had found their own mother. Ever capricious, the gods, however, caused mother and sons not to recognize one another, and the queen made plans to marry the boys to her daughters. Only the youngest son seems to have been aware of the potential incestuousness of the situation, as he warns, "It is not right!" Apparently his admonition goes unheeded, but the text breaks off at this point. The Zalpa Legend helps to elucidate two passages associated with Israel's the minor judges: Judg 10:3–4, which mentions Jair the Gileadite with his thirty sons who rode on thirty donkeys; and Judg 12:8–9, which lists Ibzan as having had thirty sons and thirty daughters. In the latter case, it is almost as if the biblical author is responding to the Zalpa Legend in pointing out that Ibzan sent his thirty daughters outside the clan to marry and brought in thirty daughters-in-law precisely in order to avoid the situation that arose in Kanes. It is difficult to believe that the author of this biblical passage was not aware of the Zalpa Legend,[120] and if he was, then the story must have been a living tale that circulated within the Hittite Empire and was not simply a canonical document of antiquarian interest.

The Appu Myth is about a wealthy but childless couple. Taking pity on them, the Sun-God descends to earth disguised as a young man and grants Appu and his wife a son, whom they name "Evil." The couple then has a second son, whom they name "Just." When the brothers grow up and divide their father's estate, Evil takes the better portion. A dispute ensues that ends in the two brothers appearing in the divine court of the Sun-God, who decides in favor of brother Just. Evil is not satified, however, and the case is referred to Shaushga, queen of Nineveh. Unfortunately, the text breaks off before we learn her judgment. The Egyptian Tale of Two Brothers shares a similar theme of two brothers (Truth and Falsehood) who are judged before a divine assembly, but the similiarity to the patriarchal narratives contained in the elements of the childless couple, the deity disguised

---

and Original Hittite Literature," *IOS* 15 [1995]: 124 n. 6) notes that the Gibeah outrage in Judg 19–21 is also a story used to serve the political purposes of the victorious party.

120. For their possible genetic connection, see Matitiahu Tsevat, "Two Old Testament Stories and Their Hittite Analogues," *JAOS* 103 (1983): 326.

as a human, and the feud between two brothers over their inheritance are even more striking.[121]

The Tale of the Sun-God, the Cow, and the Fisherman is similarly concerned with a childless couple, in this case a fisherman and his wife. The myth begins with the Sun-God's love for a cow, which results in the birth of a human child. The child is rejected by his confused mother, forcing the Sun-God to take the child and place him where he is found by the fisherman. Rejoicing in his good fortune, the fisherman returns home with the baby and instructs his wife to feign birthing pains so that their neighbors, believing she has just given birth, will bring them bread and beer. The tablet containing the next part of the story has not been recovered, but it has been suggested that the tale concerns the child coming of age and becoming a great leader, a common literary motif in antiquity.[122]

The Story of Kessi the Hunter is attested in Hurrian as well as Hittite, and a copy in Akkadian has even been found at El Amarna in Egypt, indicating that Hittite myths and stories were circulating outside of Anatolia. The myth revolves around Kessi's obsessive love for his beautiful wife. He is so absorbed with her that he neglects his hunting, as a result of which not only does his mother go without food but the gods are denied their offerings. Prodded by his mother, Kessi takes up his spear, calls his dogs behind him, and heads to the mountains to hunt, but the gods, angry at his neglect, hide the game from him. Kessi wanders in the mountains for three months, afraid to return home empty-handed. When he finally does return home, he is visited by a series of seven ominous dreams. His mother's interpretation of these dreams, as well as the rest of Kessi's adventures, are lost.

Myths of Hattian, or native Anatolian, origin are the most numerous in quantity but are limited in scope. It seems that the Hittite scribes recorded and preserved only those Hattian myths concerned with the disruption of order in the world and its ultimate restoration, a theme that suited their own sensibilities. The defection of the god Telipinu from his place in the cosmos brought the natural world to a halt: "Mist siezed the windows. Smoke [seized] the house. In the fireplace the logs were stifled. [At the altars] the gods were stifled. In the sheep pen the sheep were stifled. In the cattle barn the cattle were stifled. The mother sheep rejected her lamb. The cow rejected her calf."[123]

---

121. See Singer, "Hittites and the Bible Revisited," 753, who also suggests that Appu (or Abu) is a hypocoristic form resembling the West Semitic name Abra(ha)m; see also idem, "Some Thoughts," 124–25.

122. Bryce, *Life and Society*, 221.

123. Translated by Harry A. Hoffner Jr., *Hittite Myths* (2nd ed.; SBLWAW 2; Atlanta: Scholars Press, 1998), 15.

Fig. 3.14. A Neo-Hittite orthostat relief from Malatya depicting the cosmic battle between the Storm-God and the dragon Illuyanka. Anatolian Civilizations Museum, Ankara. Photo by the author.

It took the efforts of a cadre of deities to bring about his return. The myths about Telipinu are but one variation on a common theme in which a variety of deities, including even the personal deities of the queens Asmunikal and Harapsili, must be restored to their places in the cosmos. For example, when it is the Sun-God who disappears, Jack Frost paralyzes the land. These myths provided the oral component to ancient rituals designed to restore order to a world that had become unbalanced. The considerable variations on this theme suggests that the myths circulated orally before they were recorded for the purposes of the state.

Another theme of the Hattian myths is the cosmic battle between the Storm-God and a mythological serpent, a Leviathan-type creature called Illuyanka (fig. 3.14). Two variations on this theme have survived, both of which were transcribed together on a single tablet by a scribe named Kella and are identified as the cult legend of the spring *purulli* festival. Their connection to the festival is clear: the Hittite Storm-God, as the chief benefactor of plant and animal life, must do battle with the chaos dragon, who symbolizes desolation and death. Only when the monster is defeated "may the land flourish and prosper" and the festival be celebrated. Both stories open with the Storm-God's initial subjugation by the dragon. In the first story, Inara, the daughter of the Storm-God, prepares a feast to which she invites Illuyanka and his offspring. They become drunk on the wine and beer and are unable to slither back into the hole from which they have emerged. Hupasiya, a mortal whom Inara has managed to entice into helping her in exchange for sexual favors, is then able to tie up the serpents, allowing the Storm-God to kill them. Hupasiya is then spirited away by Inara to her heavenly abode but finds himself unable to obey her command not to pine for his family. The text breaks off at this point, but we may assume that Hupasiya's fate was to die for his disloyalty to the goddess.

In the second version, the dragon steals the Storm-God's heart and eyes, incapacitating him. The Storm-God then takes the daughter of a poor man as wife and has a son. The son grows up to marry the daughter of the dragon and, when he enters the household of his father-in-law, asks for the Storm-God's heart and eyes as a wedding gift. The dragon has no choice but to agree, but the son, having betrayed his new loyalties, asks to be killed along with his father-in-law the dragon, which the Storm-God does. Once again the mortal, so vital in bringing about the Storm-God's victory, is sacrificed, a moral about the insignificance of human life in the face of divine power.

The cycle of songs about the god Kumarbi and his battle with Teshub for the kingship of heaven entered Anatolia from Hurrian Syria or perhaps Kizzuwatna (Kumarbi's hometown was Tell Mozan-Urkesh in Syria) sometime in the empire period and was preserved by the religious establishment in Hattusa. The individual songs that make up this cycle provided a primeval history of the Hurrian gods whose cults were becoming increasingly important to the Hittite state. At the same time, some evidence indicates that the songs circulated orally in the region and, contrary to received wisdom, were probably sung in the course of the performance of various festivals and rituals both within and outside of the Hittite capital.

The cycle shares with old Anatolian myths the pitting of the gods of heaven against those of the netherworld, although the Hurrian myths, which are thought to offer a more sophisticated approach to mythic narrative, are generally given higher marks for literary merit than the Anatolian myths. Such judgments are, of course, subjective. The cycle as a whole concerns the competition between Kumarbi, an underworld deity, and Teshub, the Hurrian Storm-God, for the kingship of heaven. The Song of Kumarbi, probably first in the cycle, relates how Alalu, father of Kumarbi, was driven from the throne by Anu. Kumarbi in turn wrests the kingship from Anu and in the struggle bites off his loins, a castration intended to prevent any future offspring of Anu from taking the kingship away from Kumarbi. Instead, Kumarbi becomes impregnated with the very offspring he hoped to forestall, eventually giving birth to his rival Teshub. In each of the subsequent songs, another of Kumarbi's own offspring—LAMMA, Silver, Hedammu, and Ullikummi—rises up to try to depose Teshub. Although it is difficult to know in which order to read the the songs,[124] Teshub's ultimate victory is assured, as it is he, not Kumarbi, who heads the Hurrian pantheon.

---

124. Hoffner (ibid., 40–42) suggests the sequence: Song of Kumarbi, Song of LAMMA, Song of Silver, Song of Hedammu, and Song of Ullikummi. Additional members of the cycle have been proposed, including the Song of Kingship, which was

There is no question that the Kumarbi cycle provided the inspiration for Hesiod's *Theogony*, with its sequence of divine kings Uranos-Kronos-Zeus. Even Anu's (= Uranos) castration is taken over into the Greek myth. Kumarbi is attested outside of these myths, even into the first millennium,[125] facilitating an identification with Kronos. The battle between Teshub and Ullikummi most likely provided the source for the Greek myth of the cosmic battle between Zeus and Typhon; both confrontations took place on Mount Hazzi (Kasios). Other elements of the story, namely, the birth of a deity from the head of Kumarbi and the Atlas-like figure of Ubelluri in the Song of Ulli-kummi, who bears the world on his shoulders, testify to the indebtedness of certain Greek mythic traditions to Hurro-Anatolian forebears.

The most recent addition to the Hurro-Hittite mythic collection is the Song of Release, a Middle Hittite–period wisdom text that was composed in Hurrian and translated into Hittite. The composition falls into four distinct parts, beginning with a proemium that introduces the divine subjects of the piece. Following the proemium are a series of seven parables each with a moral, such as the importance of loving one's homeland, being satisfied with what one has, honoring one's parents,[126] and fulfilling one's duty. There follows an incomplete description of a feast in the palace of Allani, goddess of the underworld, at which Teshub is the guest of honor. The composition concludes with an allegory situated in the Syrian city of Ebla, in which one of its prominent citizens, Megi, unsuccessfully beseeches the city council to issue a debt remission. The council refuses despite Teshub's threats of divine retribution.[127] The poem would seem, then, to serve as an etiology for the destruction of Ebla, which in fact occurred during the Syrian campaigns of

---

performed in connection with the cult of Mount Hazzi (Ian Charles Rutherford, "The Song of the Sea [ŠA A.AB.BA SÌR]: Thoughts on KUB 45.63," in Wilhelm, *Akten des IV. Internationalen Kongresses für Hethitologie*, 599); the Song of the Sea, also connected with Mount Hazzi (Rutherford, "The Song of the Sea," 598–609); and the Hurrian-language Song of Oil (Yakubovich, "Were Hittite Kings Divinely Anointed," 134).

125. In the Luwian inscription TELL AHMAR 1, §2: (DEUS.BONUS) Ku-pá?+ra/i-ma-sa$_5$. Hawkins proposes that the divine name Kuparmas invoked in this inscription is a late and deformed Luwian form of Kumarbi (*CHLI* I.1, 240–41).

126. In this instance, the parable involves a coppersmith who fashions a cup that then curses its maker; compare the biblical topos of the potter and his clay creation in Isa 29:16; 45:9; Jer 18:6; Rom 9:20–21 (Harry A. Hoffner Jr., "Hittite-Israelite Cultural Parallels," *COS* 3:xxxiii).

127. Hoffner (*Hittite Myths*, 76) compares 2 Chr 36:17–21, which attributes the destruction and exile of Judah to the people's failure to observe Yahweh's sabbatical year remissions. We may also note similar ideas about redemption and forgiveness of debt found in the Pentateuch.

Hattusili I and Mursili I in the seventeenth century B.C.E.[128] The composition as a whole is connected by the common theme of defining what is good and right behavior.

PRAYERS

The earliest surviving prayers from the Hittite world are invocations to the gods embedded within rituals belonging to the Old Anatolian cult layer. These typically appear in the form of short benedictions for the royal couple. Longer invocations (*mugawar*) forming independent compositions that were spoken by an officiant on behalf of the king developed from these.[129] In the early empire period (early fourteenth century), Kantuzili, a Hittite prince (son of Tudhaliya II and Nikkalmati) who served as high priest in Kizzuwatna, introduced the personal prayer to Anatolia.[130] Although the Hittites borrowed hymns from Mesopotamia into their scribal curriculum,[131] these were never adopted as part of Hittite religious observance. Personal prayers, on the other hand, like the earlier Anatolian prayers, were accompanied by ritual actions (see ch. 4). Kantuzili's Prayer to an Angry God is a rare example of a prayer composed by a member of the royal family other than the king (or queen).[132]

Where earlier prayers were general requests for divine succor, the personal prayers sought divine intervention in specific situations resulting from the anger of a particular deity. Arnuwanda I and his queen Asmunikal prayed to the Sun-Goddess of Arinna for relief from the ravages of the Kaska. Itamar Singer notes the thematic similarity of this prayer to Mesopotamian lamentations over the destruction of cities and with the book of Lamentations in the Hebrew Bible.[133] Taduhepa, wife of Tudhaliya III, composed a prayer in Hurrian on behalf of her ailing (?) husband. Mursili II, whose reign was frought with challenges both personal and official has left behind the greatest number of prayers. Most of these are concerned with the plague that had been decimating the kingdom since his father's reign; the remainder are a touching, albeit futile, appeal to the gods for the recovery of his wife Gassulawiya.

---

128. Volkert Haas and Ilse Wegner, "Baugrube und Fundament," *IstMitt* 43 (1993): 57.

129. Singer, *Hittite Prayers*, 13, and see nos. 1–3.

130. Itamar Singer, "Kantuzili the Priest and the Birth of Hittite Personal Prayer," in *Silva Anatolica: Anatolian Studies Presented to Maciej Popko on the Occasion of His 65th Birthday* (ed. Piotr Taracha; Warsaw: Agade, 2002), 301–13.

131. *CTH* 312–314, 792.I, 793–795; see Singer, *Hittite Prayers*, 3.

132. Singer, *Hittite Prayers*, 7.

133. Ibid., 40.

Muwatalli's Prayer to the Assembly of Gods, in contrast, served as a model prayer to be used in any situation, while his Prayer concerning the Cult of Kummanni was composed as a promise of restitution for past neglect. The prayers of Hattusili III and Puduhepa (for the health of Hattusili III) are the most intimate in tone of all the personal prayers. The latest preserved prayer is a plea by Tudhaliya IV to the Sun-Goddess of Arinna for military success.

A prayer might include an invocation for attracting the god's presence through words and ritual acts (*mugawar*); a hymn of praise, adulation, and adoration (*walliyatar*); and a petition for divine favor (*wekuwar*). The most common element in a Hittite personal prayer, however, was the *arkuwar* or "plea," a juridical term referring to a defense or self-justification against an accusation. This tells us that royal prayers essentially served as a formal defense presented on behalf of the king in a legal proceding before the divine court. A deity, usually the Sun-God or Sun-Goddess or a storm-god, is invoked to intercede with the angry deity, whose identity the petitioner does not know. The petitioner's defense often comprised a lengthy denial of responsibility and a reminder of the gods' dependence on the humans who serve them so well, but ultimately, the acknowledgment of the sin, even for the innocent, was a necessary prerequisite for redemption in the prayers. At the same time, the petitioner was not above bribing the gods. Queen Puduhepa, for example, vowed to bestow gifts on the goddess Lelwani if she would give health and long life to Hattusili III.

As literature, the Hittite personal prayers are rich in poetic language, metaphors and similes, and reflections on the human condition. In the face of divine anger, humans are helpless: "Wherever I flow like water, I do not know my location. Like a boat, I do not know when will I arrive at land."[134] Free for the most part of political rhetoric, the prayers provide as honest a glimpse into the hearts and minds of the Hittite kings as we can hope to find. Mursili II unabashedly complains of his weariness of constant conflict: "Rested are the belligerent lands, but Hatti is a weary land. Unhitch the weary one, and hitch up the rested one."[135] Even the righteous cannot expect to be rewarded: "To mankind, our wisdom has been lost, and whatever we do right comes to nothing."[136] Mursili II concedes that the innocent must pay restitution for the sins of their fathers: "It so happens that the father's

---

134. Singer, *Hittite Prayers*, 35 (no. 4b, §26").
135. Ibid., 52 (no. 8, §7).
136. Ibid.. Compare the book of Job and the Mesopotamian Poem of the Righteous Sufferer.

sin comes upon his son, and so the sin of my father came upon me too."[137] In the end, the only alternative to death is a life filled with misery: "Life is bound up with death and death is bound up with life. A human does not live forever. The days of his life are counted. Even if a human lived forever, and evil sickness of man were to be present, would it not be a grievance for him?"[138] Whether members of Hittite society other than its royal family found a similar emotional release from their suffering through prayer we may never know.

---

137. Singer, *Hittite Prayers*, 59 (no. 11, §8). Cf. Exod 20:5; Deut 5:9. Note also the motif of the wicked father and the righteous son in Ezek 18, which has a parallel in Mursili II's treaty with Kupanta-Kurunta of Mira (John B. Geyer, "Ezekiel 18 and a Hittite Treaty of Mursilis II," *JSOT* 12 (1979): 31–46.

138. Singer, *Hittite Prayers*, 32 (no. 4a, §5).

4

RELIGION

RELIGION ANIMATED EVERY FACET OF LIFE IN HATTI. This simple truism applied
equally to the king and to his subjects and explains why texts of a religious
character constitute by far the largest percentage of the documents recovered
from the Boghazköy-Hattusa libraries. These religious compositions are
official in nature, not canonical or theological, and certainly were not
written to aid in private devotion. Instead, the records were intended to
aid the bureaucracy in the organization and maintenance of the religious
responsibilities of the king and so are purely practical documents, including
regulations to guide the temple personnel in the performance of their duties,
records of cultic administration, prescriptions for the proper performance
of ceremonies, reports of diviners, religious compositions used in scribal
education, and so on. Despite their limitations, these texts offer a wealth of
information about religious life in Late Bronze Age Anatolia.

The material record also provides important clues to religious activities.
Small figurines in precious metal and stone of divine beings and other cult
objects, images carved into living rock, and scenes on seals reveal how the
Hittites conceptualized the divine. Ground plans of temples allow us to
imagine the daily activities of the priests and other temple personnel as they
went about the business of maintaining the cults of the gods. The remains of
ancient waterworks (e.g., pools and wells) and the religious structures built
in and around natural water sources, such as springs and rivers, are vivid
reminders of the role of water as a conduit to the world below the earth and
to the beings that inhabited that world. With these tools in hand, it is possible to piece together the beginnings of a framework for religious expression
in Hatti.

THE OFFICIAL RELIGION

The Hittite kings were devoutly religious, even if, more often than not, politics
played a key role in how their piety was articulated. Decisions regarding the

cult were rarely made independently of political concerns. Tudhaliya II's adoption of the cult of the goddess of the night in Samuha as relations with her home territory of Kizzuwatna were warming up, the promotion of the cult of the Storm-God of Aleppo as Hatti's empire in Syria grew, Muwatalli II's move of the capital to Tarhuntassa as part of a refocusing of the state religion on southern cults, and Tudhaliya IV's introduction in Hurma, an ancient town in central Anatolia, of cults of deities connected with the kingship are just a few examples of the interconnectedness of politics and religion. Polytheism by definition precludes religious dogma and orthodoxy, and the religion pro-moted by and for the Hittite ruling elite reflects the expansiveness inherent in such a system even as it accommmodated reforms initiated by individual kings to promote favored cults.

THE PRIESTHOOD

Maintaining the cult of a pantheon as expansive and complex as that of the Hittites required the services of numerous priests and support personnel. Priests (SANGA, Hittite *sankunni*) were responsible for the daily care of the gods in the form of their cult images.[1] Also serving the gods directly were the "anointed" priests (GUDU$_{12}$, Hittite *kumra*?) and the "mother of the deity" (AMA.DINGIR-*LIM*, Hittite *siwanzanna*) priestesses. The reigning queen held the latter title. These, however, seem to be fairly generic designations masking what was a far more complex religious bureaucracy, as far more priestly titles are known from the texts.[2] Despite the large numbers of priests and priestesses with various labels, we know remarkably little about how the priesthood was structured, what specific responsibilities accompanied which title, and where they fell within the temple hierarchy. We might assume, for example, priests who had direct contact with the deity, and thus were held to the highest levels of cultic purity, also enjoyed the highest status in the temple bureaucracy, but we have no way of identfying who fell into this category. Some priestly offices were cult-specific, such as those of the *alhuitra* and *huwassanalli* priestesses connected to the cult of the goddess Huwassanna at Hupisna in the Lower Land. Others, such as the *patili*-priests who offici-ated over rituals connected with birth and pregnancy, had clearly demarcated spheres of activity. Still others bore titles derived from specific locations in

---

1. For the full range of the *sankunni*'s (both male and female) cultic role, see *CHD* Š/1, s.v. For a survey of the role of Hittite priests and priestesses in Hittite society, see Ada Taggar-Cohen, *Hittite Priesthood* (THeth 26; Heidelberg: Universitätsverlag, 2006)

2. See Jörg Klinger, "Zum 'Priestertum' im hethitischen Anatolien," *Hethitica* 15 (2002): 93–111.

the temple (e.g., the *hilammatta* and *karimnala* priests, from *hilammar* "gate-house" and *karimmi* "shrine," respectively), and we might assume, although we cannot be certain, that their duties were correspondingly focused.

We also know little about the circumstances under which individuals came to the priesthood. Members of the royal house were given in service to various deities, particularly in their youth, but what this meant exactly in terms of their duties and whether they continued actively in these roles throughout their lives is unclear. A celebration of the "festival of the lots" involved the casting of lots to select the new priests, as well as the anointment (with water) of the chosen, but who the candidates were, where they came from, and why is not revealed.[3] The relative anonymity under which priests and priestesses other than the king and queen—who sat at the top of the priestly hierarchy—operated is another reflection of the control exerted by the state over the religious structures of the kingdom. The priesthood was a state-sponsored profession, albeit one to which certain privileges, such as exemption from taxes, were attached.

While priests of temples in major cities were often of royal lineage, village priests may have been commoners occupying a relatively low rung in Hittite society. Even small local temples required a minimum staff of two or three priests. Hittite priests received instruction in the proper maintenance of the cult and conduct befitting their status within the temple hierarchy. So far as we know, being in service to the gods was a full-time job; there is no indication that even the humblest of priests went home at the end of his shift to attend to his crops, although according to the Instructions to Priests and Temple Officials priests were not barred from having a family.

Besides the priests and priestesses, the personnel required to run the main temple at Hattusa included those who had what we would think of as religious duties, such as musicians, dancers, augurs, and diviners, as well as many occupations that were more "secular" in nature, including scribes, cooks, leather workers, potters and other artisans (goldsmiths, silversmiths, stonecutters, engravers, weavers), herders for the temple flocks, farmers who tilled the temple lands, and kitchen personnel, as well as the temple guards.[4] One of these support personnel was the *haliyatalla* "keeper, guard," whose duties are described in the Instructions to Priests and Temple Officials:

---

3. Ada Taggar-Cohen, "The EZEN *pulaš* (a Hittite Installation Rite of a New Priest) in Light of the Installation of the dIM priestess in Emar," *JANER* 2 (2002): 126–59.

4. Hans G. Güterbock, "The Hittite Temple according to Written Sources," *Le temple et le culte* (CRRAI 20; Istanbul: Nederlands Historisch-Archaeologisch Instituut, 1975), 129–32.

Further, let sentries be posted at night and let them continue to make the rounds all night. Outside let the guards (*haliyatalla*) keep their watch. But inside the temples let the temple officials make the rounds all night. Let there be no sleep for them. Each night one high priest is to be in charge of the sentries. And further, of those who are priests, someone shall be (assigned) to the temple gate and shall guard the temple.[5]

Jacob Milgrom has compared the role of the Hittite guard with that of the Levites as described in the Priestly Code.[6] Here the priests and Levites are sharply distinguished from each other in all their functions save one: they share custody of the tabernacle, priests within the sacred area and Levites without. Like the Levites, the Hittite guard "is under command of a high priest, is stationed outside the sacred area, escorts the layman requesting a rite into the sacred area, pursues or guards against an intruder into the sacred area at the command of the priests, and suffers death if he is responsible for unlawful trespass."[7] Similarly, the Hittite priest guards the temple within the sacred area, its sacred court, and its entrance and pays with his life for any sin that takes place on his watch. Milgrom concludes from this striking parallel that the sacred function of guarding the sanctuary (although not necessarily the antiquity of the priests and Levites themselves) must hark back to the late second millennium.

PLACES OF WORSHIP

Temples served to house not only the statue of the deity but the priests and craftsmen who were in service to the deity. The Great Temple dominating the "old city" of Hattusa to the north must have been a magnificant structure, with a large area set aside as offices and residences for temple dependents. None of the structures situated on the acropolis appears to have served solely as a temple; rather, small shrines to various deities were incorporated within the palace complex.[8] The main temple quarter was located in the Upper City. Here sanctuaries of various sizes, but following a consistent architectural plan, were dedicated to the cults of the state gods (fig. 4.1). Every town and village of any size within the Hittite domain had at least one temple staffed with cult

---

5. "Instructions to Priests and Temple Officials," translated by Gregory McMahon (*COS* 1.83:219, §10).

6. Outlined in Num 3:6–7, 32, 38; 16:9; 18:2–4, 26–28; 2 Kgs 10:24.

7. Jacob Milgrom, "The Shared Custody of the Tabernacle and a Hittite Analogy," *JAOS* 90 (1970): 207.

8. Maciej Popko, "Zur Topographie von Ḫattuša: Tempel auf Büyükkale," in Beckman, Beal, and McMahon, *Hittite Studies in Honor of Harry A. Hoffner Jr.*, 315–23.

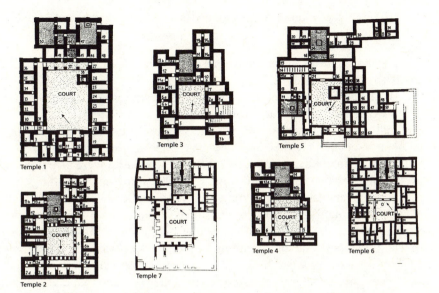

Fig. 4.1. Plans of some of the temples in Hattusa. The Great Temple is on the upper left. The gateway, courtyard, and cellas of the main temple structure, as well as the storerooms and archives are visible. The remaining plans belong to temples in the Upper City. From *Across the Anatolian Plateau* (AASOR 57; Boston: ASOR, 2000), 96.

personnel. Excavations at Kuşaklı-Sarissa, considered to be a medium-sized Hittite town, have revealed a temple in the lower city whose plan resembles those of the temples in Hattusa's temple quarter. Another religious complex on the acropolis bears architectural similarities to the Great Temple in Hattusa and was similarly dedicated to the local storm-god.

The image of the god was housed in the cella, or main shrine of the temple. Hattusa's Great Temple had two cellas, one for the Storm-God and one for the Sun-Goddess. Each temple had a central courtyard. Worshipers crossing the courtyard from the temple entrance passed through a portico into the cella, which could accommodate only priests and a small number of worshipers. Corkscrew access (i.e., locating the cella so that it was not in the direct line of sight of the entry) limited the number of people who could enter the cella. The temples had to accommodate worship by the king, queen, and high officials, but ordinary people were not allowed within the temple precinct to worship, and even the temple personnel would have had restricted access. An oracular inquiry conducted at Alalakh reveals that trespass by unauthorized persons was an offense to the gods:

> Since it has been established (by oracle) that the god was desecrated by a ritual offense, we asked the temple officials, and Tila said: "People should

not look at the Storm-God; but a woman looked in at a window and a child
went into the temple."[9]

Clearly, the cella was the exclusive purview of the gods and their immediate
caretakers.

Worship of the Hittite gods was not restricted to the large city temple
complexes with their many rooms and large courtyards but was also
frequently carried out in sacred precincts on rocks or mountains—with or
without associated architecture. The most important of these was the rock
sanctuary at Yazılıkaya (see ch. 3). Open-air sanctuaries were commonplace
in Anatolia, particularly where some natural feature, such as a large rock
outcropping, lent itself to the numinous. The texts often refer to rituals taking
place on mountains, which were considered from early Hittite times to be
the place where the presence of the celestial deities could be felt and where
special ceremonies devoted to their worship were performed. A common
element of open-air worship was the standing stone, called *huwasi*. These
stelae were similar, at least in appearance, to the *maṣṣebot* found in Palestine
but were sometimes also engraved with a relief or an inscription. Each stela
belonged to a specific deity, for which it was a representation, functioning in
this respect just as the god's statue functioned in his temple. Such open-air
sanctuaries may have been standard equipment for most towns, as suggested
by the *huwasi*-complex with its sacred pool discovered by the excavators two
and a half kilometers south of the Hittite town of Kuşaklı-Sarissa.

Finally, the importance given to provisioning the gods of the underworld
cannot be overlooked. Chapter 2 mentioned the vaulted stone chamber of
Suppiluliuma II that provided him access to the underworld. Considerably
older, a grotto with steps leading to an underground chamber once filled with
water was constructed outside of the Great Temple, allowing temple func-
tionaries to see to the needs of the gods beneath the earth without having
to inconvenience themselves too greatly. Such structures, both within and
outside of the capital, were important channels for communicating with, and
propitiating, potentially malevolent forces.

FESTIVALS

Festivals punctuated the cultic calendar at regular intervals throughout the
year. The major yearly festivals, the festival of the crocus (AN.TAḪ.ŠUM),

---

9. AT 454 ii 7–10; Oliver R. Gurney, "A Hittite Divination Text," in *The Alalakh Tablets* (ed. D. J. Wiseman; London: The British Institute of Archaeology at Ankara, 1953), 116–18.

celebrated in the spring, and the festival of "haste" (*nuntarriyashas*), celebrated in the autumn, kept the king and his entourage on the road traveling
from town to town visiting temples within the religious district of north-central Anatolia for weeks at a time. The very ancient KI.LAM festival (Hittite
hilammar), on the other hand, involved the hosting in Hattusa of delegations
from towns participating in this religious network. Among the many
highlights of this festival was a lengthy parade before the king that included a
troop of dancers and a display of images of wild animals in precious metal.

The spring *purulli*-festival was celebrated throughout Hittite times.
Recorded on no fewer than thirty-two tablets, it celebrated the regeneration of
life at the beginning of the agricultural year. The festival schedule included a
recitation of the myth about the conflict between the Storm-God and a dragon,
Illuyanka. Because the festival celebrates the Storm-God's victory over the
serpent, which he achieved only with the aid of humans, it also served to
reinforce the symbiotic relationship between the human and divine realms.

Each of these state-sponsored festivals served for the participating towns
and their representatives as an expression of allegiance to the king and for
the king as a means of forging a collective religious identity and unity.[10]
In a society whose religion was constantly being transformed by external
influences, most notably Hurrian, it is worth noting that the major Hittite
festivals, with their deep Anatolian roots, apparently continued to be carried
out unchanged until the end of Hittite history. One major yearly festival,
however, was introduced from Kizzuwatna, where Hurrian beliefs and
practices were most strongly felt. The nine-day-long *hisuwas* festival was not
season-dependent and was performed to honor the Storm-God of Manuzziya
(a mountain in Kizzuwatna) and his circle. Eagles, which were sacred to this
deity, played a prominent role in the festival and may have given it its name.
It included a ceremony for the military success of the king.[11]

In addition to the major yearly festivals, there were also festivals
commemorating other aspects of agrarian life, including festivals of the grape
harvest, of the sickle, of a pile of grain, of bathing, of the year, of the month,
of the old men, and so on. More than eighty Hittite festivals are known by
name. They are usually named for an agricultural event, or after the season, or
after the main practitioners in the activities. Generally speaking, fall festivals
celebrated the harvest in the filling of the storage vessels, while the spring

10. Gilan, "Hittite Ethnicity?"; Ian Rutherford, "The Dance of the Wolf-Men of
Ankuwa: Networks, Amphictionies and Pilgrimage in Hittite Religion," paper delivered
at the 5th International Congress of Hittitology, Corum, 4 September 2002.

11. Haas, *Geschichte der hethitischen Religion*, 848–75.

festivals celebrated breaking open these stored goods. The most frequently repeated festival was the "festival of the month," by which we are probably to understand a festival marking the new moon.

As monotonous as the festival prescriptions can seem at times, they are certainly not without their interesting peculiarities. In an episode in the Kizzuwatnean festival of Teshub and Hebat celebrated in Lawazantiya, the king at one point restrains the goddess Hebat in the form of her statue. In a ritualized verbal exchange in which the priest takes the role of the goddess, the king demands, and presumably receives, a blessing, before releasing her. This brief ritual clarifies the nature of Jacob's strange encounter when fording the Jabbok River in Gen 32:23–32.[12] The text tells us that a man wrestled with Jacob until daybreak, with neither party able to overcome the other. When the man asked to be released, Jacob refused to do so until he had blessed him. The encounter is usually taken to be a supernatural one, the man perhaps representing the numen of the river, and the Hittite ritual confirms this understanding.

THE SACRIFICIAL CULT

To ensure that the gods continued to attend to their human charges, it was sometimes necessary to perform elaborate rituals of attraction to draw them to whatever festivities were being held in their honor. In addition to laying out honey, wine, milk, butter, and other irresistible offerings, ritual specialists drew paths with colorful textiles and branches to attract the gods and to assist them in finding their way. These efforts were supplemented by incantations summoning the gods: "[If you are in Nineveh] then come from Nineveh. If you are [in] R[imushi, then come from Rimushi].... If (you are) in the rivers and streams [them come from there].... If you are with the Sun Goddess of the Earth and the Primor[dial Gods] then come from those. § Come away from these countries."[13] On arriving at the festival, the deity took up residence in his or her statue, to which the offerings would be presented.

These offerings featured a variety of baked goods and libations of beer and wine, as well as firstfruits offerings, depending on the time of year. In

---

12. For the comparison, see Matitiahu Tsevat, "Two Old Testament Stories and Their Hittite Analogues," *JAOS* 103 (1983): 321–26; for the Hittite text, see Heinrich Otten, "Kampf von König und Gottheit in Einem Hethitischen Ritualtext," *BagMitt* 7 (1974): 139–42; René Lebrun, "Textes religieux hittites de la fin de l'empire," *Hethitica* 2 (1977): 116–42.

13. "Ritual and Prayer to Ishtar of Nineveh," translated by Billie Jean Collins (*COS* 1.65:164, §§4–7).

the daily care of the gods, animals were also regularly sacrificed for their table. The blood sacrifice of a sheep or goat or, less often, cattle was the high point of most offering rituals. The prospect of a feast attracted the deity to his or her temple, where the participants in the ritual (usually temple personnel) could join him or her in a communal meal.

The preparations for the sacrificial ritual typically began with the consecration of the animal and the cleansing of the participants, the image of the deity, and the space in which the sacrifice would occur. A liturgy might be recited and incense burned. The animal was brought in, sometimes with great fanfare. Only top-quality items could be given to the deity. The substitution of a scrawny animal for a healthy one left the offerant vulnerable to divine retribution. The procession could include singers and musicians as well as other participants in the ritual, such as the cook. The moment of slaughter, for which a special knife was used, was one of jubilation. The animal was then butchered and the deity given the roasted heart and liver. The cook used the remainder of the animal to make a stew to be shared by the participants. The food was set out, libations poured, and the feasting began. At this point the king might "drink the god," that is, toast him, a practice unique to the Hittites. Ceremonies of this kind correspond most closely to what are termed "fellowship" offerings (*šelāmîm*) in the Hebrew Bible, the primary purpose of which was the communal meal with the deity.

Sacrificial rituals were performed privately as well. In a ritual for the Storm-God of Kuliwisna, the actions of the master of the household, who officiated during the ritual, are described in detail:

> The master of the household presents them (the ram and bull) to the Storm-God of Kuliwisna. The cooks elevate (the heads of) the ram and the bull and they give the bronze knives to the master of the household. The master of the household places the hand with the bronze knife on the jugular vein of the ram and the bull. The cooks kill them on the altar. They give those knives to the cook who completes the killing.[14]

Although the master of the household did not perform the actual slaughter, by placing his weaponed hand on the animal's throat he established that the offering was his and that the slaughter was being performed on his behalf. The meaning of the Hittite gesture is similar to that of the laying on of hands performed in biblical sacrifice, for it also served to attribute the animal and accompanying sacrificial acts to the one who did the hand placement or

---

14. *KBo* 15.33 (*CTH* 330) iii 9–14.

conferred authorization on another to act on behalf of the person making the gesture.[15]

A less common form of sacrifice in Anatolia proper were burnt offerings, which were introduced from Hurrian Kizzuwatna. Birds were the most frequent victim in such sacrifices, although lambs and kids might also be offered. Burnt offerings were often directed to the gods of the underworld: "He takes three birds and offers two of them to the Anunnaki deities, but the other bird he offers to the Pit and he says as follows: 'For you, O Primordial Deities, cattle and sheep will not be forthcoming. When the Stormgod drove you down to the Dark Underworld he established for you this offering.' "[16]

DIVINATION

Mursili II addressed the gods in one of his prayers asking for abeyance of a plague: "if people have been dying because of some other matter, let me either see it in a dream, or [let] it [be discovered] by means of an oracle, or let a prophet speak of it. Or the priests will sleep long and purely (in an incubation oracle) in regard to that which I convey to all of them."[17] Divination, the science of determining future events by means of signs sent by the gods, in all its forms is a key part of the human-divine relationship within polytheistic societies. It presupposes, moreover, that the gods care enough about the welfare of humans to make these signs available to them, if they only have the special knowledge required to read them. Oracles are deliberate attempts to determine the will of the gods—they are solicited portents. Omens, on the other hand, are unsolicited or offered portents in which the deity takes the initiative by sending a sign.[18]

The Hittites practiced several kinds of oracles, in each of which the diviner asked a question, and the deity was expected to answer in the particular divinatory language chosen (see further below). The questions asked were not open-ended; they required only positive or negative responses, so the practitioner had to continue asking questions until he had arrived at the correct one. Tablets recording oracles often survive as notes hastily taken

---

15. Lev 1:4; 3:2, 8, 13; 4:4, 24, 29, 33. See David P. Wright, "The Gesture of Hand Placement in the Hebrew Bible and in Hittite Literature," *JAOS* 106 (1986): 433–46.

16. "Purifying a House: A Ritual for the Infernal Deities," translated by Billie Jean Collins (*COS* 1.68:170, §34).

17. "Plague Prayers of Muršili II," translated by Gary Beckman (*COS* 1.60:159).

18. For a detailed discussion of Hittite divination, see Richard H. Beal, "Hittite Oracles," *Magic and Divination in the Ancient World* (ed. Leda Ciralo and Jonathan Seidel; Leiden: Brill-Styx, 2002), 57–81

during the course of the inquiry. Subjects of inquiry might include the optimum time for the inauguration of a monarch or approving changes in a festival program.[19] Oracles do not appear to have been used to determine policy, however. In other words, diviners could perform an extispicy to determine from which direction to attack a city or which general should lead the attack, but the decision about whether to attack in the first place was not put before the gods.

Most frequently, oracular investigations were conducted not for advice but for the purpose of determining the source of divine anger or impurity. In these cases, the diviner would set about first to establish the identity of the deity who was causing the particular problem, then to determine the reason for his or her anger, and finally to ascertain what restitution was required to satisfy the deity. Tudhaliya IV's accession to the throne of Hatti was a particularly contentious event and one that was therefore accompanied by an extensive oracular investigation designed to cleanse the kingship of the curses of now-deceased political antagonists such as Tawananna, Danuhepa, Arma-Tarhunda, and Urhi-Teshub. In this process, the diviners checked and double-checked the results by putting the same questions to a series of oracle types.

Extispicy, or "flesh oracles," involved the examination of sheep exta. This type of divination had its origin in Babylonia and was transmitted to Anatolia through the Hurrians. A diviner (HAL, Akkadian *barû*) trained in this particular form of inquiry examined the animal's liver, gall bladder, or intestines for any marks, such as creases, bumps, spots, or discolorations, that might have significance. Associated with extispicy, but much less common, were the "bed" oracles, which involved the observation of the animal as it was led to slaughter for the "flesh" oracles. Observations relating to how an animal moved its tail or tongue or where it lay down in its pen were combined with the examination of the exta to produce a final result.

Symbol (KIN) oracles are distinctly Hittite in origin and involved the manipulation of symbolic tokens with names that represented personages (Heart of the King, Enemy, Storm-God) or concepts (Wealth of the Land, Emptiness, Desire). The "active" tokens (perhaps an animal?) took one or more "passive" tokens and gave them to a third symbolic object, known as the "receptive" token. For example: "His Majesty will go up (on campaign) into the Haharwa mountains and will spend the night there. If we have nothing to fear regarding his person, let (the oracle) be favorable. The 'gods'

---

19. Gary Beckman, "The Tongue Is a Bridge: Communication between Humans and Gods in Hittite Anatolia," *ArOr* 67 (1999): 526.

stood up and took 'fire' and 'great sin.' They were given to 'the overseer.' (Result:) Unfavorable."[20] The tokens were either positive (e.g., Rightness, Good, Will) or negative (e.g., Enemy, Evil, Failure), and the overall outcome was determined by the balance of positive tokens to negative ones. The tokens could also be customized to the subject of the specific inquiry; so, for example, if the question were about whether the king would prevail over the Assyrians, one could insert a token with the name "King of Assyria." This particular type of divination was usually performed by the ritual experts known as "Wise Women" (see below).

Augury entailed the observance of bird behavior by someone specially trained in the art. Twenty-five types of fowl are recorded in these documents. Augurs (bird watchers) read a bird's movements and behavior within a demarcated area with regard to whether it flew off to the right or left, perched on a roof, turned its head, flew over a river, and so on. The technical aspects of interpreting these behaviors is obscure, but the practice was again a native Anatolian invention that eventually made its way to Rome, where it was a well-developed art.

Similar in concept to the symbol oracles, albeit much more rare, snake oracles were also native to Anatolia. Owing to their arcane vocabulary, they are poorly understood, but we do know that they involved the observation of the movement and behavior of snakes in a water basin. As with symbol oracles, symbolic names were applied to areas in the basin and to the snakes so that the meaning of the snake's movements and behavior from place to place could be read. Lecanomancy, interpreting the motion of oil in water, is also known to have been used.

Having received insight into some future event either by oracle or by omen, a person could move to avert the evil, if indeed it was evil that was portended. One could alter the predicted outcome by changing one's plans, by performing magic or making offerings to avert the evil, or by soothing the god whose anger was the cause of the problem. Because the future was not fixed, but could be altered, divination gave humans some control over their destiny. Although the omens and oracles that have come down to us pertain exclusively to the operations of the state and its priesthood, the average individual is also likely to have sought out the superior knowledge of the gods, but the means by which one did this or how one might have interpreted signs from heaven we do not know.

---

20. *KUB* 5.1 (*CTH* 561) i 32–33; translated by Gary Beckman, "The Tongue Is a Bridge," 530.

Dreams as a means by which the gods communicated their will to humans were the most common form of omen in Hittite texts of the empire period. The deity could either speak to the dreamer directly or send a messenger in the form of someone known to the dreamer, as when the goddess Shaushga sent Muwatalli II to Mursili II in a dream to tell him to give Hattusili to her as a priest. Dreams could also be oracles, if they were solicited by dream incubation, that is, by sleeping in the temple in the hopes of receiving a message from heaven. Although Deut 18:10 condemned divination generally, dreams and prophecy were not denounced in the Hebrew Bible. While the Hittites shared an interest in dreams, they did not rely heavily on prophecy as a means of communication with the divine. Mursili's prayer, cited above, refers to a "man of god" (*siuniyant*) who might "(come and) declare" the cause of suffering, while in another prayer the priest Kantuzili refers to consulting the will of the deity by means of a seeress (ENSI). Clearly, then, prophets were active in parts of Anatolia in the Late Bronze Age, but we know nothing about who they were or how and where they might have functioned.

EXCURSUS
DID THE HITTITES PRACTICE NECROMANCY?

The Hittites maintained an active line of communication with the deities who lived beneath the earth in order to retain their goodwill. Without the assistance of the chthonic gods in confining pollution and other evils to their underground realm, all hell would break loose, literally. The rituals by which humans were able to "link up" with the underworld divinities are closely related to necromantic practices known in the eastern Mediterranean world in the first millennium, including the episode of the witch of Endor, who called up the ghost of the prophet Samuel at Saul's request to learn how he should proceed against the Philistines (1 Sam 28:8).[21] In one such Hittite ritual, which takes place on the bank of a river, the ritual specialist sprinkles oil and honey on the clay that forms the bank, from that clay makes figurines of the gods of the underworld in the shape of daggers (as symbols of the

---

21. For a discussion of Hittite *api-* "pit" and its possible connection to Hebrew *ʾôb*, found in 1 Sam 28, see Harry A. Hoffner Jr., "Second Millennium Antecedents to the Hebrew *ʾôb*," *JBL* 86 (1967): 385–401. For the case against *api-* = *ʾôb*, see Frederick H. Cryer, *Divination in Ancient Israel and Its Near Eastern Environment* (JSOTSup 142; Sheffield: JSOT Press, 1994), 260 n. 1; Brian B. Schmidt, *Israel's Beneficent Dead: Ancestor Cult and Necromancy in Ancient Israelite Religion and Tradition* (Winona Lake, Ind.: Eisenbrauns, 1996), 151

underworld), then spreads them out on the ground.[22] In front of them he uses a dagger to open up a pit in the ground into which he pours oil, honey, wine, and other libations. He throws a piece of silver as payment into the pit before covering it over to the accompaniment of an incantation. Such rituals typically included sacrificing an animal over the pit as well. Odysseus performs a remarkably similar ritual when seeking out the ghost of the seer Teiresias for advice on his journey in book 11 of the *Odyssey*, the main difference being that the Hittite ritual was performed to pacify demons, not to gain special knowledge from them.

The living could on occasion make contact with the dead. One oracle question, in fear of the anger of a ghost, asks "Do her (Shaushgatti's) children utter curses and stir up the deceased? Then, let the KIN be unfavorable."[23] In instances such as this, the method for making contact with the dead is unknown, but, more importantly, the purpose of the solicitation again was not divinatory but rather to tap the power of the angry ghost to harm one's enemies or, more likely, to pacify it.

Another line of inquiry in this regard has followed a pair of Hittite demons known as *annari* and *tarpi*, the former benevolent and the latter maleficent. The Hittites identified these entitites with the Mesopotamian classes of demons called *lamassu* and *shedu*, who also could be both good and bad. In an old Hittite myth, demon *tarpi* is placed along with other malevolent and undesirable things inside a bronze cauldron sealed with a lead lid and placed on the bottom of the sea.[24] This passage reminds one of the seventh vision

---

22. This is a reversal of the creation of humanity by the gods, specifically the mother goddesses, and the irony is not lost on the author of the text, who remarks, "as Hannahanna takes children from the river bank and I, a human being, have come to summon the Primordial Deities of the river bank, let the Sun-Goddess of the Earth open the Gate and let the Primordial Deities and the Sun God(dess) of the Earth up from the Earth." "Purifying a House: A Ritual for the Infernal Deities," translated by Collins (*COS* 1.68:169, §12).

23. *KBo* 2.6 (*CTH* 569) ii 55–56, translated by Theo van den Hout, *Purity of Kingship: An Edition of CTH 569 and Related Hittite Oracle Inquiries of Tuthaliya IV* (DMOA 25; Leiden: Brill, 1998), 204–5. On contacting the dead, see idem, "Death as a Privilege: The Hittite Royal Funerary Ritual," in *Hidden Futures: Death and Immortality in Ancient Egypt, Anatolia, the Classical, Biblical and Arabic-Islamic World*, (ed. Jan M. Bremmer, Theo van den Hout, and Rudolph Peters; Amsterdam: Amsterdam University Press, 1994), 44–48; Giuseppe del Monte, "Il terrore dei morti," *Annali dell'Istituto Universitario Orientale di Napoli* 33 (1973): 373–85; Alfonso Archi, "Il dio Zawalli: Sul culto dei morti presso gli Ittiti," *AoF* 6 (1979): 81–94; Heinrich Otten, *Hethitische Totenrituale* (Institut für Orientforschung, Veröffentlichung 37; Berlin: Akademie-Verlag: 1958), 143–44.

24. "The Storm God at Liḫzina," translated by Billie Jean Collins (*COS* 1.69:172, §4'–5').

of Zechariah (5:5–11), where a female figure symbolizing evil witchcraft is placed inside an *ephah* (a vessel) with a lead lid and carried off to Babylon.[25] Hoffner has suggested that Hebrew *teraphim*, a word of ambiguous meaning used in the Hebrew Bible possibly in reference to ancestor figurines that functioned in divinatory practices, particularly in necromancy (2 Kgs 23:24), derives from Hittite *tarpi*.[26] The proposed linguistic connection has been challenged, however,[27] and there is no evidence linking the Hittite *tarpi*-demon (or the Mesopotamian *shedu* and *lamassu*, for that matter) with necromancy, divination, or the ancestors.[28]

In sum, although all the elements of later necromantic rites were present in Bronze Age Anatolia, and although the dead could be contacted when it was necessary to appease them, the calling up of the dead for the purpose of predicting the future was not demonstrably a part of Hittite religious practice, either public or private.

PRAYER

Personal prayers allowed the kings to communicate directly with the gods regarding the anger of some deity and the grave circumstances resulting from that anger. Since the identity of the angry deity was unknown, the kings invoked the supreme deities of the land, most often the solar deities—the Sun-Goddess of Arinna, the Sun-Goddess of the Earth, and the Sun-God of Heaven—that is, the all-seeing guarantors of justice for every living creature. Various storm-gods were also approached, including the Storm-God of Hatti

---

25. Volkert Haas, "Ein hurritischer Blutritus und die Deponierung der Ritualrück-stände nach hethitischen Quellen," in *Religionsgeschichtliche Beziehungen zwischen Kleinasien, Nordsyrien und dem Alten Testament* (ed. Bernd Janowski, Klaus Koch, and Gernot Wilhelm; OBO 129; Fribourg: Universitätsverlag, 1993), 77–83. Singer, ("Hittites and the Bible Revisited," 750) compares Pandora's box in Greek tradition.

26. Harry A. Hoffner Jr., "Hittite *tarpiš* and the Hebrew Teraphim," *JNES* 27 (1968), 61–68.

27. H. Rouillard and J. Tropper, "*TRPYM*, rituels de guérison et culte des ancêtres d'après 1 Samuel XIX 11–17 et les textes parallèles d'Assur et de Nuzi," *VT* 37 (1987): 340–61; F. Josephson ("Anatolien *tarpa/i*, etc.," in *Florilegium Anatolicum*, 181) suggests instead a derivation from Hittite *tarpalli*- "substitute."

28. *KBo* 23.4:5, a join to *KUB* 33.66 (*CTH* 331), lists a similar set of evils to be disposed of but replaces *tarpis* with *hinkan* "disease, plague, death," suggesting its role as a demon had more to do with death and destruction than with divination. For additional arguments against Hoffner's interpretation, see Rouillard and Tropper, "*TRPYM*, rituels de guérison et culte des ancêtres," 360–61; Otto Loretz, "Nekromantie und Totenevokation in Mesopotamien, Ugarit und Israel," in Janowski, Klaus, and Wilhelm, *Religiongeschichtliche Beziehungen*, 303; Cryer, *Divination in Ancient Israel*, 272 n. 2.

and his Hurrian counterpart Teshub, the Storm-God of Nerik, Telipinu, and the Storm-God of Lightning, who was Muwatalli's personal deity. Lesser deities were often asked to intercede on behalf of the suppliant with the supreme deity whose favor was sought. Puduhepa, for example, invoked Lelwani, Zintuhi, Mezzulla, and the Storm-God of Zippalanda in her prayer to the Sun-Goddess of Arinna for the health of Hattusili III. Occasionally the entire assembly of gods was invoked, perhaps as a last resort when all other attempts at redress had failed.[29]

Prayers were probably always accompanied by a ceremony that, with some exceptions, the king himself performed. Muwatalli's prayer to the Storm-God of Lightning provides a rare description of the scene, which takes place on the roof of the temple:

> Thus says *tabarna* Muwatalli, Great King, king of Hatti, son of Mursili, Great King, king of Hatti, the hero: If some problem burdens a man('s conscience), he makes a plea to the gods. He places on the roof, facing the Sun, two covered wickerwork tables: He places one table for the Sun-goddess of Arinna, and for the male gods one table. On them there are: 35 thick breads of a handful of moist flour, a thin bowl of honey mixed with fine oil, a full pot of fat-bread, a full bowl of groats, thirty pitchers of wine. And when he prepares these, the king goes up to the roof and he bows before the Sun-god of Heaven.[30]

During the recitation of the prayer, the king might raise his hand to the deity or bow or go down on his knees in a position of supplication. Although the prayers can be very personal in tone, these ceremonies were not held in private. In addition to the priests assisting with the ritual activity, there is evidence in the prayers themselves of audiences, as in the words "So be it," spoken by the congregation at the end of two of Mursili's prayers.[31] Some prayers were performed on a daily basis (probably by a representative of the king),[32] while those addressing a specific situation such as an illness might be performed only once.

---

29. See Singer, *Hittite Prayers*, 9.

30. Translation by ibid., 86 (no. 20, §1).

31. Ibid., nos. 8, 9.

32. In Mursili's case, a scribe, indicating that the prayer was read out rather than memorized and recited by a priest.

DEITIES AND DEMONS

"May the thousand gods give you life," wrote a scribe to his father and mother who lived in Tapikka.[33] Their expansive pantheon was a point of pride for the Hittites, and they invoked them collectively in blessings and as witnesses in their treaties. The actual number of deities attested in the surviving Hittite documents has not yet reached the canonical one thousand, but the number was hardly an exaggeration.[34] The pantheon in its final form evolved through a process of territorial expansion and assimilation, over time absorbing the gods of the Hattians, Palaians, and the Luwians. Eventually the expansion of the Hittite state resulted in the introduction of gods not only from other parts of Anatolia but also from Hurrian Syria and Mesopotamia.

The size of the Hittite pantheon may be attributed to a resistance to syncretism, since in general the Hittites tended not to identify their own gods with either foreign or native deities of a similar type, in the way, for example, that members of the Greek pantheon were identified with those of the Roman. Scribes brought a certain order to the system by grouping together local deities who showed a common character. For example, they designated all bringers of rain and thunder with the same Mesopotamian ideogram (U) indicating a storm-god. This system, however, renders it difficult to tell which deity is meant by the generic designation—the sign for tutelary deity (LAMMA) could refer to any number of deities, including Zithariya, Hapantaliya, and Inara—and often the original names of the deities are entirely lost. So, to distinguish deities belonging to a particular "type," the scribes sometimes attached the name of the city that served as the deity's cult center. Thus are attested the Storm-Gods of Nerik, Zippalanda, and Aleppo. We know, however, that these gods were worshiped individually because they appear side by side in the texts as separate divinities. Where the original names of the gods do survive, it is often a result of the fact that the Hittites sometimes addressed them in the gods' native tongue in an effort to please them. For this reason we know that the Sun-God of Heaven in Hittite is called Istanu but in Hurrian is worshiped as Shimegi, in Luwian as Tiwat, in Palaic as Tiwaz, in Hattian as Eshtan, and in Akkadian as Shamash.

The myths and iconography indicate that the gods of the Hittites were conceived of in human terms. They required sustenance, exhibited a range

---

33. *HKM* 81:5.

34. Itamar Singer, "The Thousand Gods of Hatti: The Limits of an Expanding Pantheon," *IOS* 14 (1994): 81. For a full listing of the gods attested in the Hittite texts, see Ben H. L. van Gessel's three-volume *Onomasticon of the Hittite Pantheon* (HdO 1/33; Leiden: Brill, 1998–2001).

of emotions, and were negatively affected by the acts of other gods—if one failed to perform his divine duties, all suffered. In the cult, their statues were subjected to a schedule probably not unlike a royal personage: they slept, arose, dressed, dined, enjoyed entertainments, and held court. No single divinity embodied goodness, and, by the same token, neither was there a divinity that epitomized or explained the existence of evil. "Evil" as one half of a cosmic duality had no place in Hittite thought. The gods were neither omniscient nor omnipotent but made mistakes and were capable of being deceived. Still, they possessed a wisdom and power that was far above that of humans. The level of wisdom and power varied widely depending on each deity's status within the pantheon, which itself often depended on the importance of the natural phenomenon that that deity represented.

Most important were the storm-gods, who brought the rain and winds to fertilize the crops. Solar deities (sun, moon) of both genders were also prominent. Deities of grain, vineyards, and orchards were directly responsible for the prosperity of the crops. There were also deities of wildlife, deities of war and pestilence, and personal protective deities who often served as intermediaries to the other gods on behalf of their mortal charges. The mother-goddesses were responsible for the creation of humanity and for birth in general, while the fate-goddesses (Gulses) determined human destiny. Other groups of gods, some whose nature can hardly be determined, are attested, including the Heptad (the "Seven") and the primordial (underworld) deities. Finally, the mountains, rivers, streams, heaven and earth, winds, and clouds are included in lists of divine witnesses to diplomatic treaties; we are not given their individual names in these contexts.

Hittite deities, particularly goddesses, were usually depicted in human form, that is, anthropomorphically, although divine representations could take a wide variety of forms. The Hittites endeavored to understand the cosmos through imagery drawn from the daily experiences of agrarian life. Hence the character of many deities was manifested through an association with some animal. They were frequently depicted standing on their associated animals, and some were even represented by their associated animals. Hence, cult images could take the form of an animal; for example, a bull often stood in for the Storm-God. In other cases, inanimate objects or fetishes could stand in for the deity, so the cult image might be a stela (*huwasi*), a weapon (mountain-gods), a rhyton in the shape of a fist (war-gods), or a solar disk (sun-gods). The Hittites did not worship the animals or objects but rather the deity that the object or animal symbolized.

The supreme male deity of the Hittite pantheon, the Storm-God of Hatti (Hittite Tarhunt) was an Indo-European import, later identified with the Hurrian Teshub. In Hurrian tradition the divine bulls Sherri and Hurri drew his wagon. The Storm-God of Hatti shared the Great Temple at Hattusa with the supreme goddess of the land, the Sun-Goddess of Arinna. Assimilated into the pantheon from the native Hattian tradition, the Sun-Goddess was the special protector of the kingship. Her Hattian name was Wurusemu, and she was later identified with the Hurrian Hebat. Their sons, the Storm-Gods of Nerik and Zippalanda, their daughter Mezzulla, and their granddaughter Zintuhi completed the divine first family in the Old Kingdom.

According to the mythological texts, Telipinu and Inara were also important in the Old Kingdom pantheon. Inara was the daughter of the Storm-God and the protective deity of Hattusa. She was a goddess of the hunt and wild animals. Some scholars identify her with Hattian Teteshapi, whose name means "Great Goddess." Telipinu, a lesser storm-god concerned with cultivation, was the main protagonist in the Missing Deity myths (see ch. 3). Kamrusepa also figures prominently in Anatolian mythology as a goddess associated with magic, while Hannahanna, the "grandmother," was consulted by the other gods for her wisdom. Her special animal was the bee, symbol of hearth and home.

Istanu, the Sun-God of Heaven, held a high status in the pantheon from the Old Kingdom on and was the all-seeing dispenser of justice to humans and animals. Because of his judicial powers, he was most frequently invoked in prayers and hymns of praise that sought some kind of legal recognition or justification. Although not the supreme deity of the land, as the dispenser of justice he was given priority in the canonical treaty god lists. His mystical relationship to the king of Hatti has already been discussed (see ch. 2).

Mesopotamian imports of the empire period included Ishtar (Hurrian Shaushga), who gained much popularity in Anatolia at the end of the Bronze Age owing to her patronage of Puduhepa and Hattusili, when a number of local deities began to appear with her name. Her role in Anatolia as a goddess of both love and war mirrors her role in Mesopotamia. Her handmaids Ninatta and Kulitta accompany her in god lists. From Syria came Ishara, whose epithet, "queen of the oath," identifies her primary role as divine witness to treaties and vows. She might have been considered an effective enforcer of these, since she seems to have been associated with both sickness and healing; in one text, diseases are called the children of Ishara.

The Hittites could have borrowed the concept of the tutelary, or protective, deity from both Hattian and Mesopotamian religious tradition. The tutelary deity (written with the Sumerogram LAMMA) had numerous manifestations, which were identified more precisely by the addition of geographic and other epithets. One manifestation, the tutelary deity of the field, was particularly popular in Hittite relief art, where he is shown standing on a hart and holding a weapon in one hand and a bird of prey and a hare in

Fig. 4.2. The relief on the silver stag rhyton on display at the Metropolitan Museum of Art depicts the tutelary deity of the field standing on his sacred animal, a stag, receiving the attention of the king and priests. Norbert Schimmel Collection, Metropolitan Museum of Art, New York.

the other (fig. 4.2). Other such deities may have protected particular locations, persons, and even activities.

The forces eminating from the underworld received considerable attention in Hittite religion. Because the Hittites feared them, they kept underworld deities well supplied with offerings to prevent them directing their noxious powers against humanity. In early tradition the deities of the underworld included Hittite Lelwani, "king (later "lady") of the underworld," and Hattian Isdustaya and Papaya, the Parcae who spun the years of human lives. The Sun-Goddess of the Earth headed the pantheon that dwelt within the earth in later

Hittite tradition. An avatar of the Sun-Goddess of Arinna, she represented the sun's course during the hours of the night. Her chthonic nature, perhaps a result of her syncretism with Hurrian Allani, who guarded the gate that separates the underworld from the upper earth, is attested by invocations directed to her in rituals performed for the dead. She conveyed the spirits of the dead to the underworld, and her worship involved placing offerings and sacrifices in the ground. With her in the regions beneath the earth lived the primordial deities, who total twelve in number in the canonical lists of divine witnesses in the treaties (their numbers vary from five to fifteen in the rituals). Their role was to "judge" the cause of an evil and to remove it to the underworld.

Under a religious reform instituted by Puduhepa and completed by Tudhaliya IV, a level of syncretism was achieved within the official pantheon through the creation of a divine family, at the head of which were Hurrian Hebat and Teshub with their son Sharruma. This divine triad was identified with the deities who headed the traditional pantheon, the Sun-Goddess of Arinna, the Storm-God of Hatti, and their son the Storm-God of Nerik. The divine figures carved into the rock sanctuary at Yazılıkaya depict this syncretism of the Hittite and Hurrian gods in its official and final form. These identifications were artifical, manufactured in the royal court as a means of promoting the Hurrian element within the empire and of encouraging religious cohesion and political unity. In spite of efforts to reshape the official pantheon, at no point was a divine hierarchy ever imposed on a wide scale, for this would potentially have undermined the king's efforts to retain the loyalty of his subjects.

Human ambition could achieve no greater purpose than to serve the gods well, as a good servant served his or her master. The pious could hope to be rewarded with a life free of illness and hardship. Humans and deities also depended on one another for survival. The gods needed the sustenance provided by humans in the daily cult. Thus Mursili II reminded the gods, "but if the gods, my lords, [do not remove] the plague [from Hatti], the makers of offering bread and the libation pourers will keep on dying. And if they too die, [the offering bread] and the libation will be cut off from the gods, my lords. Then you, O gods, [my lords], will proceed to hold the sin against me."[35] At the same time, humans were dependent on the beneficence of the deities who controlled the forces of nature that ensured agricultural bounty and the growth of the herds.

---

35. "Mursili's Third Plague Prayer," *CTH* 378.III; translated by Singer, *Hittite Prayers*, 57 (no. 10).

If a deity such as Telipinu left his post out of anger or confusion, the natural world could not function:

> Telipinu too went away and removed grain, animal fecundity, luxuriance, growth, and abundance to the steppe, to the meadow. Telipinu too went into the moor and blended with the moor. Over him the *halenzu*-plant grew. Therefore barley (and) wheat no longer ripen. Cattle, sheep, and humans no longer become pregnant. And those (already) pregnant cannot give birth.[36]

Even the gods were adversely affected: "[The Sun God made] a feast and invited the Thousand Gods. [They ate], but couldn't get enough. They drank, but couldn't quench their thirst."[37] But a ritual, performed by a human practitioner in the guise of the goddess of magic, Kamrusepa, was effective in restoring the deity to his or her place in the cosmos, and with him or her the cosmic balance: "The mist released the windows. The smoke released the house. The altars were in harmony again with the gods.... Then the mother looked after her child. The sheep looked after her lamb. The cow looked after her calf. And Telipinu too looked after the king and queen and took account of them in respect to life, vigor, and longevity."[38] The collection of compositions known as the Missing Deity myths were ritual tools for coping with deities who failed adequately to maintain their role in the human-divine continuum.

Sin and Pollution

When bad things happened to good people, the cause was sought either in some accidental transgression on the part of the afflicted individual or in the form of a sorcerer, demon, or angry deity. Whether committed willfully or accidentally, transgressions (sins) aroused the displeasure of the divine

---

36. Translation by Hoffner, *Hittite Myths*, 15.

37. Translation by ibid., 21. This mythologem appears as a curse formula in Lev 26:26: "though you eat, you shall not be satisfied" (see also Mic 6:14–15). The mythologem could have made its way into Israelite thought via the Neo-Hittites, in whose inscriptions (e.g., ÇIFTLIK §§15–16 [*CHLI* I/2, 449]; SULTANHAN §36 [*CHLI* I/2, 467) we see its further development; see Manfred Hutter, "Widerspiegelungen religiöser Vorstellungen der Luwier im Alten Testament," in *Die Außenwirkung des späthethitischen Kulturraumes: Güteraustausch–Kulturkontakt–Kulturtransfer: Akten der zweiten Forschungstagung des Graduiertenkollegs "Anatolien und seine Nachbarn" der Eberhard-Karls-Universität Tübingen (20. bis 22. November 2003)* (ed. Mirko Novák, Friedhelm Prayon, and Anne-Maria Wittke; Münster: Ugarit-Verlag, 2004), 432–34.

38. Translation by Hoffner, *Hittite Myths*, 17–18.

and could manifest themselves in pollution or impurity (*papratar*) adhering to an individual. Social sins, such as murder or theft, brought on impurity and might be dealt with by ritual means, in addition to whatever legal punishment awaited the guilty party. If one was lucky, a monetary settlement would suffice. Sources of accidental or unwillful impurity included sorcery, stumbling upon an unclean object or location, or unknowingly transgressing a taboo. Potential ritual defilement stemming from a number of unavoidable sources had to be reckoned with. The burden for an offense ignored by the transgressor passed to the next generation, so once pollution had accrued to the individual, from whatever direction it may have come, it had to be dealt with by magico-ritual means. Identifying the sin, confessing it, and correcting it were the necessary steps to pacifying the deity's anger.

Sometimes pollution was simply unavoidable, particularly in connection with birth and death. The Hittites observed prescribed purity rules in these situations, although for the latter we are poorly informed. A pregnant woman was expected to adhere to certain dietary and sexual restrictions, and she was to eat using separate utensils and at a table separate from her husband. The birth was followed by a period of ritual separation of the mother and child from the community, followed by a ceremonial reentry.

The purity of the king and his family was a major preoccupation of the state religion, as we have seen. His well-being was connected to the well-being of the entire land, and he of all humans operated in closest proximity to the gods. In this connection, two compendia of purification rituals deriving from Hurrian tradition, called *itkalzi* and *itkahhi* (Hurrian *itki* means "pure"), must be mentioned. These compendia belong to the earliest layer of Hurrian religious influence, that is, to the reigns of Arnuwanda I, whose queen Asmunikal is mentioned, and of Tudhaliya III and his queen Taduhepa. The *itkalzi* rituals, which originated in Sapinuwa (modern Ortaköy) combine incantations employing analogy ("As water is pure…, so [may the sacrificer] Taduhepa [be pure] before gods [and men]"[39]) with rites of contagion. The *itkahhi* compendium, on the other hand, is made up of hymn-like recitations. In both cases, the rites were administered by a divination priest (AZU).

The Instructions to Priests and Temple Officials provide guidelines for maintaining appropriate levels of purity among the temple servants and within the temple precinct itself. Temples underwent a regular regimen of ritual cleansing, but one form of purification is worth noting in particular. The ritual for establishing a new temple for the goddess of the night

---

39. Gernot Wilhelm, *The Hurrians* (trans. from the German by Jennifer Barnes; Warminster: Aris & Phillips, 1989), 72.

used blood to purify the statue and cella of the new deity.[40] To counter a bad omen preceding a birth, Papanikri, a Kizzuwatnean priest, "smears the birth-stool and the pegs with the blood of two birds, each separately. And he twice makes meat offerings of two sheep and four birds before the birth-stool."[41] The use of blood as a detergent was rare in the Hittite cult and was introduced from Hurrian Kizzuwatna, along with burnt offerings and bird sacrifice. We may note a biblical parallel not only in the *kippēr* rite described in Lev 16:1–19 but also in Lev 14, which provides instructions for the purification of afflicted persons (14:1–32) and houses (14:33–57).[42]

RITUAL POWER

The character of Hittite society was shaped by the ideology of its kings, so it is remarkable that we can speak at all about popular religion in Hatti. In fact, our investigations are made possible primarily by the interest that the kings took in gathering, recording, and using ritual remedies for their own needs. In the sense that many of the surviving rituals were performed for the royal family, they are not "popular," but because we may assume that these rituals were drawn from the world of folk religion, they do give us information about the sorts of rituals ordinary people would have used. Further, because the authors of the texts, who hailed from all corners of the empire, are identified along with their place of origin, we are even able to reconstruct regional practices to some extent.

Magic and medicine were not separate categories in Hittite thought or practice, and purely medical approaches to physical ailments are rare. Hittite medical texts attest to treatments for disorders of the eyes, intestine, throat, and mouth, among other things, and medical cures included the use of honey, wine or beer, plants, animal substances, and minerals. A number of physicians (A.ZU) are known by name, and, while female physicians are attested, most often women in Hatti's "healthcare system" performed the role of midwife. Hittite doctors, however, rarely limited themselves to purely medical

---

40. "Establishing a New Temple for the Goddess of the Night," translated by Billie Jean Collins (*COS* 1.70:176, §32).

41. *KBo* 5.1 (*CTH* 476) i 25–27; translated by Gary Beckman, "Blood in Hittite Ritual," Gedenkschrift for Erich Neu, forthcoming.

42. For a detailed comparison of the Hurrian "ritual of blood" with Lev 14, see Haas, "Ein hurritischer Blutritus," 67–77. See here also (69) on the use of cedar and red wool in Lev 14 and in Hurro-Hittite rituals; cf. Hoffner, "Hittite-Israelite Cultural Parallels," *COS* 3:xxx; and see also Ida Zatelli, "The Origin of the Biblical Scapegoat Ritual: The Evidence of Two Eblaite Texts," *VT* 48 (1998): 254–63, esp. 260.

treatments. Most often we see treatments that combine magical and medical means or that are purely magical, as when the physician Zarpiya performs an elaborate sacrifice to ward off demons responsible for an epidemic.

For the Hittites, the rituals that fall into the category that today we call magic constituted an acceptable, even necessary, form of communication with the divine world. Magic rituals are distinguished from regular offering rituals and from festivals in that they were not carried out at regular intervals by official priests and royal attendants but were performed when circumstances dictated. The full range of concerns evidenced includes a variety of illnesses, impurity, family discord, bad years, infertility of the fields, birth, death, sorcery and other criminal offenses (e.g., perjury, physical injury, or murder), human fertility, and impotence. These problems were solved by means of rituals tailored to address specific situations. Rituals also addressed crises that affected the community as a whole, such as plague, military defeat, bad omens, building rites, and cultic events, which included attracting absent deities, erecting divine images, and correcting offenses against the gods.

A variety of professional ritual practitioners were qualified to oversee the appropriate ritual performance on behalf of a client. Physician-exorcists (A.ZU), augurs (AZU), and ritual experts called "Wise Women," (ŠU.GI) are found. The exorcists and augurs were skilled professionals trained in ritual and divinatory techniques, while the Wise Women were repositories of folk knowledge. Whatever practitioner was in charge, he or she was typically identified by name in the incipit of the tablet. This practice is unusual in the Near East, where such compositions are usually anonymous, and suggest an individual stamp on the rituals themselves. Some of these practitioners, like the Wise Women Anniwiyani and Ayatarsha, were slaves, but through service to the royal family some did quite well for themselves. Kuwattalla, authoress of a magic ritual, was even granted land by Arnuwanda I and Asmunikal in gratitude for her expertise.[43]

The documents that record these rituals were more or less standardized in their format, beginning with an introduction identifying the professional practitioner and his or her place of origin. A statement of the problem and a list of ingredients (*materia magica*) that used to address the problem followed. Finally, the ritual recipe itself was written out in detail. These ritual prescriptions must have been used over and over again, judging by the fact that they exist in several copies (although always retaining the identity of the original author).

---

43. Hutter, "Aspects of Luwian Religion," 253.

They reveal that the primary means of treating problems were analogic magic (sympathy), transference of contagion, and substitution. In the course of a given ritual, any combination of these elements might be employed, repeated, or embellished to achieve the desired end. Although apotropaic, that is, preventive, magic did occur, Hittite rituals for the most part focused on curing problems that already existed rather than on preventing them.

Analogic (sympathetic) magic combines ritual action with an incantation that links that action to the desired outcome.[44] For example, male impotence could be cured by restoring a man's masculinity literally by taking from him the attributes of a woman (spindle, distaff) that he had been given and restoring to him the attributes of a man (bow, arrows). Indeed, the threat of femininity in curse formulas was considered to be an effective preventative against disloyalty among the troops and was incorporated into the Hittite soldiers' oath:

> He who transgresses these oaths and takes part in evil against the king, queen, and princes, may these oath deities make (that) man (into) a woman. May they make his troops women. Let them put a scarf on them. Let them break the bows, arrows, and weapons in their hands and let them place the distaff and spindle in their hands (instead).[45]

The actions embedded in the incantation were carried out in reality as the words were recited. Such incantations were one of the most common and simple components of Hittite ritual and, some have argued, its key concept.

The vehicle of the analogy might be an animal, human, god, plant, foodstuff or other substance, or natural process. From the same text, for example, the ritual specialist "places wax and sheep fat in their (the soldiers') hands and he casts (some) on the flame and says, 'just as this wax melts and just as the sheep fat is rendered, who breaks the oath and takes deceptive action against the king of Hatti, may he melt like the wax and may he be rendered like the sheep fat.' They (the soldiers) say, 'so be it.'" Oath magic

---

44. For a comparison of Hittite and biblical analogy, see David P. Wright, "Analogy in Biblical and Hittite Ritual," in Janowski, Koch, and Wilhelm, *Religionsgeschichtliche Beziehungen*, 473–506.

45. "First Soldiers' Oath," translated by Billie Jean Collins (*COS* 1.66:166, §9). Compare the prohibition in Deut 22:5 against dressing in the attire of the opposite sex, which is to be understood as a prohibition against rituals such as that in the soldier's oath designed to restore masculinity; see James C. Moyer, "Hittite and Israelite Cultic Practices: A Selected Comparison," in *Scripture in Context II: More Essays on the Comparative Method* (ed. William Hallo, James C. Moyer, and Leo G. Perdue; Winona Lake, Ind.: Eisenbrauns, 1983), 29.

like this anticipates an undesirable event in the future (in this case treason) and directs the gods automatically to intervene should it occur. But desirable events can be secured just as easily: "Just as a single pig gives birth to many piglets, let every single branch of this vineyard, like the pig, bear many grape clusters!"[46]

The images used were ones that would have been familiar to the participants. Thus the anger of the deity Telipinu was dissipated with the following words and accompanying actions:

> Telipinu is angry. His soul and essence were stifled (like burning) brushwood. Just as they burned these sticks of brushwood, may the anger, wrath, sin, and sullenness of Telipinu likewise burn up. [And] just as [malt] is sterile, so that they don't carry it to the field and use it as seed, (as) they don't make it into bread and deposit it in the Seal House, so may the anger, wrath, sin, and sullenness of Telipinu likewise become sterile.[47]

As a final example of analogic magic, consider the following metaphorical incantation that the Wise Woman Alli recites against a female sorcerer: "Let [it] (the sorcery) be a headdress and may she (the sorceress) wear it on her head. May she take it (the spell) back. Let it be a girdle for her. May she bind it on herself. Let it be shoe(s) for her. May she put it on herself."[48] To this incantation we may compare Ps 109:17–19, in which the malefactor's curses are compared to clothing that he is to wear: "He loved to curse; let curses come on him. He did not like blessing; may it be far from him. He clothed himself with cursing as his coat, may it soak into his body like water, like oil into his bones. May it be like a garment that he wraps around himself, like a belt that he wears every day."[49]

A number of techniques were used to transfer an affliction from the patient to another object. These included waving an object or animal over the patient, touching or rubbing the patient with an animal or power-laden substance such as bread, meal, honey, or mud, or passing through the severed parts of animals or through a gate made of hawthorn (which had the ability to scrape off and retain the malignancy). To extract illness from an individual, the Wise Woman Tunnawiya arranged the twelve (a standard magical number) body parts of a ram against the patient's twelve body parts, top to bottom: "Head is arranged against head. Throat is arranged against throat. Ear is arrang[ed] against ear. . . .

---

46. *KUB* 43.23 (*CTH* 820) rev 19'–22'.
47. *KUB* 17.10 (*CTH* 324) iii 13–20, translated by Hoffner, *Hittite Myths*, 16–17.
48. *KBo* 12.126 (*CTH* 402) i 16–19.
49. Wright, "Analogy in Biblical and Hittite Ritual," 503.

Fi[nger] against finger likewise.... [Foot] against foot likewise.... Blood is arranged against blood." Tunnawiya revealed the purpose of this rite: "For his twelve body parts I have arranged. Right now the body parts of the ram are claiming the sickness of the body parts of this mortal."[50] Elisha performed a similar healing ritual on a sick child by laying his own body upon the child's, mouth upon mouth, eyes upon eyes, hands upon hands, thus restoring his life (2 Kgs 4:32–35; see also 1 Kgs 17:21). Similar healing rituals are known from Mesopotamia as well, so it seems that Elisha's miracle must be understood in the context of ancient Near Eastern, if not specifically Anatolian, folk medicine.[51]

If the army was suffering defeat, a more drastic form of transference was used:

> Behind the river they sever a human, a billy-goat, a puppy (and) a piglet. On one side they set halves and on the other side they set the (other) halves. In front (of these) they make a gate of hawthorn and stretch a *tiyamar* up over it. Then on one side they burn a fire before the gate (and) on the other side they burn a fire. The troops go through, but when they come alongside the river, they sprinkle water over them(selves).[52]

Several instances of cutting animals in half and passing between their parts are attested in the Hittite texts, and when, as in this example, the occasion was serious enough to require it, a prisoner of war was included among the sacrificial victims. A late example of the motif in Herodotus (*Hist.* 7.39), although attributed to the Persians, indicates the long history and wide distribution of the rite in the eastern Mediterranean, and Achilles' sacrifice of twelve Trojan warriors along with nine dogs on the funeral pyre of Patroklos (Homer, *Il.* 23.172–177), although fictional, suggests that this ritual motif was well-known. The human sacrifice mentioned in Isa 66:3 probably alludes to such extreme forms of ritual killing as these performed in military contexts. Genesis 15:9–10 and Jer 34:18–20 both refer to a covenant-sealing ceremony that involves passing between the parts of severed animals. Although similar in form to these biblical examples, the function of the Hittite ritual was not to serve as a warning to those who would break a covenant but to purify

---

50. *KUB* 55.20 + *KUB* 9.4 + Bo 7125 + Bo 8057 (*CTH* 760) ii 1–22; translated by Gary Beckman, "The Hittite 'Ritual of the Ox' (*CTH* 760.I.2–3)," *Or* 59 (1990): 45.

51. For the argument that Elisha's miracle more closely resembles the Luwian than the Mesopotamian praxis, see Hutter, "Widerspiegelungen religiöser Vorstellungen der Luwier," 434–37, with references.

52. *KUB* 17.28 (*CTH* 730) iv 44–55.

those who passed between the parts of the animals.[53] The kind of animal used also differed, the Hittites preferring puppies, piglets,[54] and sometimes a young goat. Nevertheless, we are clearly dealing with an eastern Mediterranean ritual koiné.

In substitution rituals, a human or animal (both live animals and models fashioned from clay or dough were acceptable) took the place of the patient so that the evil or impurity accrued to it, freeing the patient from its damaging effects. For the substitution to be effective, the animal first had to be identified with the person to be purified. We read of the Wise Woman Mastigga doing this orally while presenting the sheep to the offerants: "Here (is) a substitute for you; let it be a substitute for your persons."[55] Once the identification was complete, the impurity was "downloaded" to the carrier or substitute. For example, in Pulisa's ritual to end a plague within the army, a ram and ewe are adorned with wreaths made from colored strands of wool that had been pulled from the mouth of the king, the wreaths being symbolic of the illness afflicting the troops. On the other hand, in Mastigga's ritual the patients simply spit into the mouth of the substitute sheep.[56] Once the evil was fully transferred, the carrier was sent away, while the substitute was destroyed, usually through burning, burial, or both. The purification was thus complete.

This form of purification enjoyed its most extreme form of expression in the substitute king rituals. The concept was borrowed from Mesopotamia and was put into practice whenever any of the usual divinatory techniques presaged the death of the king. In these rituals a prisoner of war was anointed with the oil of kingship while the king spoke as follows:

> Behold, this one is the king. [I have bestowed] the name of kingship upon this one. I have clothed this one in the [garments] of kingship, and I have put the cap (kingship) on this one. Evil omen, short years, short days take note [of this man] and go after this substitute![57]

----

53. For a similar ritual from Mari, see Jack M. Sasson, "Isaiah LXVI 3–4a," *VT* 26 (1976): 199–207.

54. Puppies and piglets were unclean; see Lev 11:7, 27; Deut 14:8.

55. Translated by Jared L. Miller, *Studies in the Origins, Development and Interpretation of the Kizzuwatna Rituals* (StBoT 46; Wiesbaden: Harrassowitz, 2004), 74.

56. See ibid.

57. *KUB* 24.5 + *KUB* 9.13 (*CTH* 419) obv. 20'–24'. Translation adapted from Yakubovich, "Were Hittite Kings Divinely Anointed," 124; see also van den Hout, "Death as a Privilege," 41.

The prisoner was then escorted back to the enemy land whence he came.[58]

Substitution and scapegoat rituals were commonplace in Anatolia, where they are attested as early as the Old Kingdom. Perhaps the most notable example of a substitution ritual was that performed for Mursili II after he suffered a speech loss possibly resulting from a minor stroke (see ch. 2). A substitute ox was adorned, and the king placed his hand upon it to identify the animal as his substitute offering. Together with the king's clothes, his chariot, and the horses that pulled it, the adorned ox was dispatched to Kummanni in Kizzuwatna, where the priests there were instructed to perform the ritual of the substitute as it was inscribed on an ancient wooden tablet.

The use of scapegoats (Hittite *nakkussi*) is particularly well-attested in Arzawa in western and southwestern Anatolia in rites performed for the removal of plague. Among these is Ashella's ritual to alleviate an outbreak in the army.[59]

§2 I (Ashella) do the following: When day turns to night, all who are army commanders, every one must prepare a ram. It does not matter whether the rams are white or black. I wind twists of white, red, and green wool, and he weaves them into one. I string one gemstone and one ring of chalcedony, and they tie them to the necks and horns of the rams. They tether them (the rams) before the tents at night, and as they do so, they say the following: "Whatever god is moving about, whatever god has caused this plague, for you I have just bound these rams. Be satisfied with these!"

§3 In the morning I drive them to the countryside. For each ram they bring along one jug of beer, one offering loaf, and one cup of.... At the tent, before the king, he seats an ornamented woman. He sets down one keg of beer and three offering loaves for the woman.

§4 Afterwards the camp commanders place their hands on the rams and recite as follows: "The deity who has caused this plague, now the rams are standing here and their liver, heart, and thigh are very succulent. May human flesh be hateful to him once again, and may you (O deity) be satisfied with these rams." The camp commanders bow to the rams, and

---

58. Whether all substitute king rituals ended with the release of the substitute is not clear, since the outcome is nowhere else preserved, but Mesopotamian parallels suggest that in some cases the death of the new "king" may have been necessary.

59. Miller (*Studies in the Origins*, 464–68) argues for the origin of the scapegoat rite in Arzawa, whence it spread west to Greece and east to Kizzuwatna and then the Levant. Cf. Hutter ("Aspects of Luwian Religion," 236), who suspects two separate scapegoat traditions. The fact that Lev 16 resembles the Arzawan tradition much more closely than the Kizzuwatnean has yet to be adequately explained. For a Greek example of a scapegoat ritual using a criminal, see Strabo, *Geogr.* 10.2.9. For additional Arzawan scapegoat rituals, see *COS* 1.62:161 and 1.63:162.

the king bows to the ornamented woman. Then they bring the rams, the woman, the bread, and the beer out through the army and drive them into the countryside. They go and abandon them in enemy territory (so that) they do not end up at any place of ours. Thereupon they recite as follows: "Behold, whatever evil was among the men, cattle, sheep, horses, mules, and donkeys of this army, these rams and woman have just carried it away from the camp. Whoever finds them, may that land receive this evil plague."[60]

The parallel to the biblical scapegoat rite described in Lev 16 has long been noted.[61] Both rites have as their goal the elimination of pollution from the community by means of a scapegoat sent into the wilderness or the enemy camp; in the case of Ashella's ritual, several scapegoats (rams) are used, along with a woman. Just as the Azazel rite is balanced with sin offerings to Yahweh (Lev 16:11–19), Ashella's ritual complements the scapegoat rite with sacrifices performed for the god who caused the plague on the third day of the four-day ritual (§7). Also, in both rites the person who performs the laying on of hands[62] is not the same as the person responsible for sending the animal away.[63] Although Ashella's ritual differs from Lev 16 in the sending of the scapegoats as a propitiatory offering to the gods who caused the plague, appeasement is not a universal element in Hittite scapegoat rites.[64]

The identity of Azazel, the demon to whom the scapegoat is offered in Lev 16, has long been a puzzle but can perhaps be explained by occurrences of the word *azuzḫi* in Hurrian purification rituals and in a late-seventeenth-century text from Alalakh in which birds, kids, and lambs are sacrificed as *azazḫum*-offerings to appease the gods of heaven and the underworld.[65] The

---

60. *KUB* 9.32 (*CTH* 394) i 4–32.

61. For a full discussion of the biblical and Hittite scapegoat rites, see David P. Wright, *The Disposal of Impurity: Elimination Rites in the Bible and in Hittite and Mesopotamian Literature* (SBLDS 101; Atlanta: Scholars Press, 1987), 15–74.

62. Wright ("The Gesture of Hand Placement," 433–46) points out that Aaron's laying of two hands on the scapegoat had a different purpose than the one hand that the army commanders placed on the rams in Ashella's ritual. In Lev 16, Aaron's act was designed to direct the sin to the goat that served as the focus of the ritual, not to identify the owner of the sacrifice, as in the Hittite scapegoat rite. Zatelli ("The Origin of the Biblical Scapegoat Ritual," 262) suggests that this element of the biblical rite (although not the transfer of impurities per se) was a late introduction.

63. Theodore J. Lewis and Raymond Westbrook, "Who Led the Scapegoat in Leviticus 16:21?" paper presented at the Annual Meeting of the Society of Biblical Literature, Washington, D.C., 20 November 2006.

64. Hoffner, "Hittite-Israelite Cultural Parallels," *COS* 3:xxxii.

65. See Singer, "Hittites and the Bible Revisited," 749.

term seems to be derived from the Semitic root '*zz*, Akkadian *ezēzu*, "to be(come) angry," with a Hurrian suffix (-*hi*).[66] If "Azazel" derives also from this root, then the sacrifice "for Azazel" was originally a sacrifice "for (the elimination of) divine anger," a common and very ancient source of impurity in ancient Near Eastern thought. Already in antiquity the original meaning was misinterpreted and the -*el* element added, after the pattern of El-names, to create a "desert demon."

In the Kizzuwatnean scapegoat tradition, a number of animals might be used as the substitute, including cows, sheep, goats, donkeys, or even mice:

> She wraps a small (piece of) tin in a b[ow]string. She wraps it around the offerant's right hand (and) foot. Then she takes it away from them and she transfers it to the mouse and she says, "I have taken away the evil from you and transferred it to the mouse, now let this mouse take it to the high mountains, the deep valleys, the long roads." Then she releases the mouse. § The one who turns before the *tarpattassa*-deities, you take this one for yourself! We will provide another for you to eat. She scatters the remains.... They bring another pure mouse and she offers it to the one who turns before the *tarpattassa*-deities (saying), "You eat!"[67]

This ritual, performed by the Wise Woman Ambazzi, finds an echo in the episode of the Philistines and the ark of the covenant (1 Sam 5–6). The presence of the ark caused a plague of tumors among the Philistines, a sign of God's anger.[68] On consultation, their priests advised the Philistines to return the ark to the Israelites laden with five gold mice and five gold tumors as a guilt offering (*'āšam*) in order to appease their God. Mice were unclean in Israel (Lev 11:29), and the offering makes little sense in an Israelite context but could reflect Philistine custom. The Philistine god Dagon is generally identified with Semitic Dagan, a popular deity of uncertain character. But if the name of Philistine Dagon derives instead from Indo-European $d^heĝ^hom$

---

66. Bernd Janowski and Gernot Wilhelm, "Der Bock, der die Sünden hinausträgt: Zur Religionsgeschichte des Azazel-Ritus Lev 16,10.21f," in Janowski, Koch, and Wilhelm, *Religionsgeschichtliche Beziehungen*, 152–58. For alternative viewpoints see Manfred Görg, "'Asaselologen' unter sich—eine neue Runde?" *BN* 80 (1995): 25–31; Henrik Pfeiffer, "Bemerkungen zur Ritualgeschichte von Lev 16," in Richter, Prechel, and Klinger, *Kulturgeschichten*, 313–26.

67. *KUB* 27.67 (*CTH* 391) iii 38–47, 52–54.

68. See John B. Geyer, "Mice and Rites in 1 Samuel V–VI," *VT* 31 (1981): 293–304, for an unraveling of the variations between MT and LXX and the reconstruction of the original text as involving only one plague (tumors) and one offering (golden mice).

(Hittite *tekan* "earth")[69] and refers to an Anatolian or Aegean deity connected with the earth (compare the Hittite deity Daganzipa), then the proposed Anatolian-Aegean ancestry of the Philistines becomes even more likely,[70] and the mice in 1 Sam 5–6 can then be explained as a "repurposing" of an Anatolian scapegoat rite. Also to be compared with 1 Sam 5–6 is the Ritual of Samuha, whose goal was the elimination of curses spoken before a deity. In this ritual the practitioner sent a model boat laden with gold and silver images of the oaths and curses down the river to the sea as propitiatory gifts for the offended deity.[71] The shaping of the offerings in the form of the calamities is a striking parallel to the mice and tumors of the Philistines.

SORCERY

If the Hittites did not have a word that correlates directly to our concept of magic, they were by no means short of ways to express acts of hostile magic, or maleficium. The Hittite word for sorcery is *alwanzatar*, and it is distinguished from other forms of magic ritual primarily by its intention to do harm. The rites of the sorceror, however, are nowhere described, and there was probably no demonstrable difference between them and the rites involved in "white" magic. More common than *alwanzatar* is the idea of the "evil tongue," a reference to the spoken spell or curse directed at harming an individual. Hexes (*astayaratar*) and curses (*hurtai*) are also attested and underscore the importance of the spoken aspect of magic in sorcery as opposed to the *praxis*, or ritual acts, that accompanied the words.

Among the laws of the Hittites are a number that concern acts of hostile magic. One law stipulates, "if anyone performs a purification on a person, he will dispose of the remnants (of the ritual) in the incineration dumps.

---

69. See the discussions in Itamar Singer, "Towards the Image of Dagon the God of the Philistines," *Syria* 69 (1992): 431–49; idem, "Semitic *dagān* and Indo-European *$d^h e\hat{g}^h om$*: Related Words?" in *The Asia Minor Connexion: Studies on the Pre-Greek Languages in Memory of Charles Carter* (ed. Yoël L. Arbeitman; Leuven: Peeters, 2000), 221–32, where he makes the connection between Semitic and Indo-European Dagan but does not distinguish Philistine Dagon.

70. Hutter, "Widerspiegelungen religiöser Vorstellungen der Luwier," 437–39. The Philistine pantheon already had one member from Anatolia: the goddess *ptgyh* is identified with *pelagia*, an epithet of Aphrodite. In terms of the connection between mice and pestilence, note Apollo Smintheus, a god of pestilence in Greek Asia Minor whose sacred animal was the mouse.

71. *KUB* 29.7 + *KBo* 21.41 (*CTH* 480) rev 48–57; edited by René Lebrun, *Samuha Foyer Religieux de l'Empire Hittite* (Louvain-la-neuve: Université Catholique de Louvain, 1976), 124, 131–32.

But if he disposes of them in someone's house, it is sorcery (and) a case for the king" (§44b).[72] The assumption here is that the unclean remains of the magic ritual have been deposited in the victim's house deliberately. Such an act constituted sorcery and was a capital crime. Law 111 concerns a case of voodoo: "[If] anyone forms (?) clay for [an ima]ge (?) (for magical purposes), it is sorcery (and) a case for the king."[73] In the sixteenth century, Telipinu ended his historical recounting of the chaos and political intrigue that plagued the Old Kingdom with an admonition against sorcery: "Regarding cases of sorcery in Hattusa: keep cleaning up (that is, investigating and punishing) instances. Whoever in the royal family practices sorcery, seize him and deliver him to the king's court. But it will go badly for that man (and for his household) who does not deliver him."[74] Telipinu does not mention sorcery among the intrigues at court until this pronouncement, but we are probably safe in assuming that, amidst the murder and mayhem of the preceding reigns, hostile magic was also being carried out for political gain. Even Hattusili I's caretaker in his final days, Hastayatar, had been known to consult the Wise Women for advice.

Certainly in the empire period members of the royal court resorted to magical rites on a regular basis. Arma-Tarhunda allegedly performed sorcery in an attempt to gain political advantage over Hattusili III. Most notoriously, Tawananna, widow of Suppiluliuma, brought about the death of Mursili II's beloved wife Gassulawiya through maleficium. According to Mursili, "She stands day and night before the gods and curses my wife before the gods. [She ...] her, and she wishes for her death saying: 'Let her die!' O gods, my lords, why do you listen to this evil talk?"[75] In this case, the alleged sorcerer was also the reigning queen, and, as priestess in charge of the maintenance of the cult of the state gods, her act was doubly troublesome and dangerous because she had the ear of the gods. Murder by prayer is difficult to prove, and it took an oracular inquiry to establish Tawananna's guilt. Mursili attempted to reassure the gods that their needs would be taken care of now that she was removed from the office of *siwanzanna* and opted to spare Tawananna's life, perhaps fearing the political and religious consequences of putting a queen to death.

---

72. Translation by Hoffner, *The Laws of the Hittites,* 52–53.

73. Translation follows Hoffner, *The Laws of the Hittites,* 107.

74. Telipinu's Proclamation, §50; translated by Hoffner in Roth, *Law Collections,* 237–38.

75. "Mursili's Accusations against Tawananna," *CTH* 70; translated by Singer, *Hittite Prayers,* 76 (no. 17).

COSMOGONY, COSMOLOGY, AND ESCHATOLOGY

The Hittites have left behind little evidence of an indigenous cosmogony or cosmology. Any ideas of a demiurge or a creation seem to be borrowings, either from Mesopotamia or from the Hurrians. A handful of allusions to cosmological ideas can be found in texts of various genres. For example, in the Song of Ullikummi, a part of the Kumarbi cycle (see ch. 3), the title character is hidden in the underworld on the right shoulder of Ubelluri. Teshub cannot defeat Ullikummi so long as he stands on Ubelluri's shoulder, so Ea advises the primeval deities to "open again the old, fatherly, grandfatherly storehouses. Let them bring forth the primeval copper cutting tool with which they cut apart heaven and earth."[76] The motif of the cutting apart of heaven and earth as the primary act of creation goes back at least to the Sumerians. Somewhat closer to the Genesis tradition, a Hittite ritual fragment, once again reflecting north Syrian tradition, contains this allusion to the creation: "The crescent moon rose, the darkness (bore) the Earth, the lightness bore the stars."[77] As in Genesis, the earth came into being from the primordial darkness with the introduction of light.

Prayers describe the Sun-God crossing "the gate of heaven" and arising from the sea.[78] One Hattian ritual relates how the gods in primeval time constructed a palace and established the kingship.[79] In another ritual the client recites an incantation: "When they took heaven and earth, the gods divided (it) up for themselves. The upperworld deities took heaven for themselves, and the underworld deities took the land beneath the earth for themselves. So each took something for himself. But you, O River, have taken for yourself purification, the life of the progeny, and procreation (?)."[80] In Mastigga's ritual magical ingredients were poured into a cow's horn, and the two persons on whose behalf the ritual was performed sealed it over. Then the Wise Woman said, "when the ancient kings return and examine the lands and

---

76. Translation by Hoffner, *Hittite Myths*, 64.

77. *KUB* 57.66 (*CTH* 670) iii 16; see Haas, *Geschichte der hethitischen Religion*, 107 with n. 8.

78. Mursili II's Prayer to the Sun-Goddess of Arinna; *CTH* 376.A §4, for which see Singer, *Hittite Prayers*, 51; and Muwatalli's Prayer to the Assembly of Gods; *CTH* 381 §66, for which see Singer, *Hittite Prayers*, 91.

79. *KUB* 29.1 (*CTH* 414).

80. Bo 3617 (*CTH* 433) i 8'–14' with dupls. For the text, see Heinrich Otten and Jana Siegelová, "Die hethitischen Gulš-Gottheiten und die Erschaffung der Menschen," *AfO* 23 (1970): 32–38.

custom(s), only then shall this seal also be broken."[81] This sentence may be intended in the sense of "when hell freezes over," but it is also possible that it should be understood as an eschatology similar to the Davidic tradition (2 Sam 7; Isa 9:2–7; 11:1–9).

Hittite art offers additional clues to a Hittite cosmology. Archaeologists have recently drained the water from around the Hittite rock monument at Eflatun Pinar in central Turkey, allowing us to see the entire installation for the first time. Taken as a whole, the relief composition represents the cosmos, with the supreme deities of the land framed by symbols of the heavens (winged sun-disks) and the earth (mountain-gods). Interspersed on either side and in between the two seated deities are genii and bull-men, poorly preserved today, but whose arms are raised to support the winged disks above the deities as well as the larger one that caps the entire monument. Between the mountain deities that form the bottom tier of relief, holes in the rock indicate that water was once channeled between them and beneath the seated deities into the pond, reminding us of the consistent grouping of sacred mountains and bodies of water in the texts. This image of the cosmos is repeated on a bronze miniature relief plaque found during excavations at Alaca Höyük, where the mountains are replaced by animals (a lion and a bull) on which stand two bull-men flanking a stylized tree of life; with raised hands they support the winged solar disk. It is also found among the reliefs on the male side at Yazılıkaya, where bull men can be seen supporting a crescent moon while standing on the hieroglyphic symbol for the earth, as well as on the Megiddo ivory plaque (fig. 3.10).

DEATH AND AFTERLIFE

When the Gulses (fate-goddesses who determined human destiny) cut the thread of an individual's life on earth and he arrived at the "day of his destiny," what kind of an afterlife could he look forward to? Textual and archaeological evidence alike suggest that upon death most people took up abode in the underworld. The Sun-Goddess of the Earth had the task of transporting souls to her realm, where conditions, according to one mythological text of native origin, were less than pleasant. In this place,

> One doesn't recognize the other. Sisters having the same mother do [not] recognize (each other). Brothers having the same father do [not] recognize (each other). A mother does [not] recognize [her] own child. [A child] does

---

81. "Mastigga's Ritual for Domestic Quarrel," *CTH* 404; translated by Miller, *Studies in the Origins*, 106.

[not] recognize [its own] mother.... From a fine table they do not eat. From a fine stool they do not eat. From a fine cup they do not drink. They do not eat good food. They do not drink my (?) good drink. They eat bits of mud. They drink waste waters (?).[82]

This bleak outlook is in keeping with Mesopotamian traditions about the underworld, and it not surprising that the Hittites would be influenced by such ideas. But there is no knowing how widespread this view was in a land whose cultural diversity precluded the development of strict religious canons. In any event, there may have been a fate worse than an eternity in this place. Suppiluliuma I threatens his vassal: "And if [you men] of Hayasa and Mariya do not observe these words which I have now placed under oath for you, then these oath gods <shall> thoroughly <eradicate> your persons, together with your wives, [your] sons, your [brothers], your sisters, your families.... They shall also eradicate them from the Dark Netherworld below."[83] To be denied an afterlife, even a bleak and depressing one, was certainly the more horrifying end.

Nevertheless, a trip to the underworld was a fate the Hittite kings actively wished to avoid. In the final words of his Edict, directed to his beloved Hastayatar, Hattusili I's fear of his own death is palpable: "[Wash me] well! Protect me on your bosom from the earth!"[84] But a king's prayer addressed to the Sun-God suggests that royalty at least had some expectation of ascending to dwell with the gods in heaven:

Sungod of Heaven, my Lord, what have I done that you have taken from me (my) th[rone] and given it to someone else? ... You have summoned me to the (ghosts of the) dead and, be[hold], (here) I am among the (ghosts of the) dead. I have shown myself to the Sungod of Heaven, my Lord, so let me ascend to my divine fate, to the gods of Heav[en] and [free] me from among the (ghosts of the) dead.[85]

For the kings, "becoming a god" meant a reunion with the ancestors and an eternity spent resting in a pastoral paradise. During the course of the fourteen-day-long royal funerary ritual, this afterlife was secured with the dedication of various objects related to agriculture, animal husbandry, viticulture, and

---

82. "The Voyage of the Immortal Human Soul," *CTH* 457.6, §4; translated by Hoffner, *Hittite Myths*, 34 (no. 11).

83. *CTH* 42; translated by Beckman, *Hittite Diplomatic Texts*, 33.

84. "Bilingual Edict of Ḫattušili," translated by Gary Beckman (*COS* 2.15:81, §23).

85. *KBo* 15.2 (*CTH* 421) rev. 14'–19' with dupl.; translated by van den Hout, "Death as a Privilege," 46.

hunting designed to ensure that the next life was as fully stocked with the boons of the earthly one as possible: "And have this meadow duly made for him, O Sun-god! Let no one wrest it from him or contest it with him! Let cows, sheep, horses, (and) mules graze for him on this meadow!"[86] The cremated remains of the king himself were deposited in a silver *huppar*-vessel and laid out on a bed in the tomb, or "Stone House," along with the objects in precious materials that were used during the rites. The ashes of the objects intended to accompany the deceased into the afterlife were burned like the corpse and scattered on "the place where the heads of horses and oxen have been burned."

While the spirits of deceased kings joined the gods of heaven, back in this world their statues stood in the temples of the gods in Hattusa ready to receive the homage of their descendants. The maintenance of an active ancestor cult was a necessary corollary to a happy afterlife, and offering lists for deceased members of the royal house going back more than three centuries were maintained to ensure their spirits remained at rest. It is in recognition of the importance of the ancestors that Muwatalli II transported their manes to his new capital at Tarhuntassa. Their cults were centered in the individual *hekur* (mausolea) of deceased kings.[87] Tudhaliya IV had both a tomb (Chamber B at Yazılıkaya) and a *hekur*, namely, the "eternal peak" constructed by Suppiluliuma II in his father's honor on top of Nişantaş (see fig. 2.2), but in other cases the tomb and mortuary shrine may have been one and the same. Gavurkalesi, with its rock relief of an unidentified king, associated "tomb" (a chamber enclosed by a cyclopean structure), and architecture indicating a small settlement, probably served as an imperial institution with sufficient land and personnel to meet not only the administrative needs of the reigning king but also the mortuary needs of one of his ancestors.[88] The reliefs at Firaktin of Hattusili III and Puduhepa and at Sirkeli of Muwatalli II, the former with an associated settlement, may have been the location of similar institutions, although there is no indication of actual tombs at these sites. Cup marks, presumably for receiving libations, were situated near the reliefs in both cases, as they are at Yazılıkaya, further suggesting their mor-

---

86. *KUB* 30.24 (*CTH* 450) ii 1–4; translated by Gary Beckman, "Herding and Herdsmen in Hittite Culture," in Neu and Rüster, *Documentum Asiae Minoris Antiquae*, 44.

87. For a discussion of the *hekur* and the "Stone House," see Theo van den Hout, "Tombs and Memorials: The (Divine) Stone-House and Ḫegur Reconsidered," in Yener and Hoffner, *Recent Developments in Hittite Archaeology and History*, 73–91.

88. For Gavurkalesi, see Stephen Lumsden, "Gavurkalesi: Investigations at a Hittite Sacred Place," in Yener and Hoffner, *Recent Developments in Hittite Archaeology and History*, 111–25.

tuary use. Finally, the likelihood that the reliefs were situated in places of strategic political and religious importance supports this interpretation.

Given that most members of the ruling class were related in some way to the king, and the ghosts of the nonroyal dead were as likely to return to do harm as the royal dead, we might expect them also to have enjoyed an ancestor cult. Certainly there is no reason to doubt the importance of ancestor cults at all levels of society in Anatolia. How the bodies of the ruling elite were disposed of is unclear; they may have had their ashes deposited in the royal mausolea.[89] The few Hittite cemeteries that have been found contain both cremations and inhumations placed in simple dirt graves, and the poor grave goods suggest they were for the use of the "ordinary" subjects of the Hittite king but also emphasize the importance placed on mortuary over funerary rites. Still, the burial of oxen, pigs, sheep, goats, dogs, and equids among the inhumations at Osmankayaşı adjacent to Hattusa indicate that even lesser individuals had a use for the trappings of this world in the next one.

---

89. Bryce, *Life and Society*, 56.

5

HITTITES IN THE BIBLE

COVENANT FORMS, RELIGIOUS PRACTICES, LITERARY TRADITIONS—how did it come about that the Hebrew Bible preserves so many echoes of the Hittite world, and how did Hittite cultural themes gain currency with the Israelites? Societies interact in many ways and on many levels, and no single mode of transmission is likely to explain every instance of influence, but one possibility in particular has engaged scholars from both sides of the academic divide.[1] The biblical writers claimed that a people, whom they identified as "Hittites," were among the pre-Israelite inhabitants of Palestine. In addition, a number of individuals in the biblical stories are given the sobriquet "Hittite." Is it therefore possible that Hittites living in Palestine wielded some cultural influence over the Israelites?

WHO WERE THE BIBLICAL HITTITES?

The answer depends, in part, on whether or not we can connect the "biblical Hittites" with the Hittites of Late Bronze Age Anatolia. The phrase *běnê ḥet* "sons of Heth" and its feminine form *běnôt ḥet* "daughters of Heth" appears in Genesis. Elsewhere, Hebrew *ḥittî* is used either as an epithet to identify the ethnicity of a particular individual, as "Uriah the Hittite," or in the plural form *ḥittîm* "Hittites," as in the lists of the inhabitants of Palestine before the Israelite settlement. It was on the basis of these "Hittites" in the Bible

---

1. Leading the discussion from the view of Hittology in recent years is Harry A. Hoffner Jr., "The Hittites and Hurrians," in *Peoples of Old Testament Times* (ed. D. J. Wiseman; Oxford: Clarendon, 1973), 196–228; idem, "Some Contributions of Hittitology to Old Testament Study," *TynBul* 20 (1969): 27–55. These works have significantly influenced subsequent discussions of the topic by Gregory McMahon, "Hittites in the OT," *ABD* 3:231–33; Bryce, *The Kingdom of the Hittites*, 355–56; see also René Lebrun, "Hittites et Hourrites en Palestine-Canaan," *Transeu* 15 (1998): 153–63. The most cogent recent reevaluation of the evidence is that of Singer, "The Hittites and the Bible Revisited," 723–56.

that Archibald Sayce and his generation were able to identify the inscribed monuments in Syria and Anatolia as Hittite (see ch. 1). Yet some have argued that the use of the appellation is merely a literary convention without ethnic or historical significance, others that the similarity of the name of the kingdom "Hatti" and Hebrew *het* is merely a phonetic coincidence.[2] Nevertheless, the Hebrew Bible seems to preserve some early traditions, as in the name of King Tid'al of Goiim (Gen 14:1). A member of a coalition of kings in the days of Abraham, his name recalls the Hittite king name Tudhaliya, which has led some to identify him with one of the three or four Tudhaliyas who sat on the throne of Hatti.[3] Whatever conclusions are drawn about isolated references, the larger question is whether or not it is possible to show that Hittites from Anatolia were living in Palestine when the Israelites came to settle there. If not, then who were the Hittites in the Bible? This concluding chapter addresses these two over-arching questions.

"All the Kings of the Hittites"

In the first centuries of the first millennium B.C.E., that is, about the time that the earliest passages of the Hebrew Bible may have been composed, the Neo-Hittite cities of northern Syria and southeastern Anatolia were enjoying a period of relative peace and prosperity (fig. 2.9). From the middle of the ninth century B.C.E., the annals of the Neo-Assyrian kings, as they regained their imperial ambitions following the collapse of Bronze Age political systems and began their push to conquer the lands to their west, refer to the region controlled by these cities as "Hatti," in apparent recognition of their cultural and historical affiliation with the Hittite kingdom of the Late Bronze Age. The southernmost of the Neo-Hittite kingdoms was Hamath, whose king, Toi, according to 2 Sam 8:9–10, sent an embassy led by his son Joram[4] to David to

---

2. As argued by Hoffner, "The Hittites and Hurrians," 214 (also McMahon, "Hittites in the OT," 3:233), and rejected by Tomoo Ishida, "The Structure and Historical Implications of the Lists of Pre-Israelite Nations," *Bib* 60 (1979): 469 n. 17.

3. For a discussion and dismissal of this identification, see Singer, "The Hittites and the Bible Revisited," 729–30. It has been variously argued that Goiim ("nations") could refer to Anatolia in the second millennium or to the Neo-Hittite states of northern Syria. For the phonetically similar personal name *tdġl* at Ugarit, see Manfred Dietrich and Oswald Loretz, "Die Soziale Struktur von Alalah und Ugarit. 1. Die Berufsbezeichnungen mit der hurritischen Endung *-huli*," *WO* 3 (1966): 201.

4. In the parallel passage 1 Chr 18:10, his name, Hadoram, switches the theophoric element. The name Toi is of Hurrian origin and is attested in the thirteenth century at Meskene-Emar in its Hurrian form Taḫ'e (see *CHLI* I, 2:400 with n. 30). Recent excavations in the temple of the Storm-God at Aleppo have turned up an inscription identifying

congratulate him on his victory against their common enemy, the Arameans. About a century later the Arameans became the allies of both the Hittites and the Israelites, and another king of Hamath, Urhilina, fought beside Hadad-idri of Aram (Damascus) and Ahab of Israel to defeat the Assyrians, under Shalmaneser III, at Qarqar in 853 B.C.E. Indeed, Hamath and the northern kingdom of Israel maintained political, economic, and cultural ties right up until the Assyrians subjugated them both and made them provinces of the new empire.

A handful of biblical passages that mention "Hittites" fits this picture of the relationship that Israel enjoyed with its neighbors in Syria. For example, 1 Kings relates that Solomon imported chariots from Egypt and horses from Cilicia and exported them to "all the kings of the Hittites and the Arameans" (1 Kgs 10:29 and its parallel, 2 Chr 1:17). These Hittite kings were the rulers of the cities of northern Syria with whom Israel maintained a healthy trade relationship. The Bible also alludes to the military aspect of that relationship. Relating an event that took place about a century after Solomon, 2 Kgs 7:6 describes how the Arameans, while besieging Samaria, heard the approach of chariots and horses, the sound of a great army. They thus fled their camp, believing that the king of Israel had hired the kings of the Hittites and of Egypt to fight against them. The Hittites and Egyptians in this passage are not the two superpowers who fought the battle of Qadesh (1275 B.C.E.) and later brought a long-standing peace to the region, but their Iron Age descendants, who were nevertheless still powerful enough to intimidate the army of their Syrian enemy.[5] Finally, the diplomatic ties enjoyed by the two powers is reflected in the story of Solomon's diplomatic marriages to "Hittite" women (i.e., women from the "Neo-Hittite" cities of northern Syria), alongside other foreign wives, including the daughter of the pharaoh (1 Kgs 11:1).

The biblical text also preserves a memory of the territory controlled by the Neo-Hittite states. Joshua 1:4 relates how, at the beginning of the Israelite conquest of the promised land, Yahweh promised Joshua that, "from the wilderness and the Lebanon as far as the great river, the river Euphrates, all the land of the Hittites, to the Great Sea in the west shall be your territory."[6]

---

a king named Tauta (= Toi?) whose kingdom encompassed a large territory in northern Syria, including Hamath.

5. For the suggestion that the passage refers to Hamath itself, see Hutter, "Wider-spiegelungen religiöser Vorstellungen der Luwier," 431.

6. Robert G. Boling (*Joshua* [AB 6; Garden City, N.Y.: Doubleday, 1982], 122–23) follows Oliver R. Gurney (*The Hittites* [4th ed.; New York: Penguin, 1990], 60) in view-ing the phrase "all the land of the Hittites" as a gloss by a late writer who was thinking of the Neo-Hittites. Aharon Kempinski ("Hittites in the Bible: What Does Archaeology

This description accords well with what we know of the geographical expanse of the cities that were heir to the Hittite culture of the Late Bronze Age.[7] The "land of the Hittites" is mentioned only one other time, in Judg 1:26, where the man who betrayed Bethel, formerly named Luz, "went to the land of the Hittites and built a city and named it Luz." Although there is no known city by this name either in Anatolia or in Palestine, several identifications have been suggested, including the Hittite town Lawazantiya, located in Cilicia (in the territory known as Kizzuwatna in Hittite times).[8] However, the fact that the man from Bethel went to Hittite territory does not necessarily mean that Bethel was a town inhabited by Hittites,[9] and this passage is of little help in our efforts to find Hittites living in Palestine.

In sum, we may safely set aside these five passages in our quest for the "Palestinian Hittites," that is, the pre-Israelite inhabitants of Canaan, as they are consistent with what we know about the later Neo-Hittites and their association with the northern kingdom of Israel of the ninth century and following. But they also account for only five of the occasions when Hittites feature in the Bible;[10] there are many others that cannot be explained as easily.

THE "NATIONS"

The most common context in which a people called "Hittites" appears in the biblical text is in the more-or-less standardized lists of nations that inhabited

---

Say?" *BAR* 5/5 [1979]: 43), on the other hand, thinks it taps into an early tradition about imperial Hatti but reflects an imperfect knowledge of thirteenth-century Hittite geography. John Van Seters ("The Terms 'Amorite' and 'Hittite' in the Old Testament," *VT* 22 [1972]: 79–80) suggests that the passage reflects Assyrian/Babylonian usage (for which see below).

7. Compare the inscription of Adad-nirari III from Calah: "I subdued from the bank of the Euphrates, the land of Hatti, the land of Amurru in its entirety, the land of Tyre, the land of Sidon, the land of Israel, the land of Edom, the land of Philistia, as far as the great sea in the west" (translated by K. Lawson Younger, *COS* 1.214G:276).

8. Benjamin Mazar, "The Early Israelite Settlement in the Hill Country," *BASOR* 241 (1981): 78.

9. Contra Mazar, "The Early Israelite Settlement," 78; Emil O. Forrer, "The Hittites in Palestine," *PEQ* 69 (1937): 200.

10. McMahon ("Hittites in the OT," 3:232) notes that these are the only five occurrences of the term "Hittites" in the Bible that use the masculine plural form *ḥittîm*. See also Mordechai Cogan, "Locating *māt Ḥatti* in Neo-Assyrian Inscriptions," in *Aharon Kempinski Memorial Volume: Studies in Archaeology and Related Disciplines* (ed. Eliezer D. Oren and Shmuel Ahituv; Beer Sheva: Ben-Gurion University of the Negev, 2002), 90.

Palestine prior to the settlement of the Israelites. Deuteronomy 20:16–17 best exemplifies these lists: "But as for the towns of these peoples that the LORD your God is giving you as an inheritance, you must not let anything that breathes remain alive. You shall annihilate them—the Hittites and the Amorites, the Canaanites and the Perizzites, the Hivites, and the Jebusites—just as the Lord your God has commanded."[11] As Itamar Singer notes, the terminology used in describing the ethnic makeup of Canaan must have had some historical credibility in the eyes of the biblical authors, or else they would not have employed it.[12] The trick is in identifying the historical setting that the lists actually reflect.

The possibility of a northern origin for the "nations" is a theory with a long pedigree.[13] Extrabiblical evidence confirms the presence of at least one of these "nations" in the region in and around the northern Levant and Syria at the end of the Late Bronze Age or in the early Iron Age, that is, roughly in the period of the settlement of the Israelites in the land. The Hivites are mentioned in a topographical list of Ramesses II at Luxor.[14] They have been connected with Kue (Cilicia) in southern Anatolia, based on the phonetic resemblance of the two words (Quwe —> *Huwe —> Hebrew ḥiwwî). The connection is corroborated by a Hieroglyphic Luwian-Phoenician bilingual discovered near Adana, in which the Phoenician Dnnym ("Danuna," or "Adana," is another name for Cilicia) is rendered as Luwian Hiyawa, from which the Hebrew form probably derives.[15]

---

11. Twenty-seven such lists of pre-Israelite nations can be found, ranging from lists of two to lists of twelve. As identified by Ishida (*"The Lists of Pre-Israelite Nations,"* 474), this number does not include the apocryphal passages Jdt 5:16 and 1 Esdr 8:69 (the Hittites are included only in the latter). Nor does Ishida include 2 Sam 24:6, which lists Hivites and Canaanites, although he does include the four passages that list only Canaanites and Perizzites (Gen 13:7; 34:30; Exod 23:28; Judg 1:4–5). The Hittites appear in the following examples of the lists of nations: Gen 10:15–18; 15:19–21; Exod 3:8, 17; 13:5; 23:23, 28; 33:2; 34:11; Num 13:29; Deut 7:1; 20:16–17; Josh 3:10; 9:1–2; 11:3; 12:8; 24:11; Judg 3:5–6; 1 Kgs 9:20–21; 1 Chr 1:13–16; 2 Chr 8:7–8; Ezra 9:1–3; Neh 9:8; 1 Esdr 8:69.

12. Singer, "The Hittites and the Bible Revisited," 755.

13. For a full bibliography, see ibid., 735, with nn. 66 and 67.

14. *ḥwt*; see Manfred Görg, "Ḥiwwiter im 13. Jahrhundert v. Chr.," *UF* 8 (1976): 53–55.

15. George E. Mendenhall, *The Tenth Generation: The Origins of the Biblical Tradition* (Baltimore: Johns Hopkins University Press, 1973), 154. For the Luwian-Phoenician bilingual, see Recai Tekoğlu in Ismet Ipek, Kazim Tosun, Recai Tekoğlu, and André Lemaire, "La bilingue royale louvito-phénicienne de Çineköy," in *Comptes rendus des scéances de l'année 2000* (Paris: Académie des inscriptions et belles-lettres, 2000),

The Jebusites, according to biblical tradition, inhabited and ruled Jerusalem (Josh 15:63) until David conquered the city (2 Sam 5:6–9; 1 Chr 11:4–9), even giving their name as an alternate designation for the city.[16] A king of Jerusalem in the second millennium correspondence from El Amarna in Egypt bore the Hurrian name Abdu-Hepa, suggesting that the Jebusite ruling class, if not the entire Jebusite population, was Hurrian.[17] "Araunah," the name of the Jebusite who sold the threshing floor to David (see below), also appears to be Hurrian.[18] If the Jebusites, or their ruling elite, were Hurrians, then, like the Hivites, they were ultimately of northern origin.[19] One piece of extrabiblical evidence has come to light, however, that suggests a different identification. A cuneiform letter from Mari (eighteenth century) refers to an Amorite tribe known as the Yabusiʾum, perhaps to be identified with the Jebusites.[20] If so, it would confirm their presence in the region in the Late Bronze Age.

981–84; for commentary, see Hutter, "Widerspiegelungen religiöser Vorstellungen der Luwier," 426 with n. 4; Singer "The Hittites and the Bible Revisited," 735. See also Görg, "Ḫiwwiter im 13. Jahrhundert v. Chr.," 53–55, who further demonstrates the northern origins of the Hivites; and Othniel Margalith, "The Hivites," *ZAW* 100 (1988): 60–70, who attempts to equate the Hivites with the Achaeans. According to the Bible, the Hivites inhabited the central and northern portions of the land from Gibeon north to Mount Hermon (David W. Baker, "Hivites," *ABD* 3:234).

16. Edwin C. Hostetter, *Nations Mightier and More Numerous: The Biblical View of Palestine's Pre-Israelite Peoples* (North Richland, Tex.: BIBAL, 1995), 77. For the case against identifying Jebus with Jerusalem, see Stephen A. Reed, "Jebus," *ABD* 3:653.

17. Although he was king of Jerusalem, there is no evidence that Abdu-Hepa was a Jebusite. On the Jebusites as Hurrians, see Hoffner, "The Hittites and Hurrians," 225.

18. The name of David's scribe, Sheva, has an Egyptian, not a Hurrian, derivation, according to David Carr, *Writing on the Table of the Heart: Origins of Scripture and Literature* (Oxford: Oxford University Press, 2005), 117.

19. Contemporaries and one-time adversaries of the Hittites in the Late Bronze Age, ethnic Hurrians inhabited much of the region that lay between Hatti and Palestine. Although certain identification of specific groups mentioned in the Bible with Hurrians has proved elusive, few would discount the idea that they found their way to Palestine in the latter part of the second millennium and that their presence continued to be felt in the Iron Age I period. On the Hurrians in Palestine, see Hoffner, "Hittites and Hurrians," 221–26; Mendenhall, *The Tenth Generation*, 158; John C. L. Gibson, "Observations on Some Important Ethnic Terms in the Pentateuch," *JNES* 20 (1961): 227–29; Ephraim A. Speiser, "The Hurrian Participation in the Civilizations of Mesopotamia, Syria and Palestine," *CHM* 1 (1953): 311–27.

20. Edward Lipinski, *Itineraria Phoenicia* (OLA 127; Leuven: Peeters, 2004), 502. He rejects the identification of the Jebusites as Hurrian but suggests that Yabusi was the name of an Amorite clan or tribe that had settled in Jerusalem.

The Perizzites are unattested outside of the Bible. Often paired with the Canaanites, it has been suggested that each symbolically embodied a larger body of nations, either the major and minor nations, or, alternatively, Semitic and non-Semitic peoples.[21] Even less can be said about the Girgashites, who appear only in the lists of nations and then only occasionally. Extrabiblically, "Girgishi" (*grgš*) is attested as a personal name at Ugarit as well as in the Punic world.[22] Attempts to connect the biblical Girgashites with Karkisa, a town in western Anatolia attested in Hittite texts of the thirteenth century B.C.E.,[23] and with the Gergithians, remnants of the Teucrians (Herodotus, *Hist.* 5.122; cf. 7.43), or Tjeker, who had settled along the northern coast of Palestine near Dor at the beginning of the Iron Age,[24] although inconclusive, cannot be dismissed outright.

The Hittites typically occupy one of the first three positions in the lists, in alternating order with the Amorites and Canaanites. All three appear to represent major population groups, whether political or ethnic, and their interchangability suggests that they shared a certain parity, at least in the eyes of the biblical authors. In cuneiform literature, the term *amurru* "west" is both a geographical designation for the lands to the west of Mesopotamia as well as an ethnic and cultural designation for the Amorite people who, speaking their own language and worshiping their own gods, lived in the west. Sometime in the fifteenth century B.C.E., a kingdom of Amurru established itself in the upper Orontes Valley region of Syria (covering some of the territory that would later become Hamath). The competition for control of this vassal kingdom, as we have seen, lay at the center of the hostilities between Egypt and the Hittites, leading up to the battle of Qadesh. Once recaptured by Muwatalli, Amurru remained loyal to the Hittite kings until the collapse of the Hittite Empire at the end of the Bronze Age.[25] In the biblical texts, "Amorites" is used primarily as a reference to the pre-Israelite

---

21. Ishida, "The Lists of Pre-Israelite Nations," 479–80. On the Perizzites, see also Nadav Naʾaman, "Canaanites and Perizzites," *BN* 45 (1988): 42–47; Hostetter, *Nations Mightier and More Numerous*, 80–83.

22. Mendenhall, *The Tenth Generation*, 145. See also the discussion in Hostetter, *Nations Mightier and More Numerous*, 62–66.

23. F.-M. Abel, *Géographie de la Palestine* (2 vols.; Paris: Gabalda, 1933–38), 1:325.

24. John Pairman Brown, "The Mediterranean Seer and Shamanism," *ZAW* 93 (1981): 399. See also Hostetter, *Nations Mightier and More Numerous*, 64–65.

25. See Itamar Singer, "A Concise History of Amurru," in Shlomo Izreʾel, *Amurru Akkadian: A Linguistic Study* (2 vols.; HSS 40–41; Atlanta: Scholars Press, 1991), 2:135–95.

inhabitants of Canaan, and although it probably means different things at different times, it is possible that in the lists of nations it refers to the population of Late Bronze Age Amurru.

Geographically, even the term Canaan (from Hurrian *kinaḫḫu* "purple") has been difficult to pin down. It appears to include, in particular, the cities in northern coastal Palestine, such as Tyre, Arvad, Ṣumur, Byblos, and Sidon, as well as inland Hazor.[26] Territorially, its northern border ended at Amurru, although at times it appears to include Ugarit.[27] Nadav Na'aman argues that the term in the Late Bronze Age referred specifically to the entirety of Egypt's Asian province and so was a specific political and geographical entity.[28] Others assert that there was no identifiable land of "Canaan" and that the use of the term in antiquity was as ambiguous and imprecise as it is today.[29] However we understand the label, Canaan, situated roughly along the eastern Mediterranean seaboard, was a major player in the politics and culture of Late Bronze Age Western Asia.[30]

In summary, although the data remain incomplete, the lists arguably reflect to some extent the ethnic and political make-up of the northern Levant and Syria at the end of the Bronze Age. The "nations" do have a basis, however attenuated by time, in historical reality for the region north of Palestine in the Late Bronze Age. Building on this conclusion, we must still account for the Hittites in the Bible, who were supposedly living in the Judean hill country (Num 13:29; Josh 11:3) and, according to Genesis, were particularly associated with Hebron (Gen 23) and Beersheba (Gen 26:34; 27:46).[31]

---

26. Gibson, "Observations on Some Important Ethnic Terms," 217–20.

27. A. R. Millard, "The Canaanites," in Wiseman, *Peoples of Old Testament Times*, 30.

28. See Nadav Na'aman, "Four Notes on the Size of Late Bronze Age Canaan," *BASOR* 313 (1999): 31–37, with bibliography.

29. Niels Peter Lemche (*The Canaanites and Their Land: The Tradition of the Canaanites* [JSOTSup 110; Sheffield: JSOT Press, 1991], 52) concludes that "to the scribe of ancient Western Asia 'Canaanite' always designated a person who did not belong to the scribe's own society or state, while Canaan was considered to be a country different from his own."

30. See Hubert Cancik, " 'Das ganze Land Ḫet': 'Hethiter' und die luwischen Staaten in der Bibel," in *Die Hethiter und ihr Reich: Das Volk der 1000 Götter*, 31, for the place name Kinahha "Canaan" in a fifteenth-century Hittite invocation; and *RGTC* VI s.v. for a list of passages in which the place name occurs.

31. The hill country south of Jerusalem in the Late Bronze Age was a very sparsely populated region. Israel Finkelstein ("The Rise of Jerusalem and Judah: The Missing Link," in *Jerusalem in Bible and Archaeology: The First Temple Period* [ed. Andrew G. Vaughn and Ann E. Killebrew; SBLSymS 18; Atlanta: Society of Biblical Literature,

For the answer, we must return to the struggle of Syria and Palestine against Assyrian aggression.

"Wicked Hittites"

Following the conquest of Samaria in 722 B.C.E., Sargon II of Assyria continued the systematic destruction of the Neo-Hittite kingdoms of northern Syria. Assyrian forces ravaged Hamath in 720, destroying its citadel and displacing its population with settlers from Assyria.[32] According to 2 Kgs 17:24, the population of Hamath was deported to Samaria, where it continued to worship its own gods beside Yahweh (2 Kgs 17:29–34). One by one the cities of Syria fell, and with them went the last vestiges of Hittite culture.[33] With the fall of Karkamis in 717, the Hittites disappeared from history. Although the term "Hittite" as an ethnicon ceased to carry any political or historical relevence after Sargon II, Assyrian records continued to employ the term *māt Ḫatti* "land of the Hittites" as a geographical designation to refer to northern Syria.[34]

Sargon's conquests had a profound impact on the inhabitants of Syria-Palestine. Overshadowed during the ninth century by the Omride dynasty in the north,[35] Jerusalem at the end of the eighth century saw an inpouring of refugees from the north who brought with them a more cosmopolitan outlook, owing to their greater political and commercial contacts, compared with the less-urbanized south, and a vigorous literary tradition—a legacy from their Canaanite forebears.[36]

As part of a pan-Levantine scribal tradition, the inhabitants of Palestine had long been exposed to the great literature of Mesopotamia and Egypt as

---

2003], 86–87) estimates the population of Jerusalem-controlled territory in the Late Bronze Age at a mere 1,500 sedentary people.

32. The Hittite citadel at Hamath remained unoccupied (*CHLI* I, 2:402), suggesting that the Assyrians did not use the city as a provincial capital.

33. Zakkur's inscription, in Aramaic, marks the end of Hamath as an "Anatolian" dynasty. See Horst Klengel, *Syria 3000 to 300 B.C.: A Handbook of Political History* (Berlin: Akademie-Verlag, 1992), 213; J. David Hawkins, "Hamath," *RlA* 4 (1972–75): 68b. Thus Sargon's conquest only completed a process that had already begun in the middle of the eight century with the loss of the Luwian language at Hamath.

34. Cogan, "Locating *māt Ḫatti*," 86–92; contra others, he does not believe that the cuneiform documents used the terms *Hatti* and *Amurru* coterminously.

35. See, e.g., Finkelstein, "The Rise of Jerusalem and Judah," 81–101.

36. William M. Schniedewind, "Jerusalem, the Late Judaean Monarchy, and the Composition of Biblical Texts," in Vaughn and Killebrew, *Jerusalem in Bible and Archaeology*, 375–93.

well as to native traditions reflected, for example, in biblical poetry, with its clear affinities to earlier Canaanite poetry.[37] The Amarna archive preserves the correspondence between the pharaoh and the Bronze Age (Hurrian) rulers of Jerusalem.[38] Like these earlier kings, David and Solomon too were attributed with having scribes.[39] However, from the twelfth century to the ninth, Israel remained largely an oral society, in which writing played a limited role, primarily for administrative purposes. The twelfth-century abecedary from Izbet Ṣarṭah, the tenth-century abecedary from Tel Zayit,[40] the contemporary Gezer calendar, a few ostraca from Arad dating to the tenth century, and a handful of monumental inscriptions from the ninth century are among the few examples of writing from the region in this period, but they are enough to demonstrate that formal scribal training, however limited, was taking place.[41] The Egyptian story of Wenamon describes the responsibilities of the scribe of the ruler of Byblos in the eleventh century B.C.E. as being correspondence and accounting.[42] However, at least from the tenth century, royal scribes also seem to have kept historical registers of some kind, as they were able to recount accurately historical events such as Pharaoh Shoshenq's (biblical Shishak) campaign two hundred years after it occurred (1 Kgs 14:25–30).[43] The epigraphic and literary evidence for the survival of an educational tradition in northern Palestine supports the likelihood that the early Israelite scribal tradition, as well as its administrative infrastructure, drew upon the traditions of the Late Bronze Age Canaanite urban centers.[44] New archaeological investigations are also revealing the extent of continuity in the northern valleys between the Late Bronze Age and the subsequent Iron

---

37. See William M. Schniedewind, *How the Bible Became a Book* (Cambridge: Cambridge University Press, 2004), 47. See also Carr, *Writing on the Tablet of the Heart*, chs. 3 and 4, on the influence of Mesopotamian and Egyptian scribal systems on Late Bronze Age Palestine.

38. EA 286–290.

39. See, e.g., Schniedewind, *How the Bible Became a Book*, 59–60.

40. Ron E. Tappy, P. Kyle McCarter, Marilyn J. Lundberg, and Bruce Zuckerman, "An Abecedary of the Mid-Tenth Century B.C.E. from the Judaean Shephelah," *BASOR* 344 (2006): 5–46.

41. Christopher A. Rollston, "Scribal Education in Ancient Israel: The Old Hebrew Epigraphic Evidence," *BASOR* 344 (2006): 47–74; Schniedewind, *How the Bible Became a Book*, 61; Carr, *Writing on the Tablet of the Heart*, 123, 163.

42. Benjamin Mazar, *The Early Biblical Period: Historical Studies* (Jerusalem: Israel Exploation Society, 1986), 133.

43. Schniedewind, *How the Bible Became a Book*, 19–20.

44. On the continuity of scribal tradition between the Late Bronze and Iron Ages in Israel, see ibid., 20, 47–49, 52, 56–57.

Age in Palestine.[45] Thus, whether transmitted orally or by means of historical records,[46] it is reasonable to assume that the Israelites retained a collective memory of the Hittites and other Late Bronze Age political and ethnic entities through the Iron I and early Iron II periods.

Along with these literary traditions, this period of upheaval brought intensified exposure to Assyrian culture and religion, in particular the official rhetoric of its kings. Sargon's inscriptions referred to the rulers of the Neo-Hittite states, including Karkamis, Kummuh, Gurgum, Melid, Tabal, and Hamath, as "wicked Hittites" (*Ḫattĕ lemnī*).[47] Embedded in these new influences from the north, therefore, could have been a rhetorical tradition about the Hittites, one drawn from the stylistic literary conventions that characterize the Neo-Assyrian royal inscriptions.[48]

In the hands of the burgeoning southern scribal institution, northern lore and Assyrian literary convention merged and were turned to a new ideological purpose. The overarching concerns of the passages invoking the lists of nations are the conquest of the nations and the prohibition against intermarriage.[49] The latter also forms the basis for Ezekiel's admonition against Jerusalem. He reminds the city of its origins in the land of the Canaanites: "your father was an Amorite and your mother a Hittite" (Ezek 16:3; see also 16:45). Ezekiel is not evoking some dim historical memory of a time when Hittites inhabited the region. The admonition begins with the words, "You are the daughter of your mother, who loathed her husband and her children; and you are the sister of your sisters, who loathed their husbands and their children" (16:45). This use of kinship terminology to underscore

---

45. Finkelstein, "The Rise of Jerusalem and Judah," 90; Robert D. Miller II, *Chieftains of the Highland Clans: A History of Israel in the 12th and 11th centuries B.C.* (Grand Rapids: Eerdmans, 2005).

46. For the Deuteronomistic Historian's reliance on annalistic materials, perhaps originating in monumental display inscriptions, see Carr, *Writing on the Tablet of the Heart*, 142.

47. Van Seters, "The Terms 'Amorite' and 'Hittite,'" 67; Cogan, "Locating *māt Ḫatti*," 89; J. David Hawkins, "Hatti" *RlA* 4 (1972–75): 154b.

48. See Cogan, "Locating *māt Ḫatti*," 86, for the stylistic nature of the Assyrian annals as opposed to archival documents. Notably, among the refugees from the northern kingdom could have been Hamathites, who, according to 2 Kgs 17:24, were deported to Samaria (see also below).

49. For the conquest theme, see, e.g., Deut 7:1–4; 20:17; Josh 24:11–12; Exod 3:8, 17; 23:23; 33:2; 34:11; Ezra 9:1; for intermarriage, see, e.g., Deut 7:1–4; Ezra 9:1–2. Van Seters ("The Terms 'Amorite' and 'Hittite,'" 67–72) argues convincingly for the rhetorical nature of the lists of nations, but note that Van Seters sees Assyrian influence only in the vagueness of their geographical use of the designations "Hittite" and "Amorite."

the sinfulness of Jerusalem also favors a figurative interpretation rather than the traditional interpretation that the use of "mother" is a historical allusion to a time when Hittites lived in Jerusalem.[50] The anxiety over intermarriage with the nations is also expressed in the patriarchal narratives (Gen 23; 26:34–35; 27:46),[51] when Esau takes as wives Judith and Basemath, daughters of the Hittites Beeri and Elon, respectively, against his parents' wishes (Gen 26:34–35; in Gen 36:2, Adah is the daughter of Elon, wife of Esau).

In the story of Abraham's purchase of the cave of Machpelah from Ephron the Hittite,[52] the seller, Ephron, is willing to turn over the cave without cost, but Abraham insists on paying and thus symbolically legitimizes his residence in the land. This motif is mirrored in the story of David's purchase of the threshing floor in Jerusalem from Araunah the Jebusite (2 Sam 24:24; see also below) and the section of the field in Shechem that Jacob purchases from the Hivite sons of Hamor (Gen 33:19; Josh 24:32).[53] Neither the ethnicity of the locals nor the towns in which the purchases occurred is coincidental. Hebron, Shechem, and Jerusalem were all major centers in the pre-Israelite period, the co-option of which by the

---

50. As argued by Van Seters, "The Terms 'Amorite' and 'Hittite,' " 80. For alternative interpretations, see, e.g., Anton Jirku, "Eine hethitische Ansiedlung in Jerusalem zur Zeit von El-Amarna," *ZDPV* 43 (1920): 58–59; Nicolas Wyatt, " 'Araunah the Jebusite' and the Throne of David," *ST* 39 (1985): 42.

51. Van Seters, "The Terms 'Amorite' and 'Hittite,' " 68. For a discussion of the patriarchal narratives and their historicity, see P. Kyle McCarter, "The Patriarchal Age: Abraham, Isaac and Jacob," in *Ancient Israel: From Abraham to the Roman Destruction of the Temple* (ed. Hershel Shanks; Washington, D.C.: Biblical Archaeology Society, 1999), 1–31.

52. The idea, suggested half a century ago, that the story of Abraham's purchase of the cave is "permeated with" elements of Late Bronze Age Hittite legal customs has been soundly disproved. See Manfred R. Lehmann, "Abraham's Purchase of Machpelah and Hittite Law," *BASOR* 129 (1953): 15–18; and the refutation by Gene M. Tucker, "The Legal Background of Genesis 23," *JBL* 85 (1966): 77–84; Hoffner, "Some Contributions of Hittitology," 33–37. But see Raymond Westbrook, *Property and the Family in Biblical Law* (JSOTSup 113; Sheffield: JSOT Press, 1991), 24–35, who argues that the story of the purchase of the cave reflects Late Bronze Age customs and that therefore its authorship is of considerably greater antiquity than its assignment to a sixth-century Priestly source would allow.

53. See Benjamin Mazar, "The Historical Background of the Book of Genesis," *JNES* 28 (1969): 82; Gene M. Tucker, "The Legal Backgrouond of Genesis 23," 78; John Van Seters, *Abraham in History and Tradition* (New Haven, Conn.: Yale University Press, 1975), 98–99. Nadav Na'aman (The 'Conquest of Canaan' in the Book of Joshua and in History," in Finkelstein and Na'aman, *From Nomadism to Monarchy*, 274–77) compares also the Gibeonite story of Josh 9.

Israelites was essential to their foundational story of Israelite origins.[54] The fact that the patriarchal stories put the Hittites in the region of Hebron (Gen 23) and Beersheba (Gen 26:34; 27:46), that is, in the Judean hill country, the very territory that the lists of nations also identify as the Hittite homeland (Num 13:29; Josh 11:3), is not evidence of their historical and geographical accuracy but of a shared literary patrimony. The two threads of tradition merged and the Hittites became, along with the Jebusites, Hivites, Amorites, and so on, a convenient "Other," imagined as living in the hill country for the "newly arrived" Israelites to conquer.[55] The Hittites and their companions offered, in short, a negative counteridentity ("indigenous" peoples) against which a collective Israelite identity could be constructed.[56] The rejection of intermarriage with these "Canaanites" was simply a necessary component in the articulation of the Other.[57] Finally, it is regularly noted that all of the "Hittites" in the patriarchal stories bear Semitic, rather than Anatolian, names,[58] but this would hardly be surprising if the Hittites were incorporated into the narrative primarily as a paradigm for the Other.[59]

---

54. On the importance of Hebron in the Iron Age, see Finkelstein, "The Rise of Jerusalem and Judah," 89 with n. 47.

55. Thus the Israelites wrote themselves into their own history as outsiders so that they could remain untainted by the inhabitants of the land they came to settle; see Peter Machinist, "Outsiders or Insiders: The Biblical View of Emergent Israel and Its Contexts," in *The Other in Jewish Thought and History: Constructions of Jewish Culture and Identity* (ed. Laurence J. Silberstein and Robert L. Cohn; New York: New York University Press, 1994), 49.

56. On the Canaanites as Other in the Hebrew Bible, see the articles by Robert L. Cohn ("Before Israel: The Canaanites as Other in the Biblical Tradition," 74–90) and Peter Machinist ("Outsiders or Insiders," 35–60) in Silberstein and Cohn, *The Other in Jewish Thought and History*. On the table of nations in Gen 10 as a tool for defining who the Other is, namely, all "relatives" of Canaan (Gen 10:15–19), see E. Theodore Mullen Jr., *Ethnic Myths and Pentateuchal Foundations: A New Approach to the Formation of the Pentateuch* (SemeiaSt 35; Atlanta: Scholars Press, 1997), 119–20.

57. See Cohn, "Before Israel," 82–83.

58. E.g., Hoffner, "The Hittites and Hurrians," 214.

59. Or, as Lemche puts it, as "a kind of pseudo-historical invention" (*The Canaanites and Their Land*, 86). Why exactly Sargon refers to the rebellious citizens of Philistine Ashdod as Hittites in his annals for the year 711 B.C.E. remains unclear. According to Josh 11:22, the Anakim, a tribe of giants, continued to occupy the Philistine cities of Ashdod, Gaza, and Gath after they had been expelled from Hebron and the hill country. The designation "Anak" is thought to be non-Semitic, as are the names of the sons of Anak, Sheshai, Ahiman, and Talmai (Num 13:22; Josh 15:14; Judg 1:10). Deuteronomy 1:28 identifies the Amorites with the sons of the Anakim. The Anakim, like the Hittites, Amorites, and Hivites, are Others. See the translation by K. Lawson Younger, *COS* 2.118A:294. For a

AHIMELECH AND URIAH

Two more persons identified as Hittites, Ahimelech (1 Sam 26:6) and Uriah (2 Sam 11), served as officers of high rank in the service of David. Uriah was among David's Thirty, the core of his warrior elite (2 Sam 23:39; 1 Chr 11:41), and, as husband to Bathsheba, is a major character in one of the Bible's most popular narratives. As this narrative does not fit the rhetorical uses described above, we must account for the presence of these Hittites by other means. Given that David was allied with the kings of Hamath, one obvious possibility is that Ahimelech and Uriah were viewed as expatriots from the Neo-Hittite kingdoms.[60] The fact that both bear apparently Semitic rather than Indo-European names (Ahimelech has been etymologized as "my brother is king," Uriah as "Yahweh is my light") need not confound this interpretation, as the tendency to convert foreign names to Israelite ones is not unusual in the early Israelite period.[61] But an alternative etymology, that Uriah is a mixed name composed of the Hittite/Luwian element *uri* "great"

---

full edition, see Andreas Fuchs, *Die Inschriften Sargons II. aus Khorsabad* (Göttingen: Cuvillier, 1994). See Aharon Kempinski, "Some Philistine Names from the Kingdom of Gaza," *IEJ* 37 (1987): 20–24, for the suggestion that the Philistines may have come from Anatolia, based on an analysis of names found on an ostracon from Tell Jemmeh. See Van Seters, "The Terms 'Amorite' and 'Hittite,'" 74–75, for a full discussion. For more on the Anatolian origins of the Philistines and other Sea Peoples, see Itamar Singer, "The Origin of the Sea Peoples and Their Settlement on the Coast of Canaan," in Heltzer and Lipiński, *Society and Economy in the Eastern Mediterranean*, 239–50.

60. Gibson ("Observations on Some Important Ethnic Terms," 226) suggests that Ahimelech and Uriah are Neo-Hittites; Van Seters ("The Terms 'Amorite' and 'Hittite,'" 80) says that by the term "Hittite" the author meant only to convey that they were non-Israelite; Richard H. Beal ("The Hittites after the Empire's Fall," *Biblical Illustrator* [Fall 1983]: 81), argues that Uriah is most likely a descendant of refugees from Anatolia after the collapse of the Hittite Empire; Mazar (*The Early Biblical Period*, 129, 136–37) believes that Uriah originated from the Jebusite aristocracy of Jerusalem.

61. Mazar, *The Early Biblical Period*, 135. Some Philistine kings also bore Semitic names in the Assyrian documents; for examples, see Kempinski, "Some Philistine Names," 24. Compare the switch from Semitic to Hurrian names among the royalty at Amurru, when its allegience shifted away from Egypt to the Hittites (Singer, "A Concise History of Amurru," 2:182). It seems that names are as much a matter of political expediency as they are of ethnicity and religious beliefs. Ilu-bi'di, the last king of Hamath, whom Sargon II labeled an evil Hittite, was also called Yaubidi. Abraham Malamat ("Aspects of the Foreign Policies of David and Solomon," *JNES* 22 [1963]: 7) argues for the conversion of the Hamathites to Yahwism based in part on this king's name. See also Stephanie Dalley, "Yahweh in Hamath in the 8th Century BC: Cuneiform Material and Historical Deductions," *VT* 40 (1990): 27–32, who is supported by Ziony Zevit, "Yahweh

and the Hebrew *nomen dei*, Yah, best suits a Neo-Hittite origin for this figure.[62] Structurally, it is the sort of name ("Great is Yah") that an ethnic Luwian living in Jerusalem and worshiping (or at least paying respect to) the Israelite god would have taken.

A much older etymology argues that hidden behind the Semitic form of his name is the Hurrian title *ewri-* "lord."[63] If this interpretation is correct, then Uriah is probably to be linked with another biblical figure, Araunah (2 Sam 24:16–25), in whose name the Hurrian title *ewri* "lord" is also apparent.[64] The Masoretic (MT) tradition of 2 Sam 24:23 designates Araunah as "king," engendering a theory as old as Martin Luther that he might have been the last Jebusite king of the city.[65] The unusual narrative describes how the plague sent by Yahweh after David's census had stopped at the threshing floor of Araunah the Jebusite (2 Sam 24:16; 1 Chr 21:15–27). David then negotiated the purchase of the threshing floor from Araunah in order to erect an altar for offerings to Yahweh. The purchase of real estate from a local as a symbol of legitimate usurpation is a motif that we have seen before and bespeaks the literary nature of the story. Nevertheless, the threshing-floor narrative may contain a kernel of historical information about the transition from Canaaanite to Judahite control of Jerusalem.[66] The NRSV translates 2 Sam 24:23 as "All this, O king, Araunah gives to the king," but if its proper translation is "All this, King Araunah gives to the king," and if it symbolizes the submission of the old order to the new,[67] then David's plot to send Uriah to his death so that he can marry Bathsheba becomes a narrative to legitimate

---

Worship and Worshippers in 8th-Century Syria," *VT* 41 (1991): 363–66. However, the alternation in the name, again, may be nothing more than political expediency.

62. Yoël L. Arbeitman, "Luwio-Semitic and Hurrio/Mitannio-Semitic *Mischname*-Theophores in the Bible, on Crete, and at Troy," *Scripta Mediterranea* 3 (1982): 50.

63. M. Vieyra, "Parallèle hurrite au nom d'Urie 'le Hittite,'" *RHA* 5/35 (1939): 113–14. The name of Uriah's wife, Bathsheba, is also suspect, as it may contain the Hurrian theophoric name Heba as the second element. Hebat was the supreme goddess of the Hurrian pantheon. See Wyatt, "Araunah the Jebusite," 42.

64. The name is also spelled Ornan (1 Chr 21) and with the variants Awarnah, Aranyah, Araunah (Richard D. Nelson, "Araunah," *ABD* 1:353). The same name, spelled *ʾwrn*, occurs in a text from Ugarit (Hoffner, "The Hittites and Hurrians," 225). Hurrian *ʾwrnh* becomes by metathesis *ʾrwnh*. Alternatively, it may derive from Hittite *arawanni-* "aristocratic, free" (Haiim B. Rosen, "Arawna: Nom hittite?" *VT* [1955]: 318–20). See also Wolfgang Feiler, "Hurritische Namen im Alten Testament," *ZA* 45 (1939): 222–25.

65. McCarter, *II Samuel* (AB 9; Garden City, N.Y.: Doubleday, 1984), 512.

66. But cf. Werner Fuss, "II Samuel 24," *ZAW* 74 (1962): 145–64.

67. Wyatt, "Araunah the Jebusite," 39–53. For the possible translations of the passage, see McCarter, *II Samuel*, 508.

his rule. In this case, the author may have labeled Uriah a Hittite simply to establish his alterity; that is, as a foreigner, he is expendable! Alternatively, he may have had in mind the Neo-Hittite states as a natural point of origin for a character who was so central to his story. Even if Uriah were historically a Neo-Hittite, though, the use of this ethnic designation has more literary overtones than historical ones.

Conclusion

The answer to the question whether the Hittites in the Bible can be identified with the Hittites of Late Bronze Age is a firm yes—but not specifically with those living in Anatolia. Rather, the biblical authors had in mind those peoples living in the Hittite-controlled territories directly to their north who did not qualify already as Canaanite or Amorite (that is, a citizen of the state of Amurru), whatever their individual ethnic affiliation might have been. If this source was a product of the northern kingdom, as is likely, then we do not need to seek these ethnicities in the Judean hill country but rather in northern Palestine and Syria. Although the lists of nations may initially have been compiled while the Neo-Hittite cities were still flourishing, the original compilation probably drew on oral traditions and/or annalistic records that commemorated the significant role that the Hittites played in the region, particularly in northern Palestine, at the end of the Bronze Age.

The lists are not, however, primarily factual accounts of the ethnic composition of the Palestinian population before the arrival of the Israelites.[68] Only with the influx of refugees from Samaria and the subsequent eruption of literary activity in Jerusalem that accompanied the urbanization of the south in the late-eighth century did the Hittites "enter" the hill country of Judah. With the Neo-Hittite kingdoms gone and their populations dispersed, the use of the term "Hittite" quickly became, under the influence of Assyrian usage, a rhetorical tool at the hands of Jerusalem-based biblical writers who retained no direct memory of a historical people called Hittites. This literary use was extended beyond the stereotypical lists of nations into the patriarchal stories and Ezekiel's admonition and explains why the biblical passages assign the Hittite homeland to the Judean hill country, an area that had remained largely unpopulated until Sennacherib's invasion in 701 B.C.E. but became of central

---

68. With Niels Peter Lemche, *The Canaanites and Their Land*, 84. However, I reject Lemche's assertion of the pointlessness of discussing the historical identity of these nations, as they "have hardly anything to contribute the actual history of the Land of Israel in the 2nd millennium B.C.E.," since this is the sort of presupposition that he rightly criticizes other scholars for making.

importance in establishing a sense of national self-identity in the late-eighth to seventh centuries.[69] This reasoning also accounts for the lack of geographical overlap between the biblical tradition, which locates the Hittites in the Judean hill country, and the meager archaeological evidence for Hittites in Palestine (see below), which follows the north–south trade routes.

This explanation of the Hittites in the Bible, however, does not require us to discount out of hand a Hittite presence in Palestine as the point of cultural transmission. As we will see in the next section, archaeological and textual evidence support an important Anatolian presence in Palestine during the Late Bronze Age, the period of the *pax Hethitica-Egyptiaca*, which provided the ideal environment for the sharing of cultural traditions.

THE CASE FOR CONTACT

If, outside of the few biblical references to the Neo-Hittites of northern Syria, the Hittites in the Bible are employed purely as a literary construct, then, as noted above, we are freed from the need to locate evidence of a major migration in the archaeological record to explain their presence. This is especially fortunate, given that there is no firm evidence for a significant Hittite populaton in southern Palestine at any time in its history.

That said, the historical sources indicate that such migrations were possible.[70] The Hittite archives record an incident that occurred some time before the reign of Suppiluliuma, when relations with Egypt were cordial, in which "the Storm-god of Hatti carried the men of Kurustamma to Egyptian

---

69. Schniedewind, "Jerusalem, the Late Judaean Monarchy," 381–82; Israel Finkelstein, "The Archaeology of the Days of Manasseh," in *Scripture and Other Artifacts: Essays on the Bible and Archaeology in Honor of Philip J. King* (ed. Michael D. Coogan, J. Cheryl Exum, and Lawrence E. Stager; Louisville: Westminster John Knox, 1994), 173–75.

70. Forced migrations, in the form of deportations, were another means by which large numbers of people moved about in the ancient Near East. Two late inscriptions of Tukulti-ninurta I claimed that he had deported 28,800 Hittites from across the Euphrates in his accession hear (J. David Hawkins, "The Political Geography of North Syria and Southeast Anatolia in the Neo-Assyrian Period," in *Neo-Assyrian Geography* [ed. Mario Liverani; Rome: Università di Roma, 1995], 87; Singer, "The Battle of Niḫriya," 100–123). Although this number may be an exaggeration, it is not impossible that residents of Hittite lands were forced, even before the fall of the Hittite Empire, to settle elsewhere. See below on the deportation of the Hamathites to Samaria at the end of the eighth century.

territory."[71] The residents of Kurustamma, a city in northern Anatolia near the Pontus Mountains, had apparently been resettled somewhere in Egyptian territory, which, of course, would have included southern Palestine. Although we do not know how many people were involved and whether they were men serving as mercenaries only or included entire families, this emigration of Hittites from Kurustamma in the fifteenth century B.C.E. establishes that such population movements did take place. However, it is unlikly that the Kurustamma emigration can account for the infiltration of Hittite cultural elements, any more than could the trade in exotic humans occasionally mentioned in the diplomatic correspondence between Egypt and Anatolia, which usually involved an exchange of Kaska warriors and Nubians.[72]

By far the most popular and reasonable migration theory is the one that assumes a stream of emigrants from Anatolia as a result of the catastrophe at the end of the Bronze Age (see ch. 2).[73] Archaeologically, a surge of people southward might be surmised from the increased importance of Hittite regional centers such as Karkamis, which appears to have been less affected by the catastrophe than surrounding territories, and by the establishment of new centers with a demonstrably Hittite character. Most notably, a Hittite dynasty was established at Hamath, where formerly there had been no Hittite population. The presence of Luwian hieroglyphs, a new ceramic repertory, Hittite architectural styles, and cemeteries with cremation burials[74] have all been thought to indicate the arrival of a new population from Hittite lands.[75] As I argued in chapter 2, these elements should be

---

71. The Kurustamma Treaty is mentioned in several documents. The quote comes from the Second Plague Prayer of Mursili II, translated by Singer, *Hittite Prayers*, 58 (§4).

72. EA 31:15–16; Emil O. Forrer, *Forschungen* (Berlin: self-published, 1926), 2:21–22; *ÄHK*, 294; cited by Singer, "The Hittites and the Bible Revisited," 731, 734.

73. See, e.g., Mazar, "The Early Israelite Settlement," 75–85; Kempinski, "Hittites in the Bible," 39–41; Na'aman, "The 'Conquest of Canaan,'" 218–81.

74. The Hamath urn field did not go out of use until 700 B.C.E. after the Assyrians destroyed the city (Marie-Louise Buhl, "Hamath," *ABD* 3:35). This means that the Hamathites had not abandoned cremation when they abandoned Hieroglyphic Luwian (on the continuity of religious beliefs at Hamath between the Neo-Hittite and Aramean phases, see Dalley, "Yahweh in Hamath," 27–28). Thus, the absence of cremation burials in Israel, where the Hamathites were forced to take up residence, is either an accident of discovery or evidence that the Hamathites changed their burial practices upon deportation. The latter would be in keeping with the caveat issued by Singer ("The Hittites and the Bible Revisited," 740) that mortuary customs are subject to additional pressures when the acculturation of migrating population groups is at issue.

75. Buhl, "Hamath," *ABD* 3:34.

understood rather as signs of a newly emergent cultural identity, but even if a massive migration did occur, there is no archaeological evidence that it extended beyond Hamath.[76]

The discovery in Israel and Transjordan of inhumations in attached jars (in which the rims and necks are removed and the jars placed shoulder to shoulder with the unburnt remains of the deceased inside), all dating to the transition between the Late Bronze and Iron Ages, has generated considerable interest among archaeologists because they are thought to be a burial type that is most at home in Anatolia.[77] Seven sites (Kfar Yehoshua, Tell es-Saidiyeh, Tel Nami, Tel Zeror, Tell el-Farah North, Azor, and Megiddo) have produced this type of burial, although only Tell es-Saidiyeh has more than one or two containing the remains of adults. However, this type of burial is not limited to Anatolia, and the funerary objects accompanying the bodies are invariably local. Thus, by themselves these finds do not support the presence of Anatolians in Palestine.[78]

Moreover, the nature of the Hittite impact on the Israelites in the areas of law, religion, literature, and mythology suggests that the cultural exchange took place at the level of the educated elite. Neither the men of Kurustamma, whether mercenaries or farmers, nor impoverished refugees from a famine-ridden land are likely to account for the intellectual capital

---

76. For a review of the limited evidence for cremation in Palestine, see Garth Gilmour, "Aegean Influence in Late Bronze Age Funerary Practices in the Southern Levant," in *The Archaeology of Death in the Ancient Near East* (ed. Stuart Campbell and Anthony Green; Oxbow Monograph 51; Oxford: Oxbow, 1995), 167–69. Gilmour argues that there are alternative interpretations for the few cremations that have been found. A single cremation burial from eleventh century (early Iron I) Azor containing the remains of two individuals has been attributed to the Phoenicians (Singer, "The Hittites and the Bible Revisited," 742). The unusual late-thirteenth-century structure excavated near the Amman airport in 1976, which was interpreted as a mortuary institution that catered to a foreign clientele (it was filled with exotic Mycenaean imports), produced no evidence of a Hittite presence (Larry G. Herr, *The Amman Airport Excavations, 1976* [AASOR 48; Philadelphia: American Schools of Oriental Research], 1983; idem, "The Amman Airport Structure and the Geopolitics of Ancient Transjordan," *BA* 46 [1983]: 223–29).

77. Jonathan Tubb, "Sea Peoples in the Jordan Valley," in *The Sea Peoples and Their World: A Reassessment* (ed. Eliezer D. Oren; Philadelphia: The University Museum, 2000), 186; Garth Gilmour, "Foreign Burials in Late Bronze Age Palestine," *NEA* 65 (2002): 117. For a reevaluation of double pithos burials, see Itamar Singer, "On a Hittite Burial," in Oren and Ahituv, *Aharon Kempinski Memorial Volume*, *54–*58, with bibliography; idem, "The Hittites and the Bible Revisited," 740–43.

78. The jar burials at Tel Zeror are all of children and thus not useful in diagnosing ethnicity, as burial customs for children differ from those for adults.

being spent in Palestine. In other words, even if we accept the possibility of a large migration of Anatolians into Palestine during the Late Bronze–Iron Age transition, such a group is unlikely to have had a significant cultural impact on the region.

On the other hand, the period of the *pax Hethitica-Egyptiaca*, which stretched over the nearly eight decades prior to the collapse of the empire is the one period in the long history of contacts between Anatolia and Palestine that can best account for the rich and varied nature of the cultural parallels described in this volume. The treaty that initiated this idyllic age was concluded in the twenty-first year of Ramesses (1258 B.C.E.) and included promises of nonaggression, of mutual assistance in case of attack, and of support for a peaceful and secure succession for each other and provided for fugitive exchange. The marriage thirteen years later of Ramesses to the Hittite princess was preceded by extensive arrangements involving the exchange of emissaries and diplomatic missions between the two courts: "Some journeys, especially of trading expeditions, took the seaway, stopping at ports along the Levantine coast. Others traveled overland through the Lebanon Valley or Damascus (Upi), passing through the major Egyptian strongholds in Palestine: Beth-Shean, Megiddo, Aphek, Jaffa, and Gaza."[79] Of course this does not mean that ideas were not making their way—along with luxury items and new technologies—around the eastern Mediterranean both before and after the peace. But the last half century of the Hittite Empire was a time of heightened contacts with Palestine and of an intensified presence not only of diplomats from Anatolia but of merchants, craftsmen, doctors, soldiers, servants, musicians, and ritual specialists. Some were passing through, but others may have settled for a time in Palestine.[80]

The scattered material evidence of these intensified contacts include a Hittite ivory panel discovered with an ivory hoard in the "treasury" in the palace (Stratum VIIA, dating to the end of the Late Bronze Age) at Megiddo, testifying to the cosmopolitan tastes of the time. Megiddo was an important station on the overland route between Hatti and Egypt (fig. 3.10).[81] The ivory piece is decorated with divine beings and symbols in Hittite style and of Anatolian manufacture and may have been acquired by an Egyptian official operating out of the palace. Excavations at Aphek in the summer of 1976

---

79. Singer, "The Hittites and the Bible Revisited," 733.

80. See ibid.

81. This view, argued by Itamar Singer, "The Political Status of Megiddo VIIA," *TA* 15–16 (1988–1989): 101–12, is rejected by Amihai Mazar, "Megiddo in the Thirteenth–Eleventh Centuries BCE: A Review of Some Recent Studies," in Oren and Ahituv, *Aharon Kempinski Memorial Volume*, 270–71.

Fig. 5.1. This Hittite seal from Megiddo belonged to a Hittite diplomatic envoy named Anuziti and attests to the lively interchange between Egypt and Hatti in the last decades of the empire. From *BA* 58 (1995): 92.

in the area of the Egyptian "governor's residency" turned up a fragment of a Hittite bulla impressed with a Hittite royal seal. Bullae were used to seal shipments of goods. Perhaps this one sealed the shipment of dyed wool sent to the Egyptian governor, mentioned in a letter from Ugarit found nearby.[82] Both of these items are undeniably connected with Egyptian-Hittite diplomatic contacts during this time of peace.

In the process of conducting their business in the region, these Hittites left behind scattered material evidence of their presence. Two private seals of Hittite manufacture have been found at Tell el-Farah South, belonging to Zazuwa and Ana, and one at Megiddo, which was owned by Anuziti, who bore the title "charioteer," thus identifying him as a diplomatic envoy (fig. 5.1).[83] Seals of this sort accompanied their owners and so are evidence of more than mere trade. A signet ring of a type that was popular in Hittite Syria was found in the cemetery at the important port town of Tel Nami adorning the hand of a man with the Hurrian name Ushe. His burial goods indicate that

---

82. As suggested by Singer, "The Hittites and the Bible Revisited," 738 n. 78.
83. Itamar Singer, "A Hittite Seal from Megiddo," *BA* 58 (1995): 91.

he was an official of some importance, possibly a priest.[84] Was he a visitor who met with an untimely death, or did he reside in Palestine?

No doubt as we begin to understand better the processes by which cultural elements migrate from one society to the next, we will make progress in identifying which cultural parallels are likely to have been the result of an intellectual partnering of the sort that occurred during this time of peace, as opposed to influences that were the result of centuries of more distant, indirect relations. Here I have argued that no migration is necessary to explain the Hittites in the Bible and that the Hittites who came to northern Palestine during the *pax Hethitica-Egyptiaca*, whether their stay was long or short, were sufficient in quantity and, more importantly, in quality to explain the level of cultural transmission that is evident. Certainly, the two regions maintained important contacts throughout history.[85] For example, the Hamathites, who were deported to Samaria after 720 B.C.E., could have transmitted elements of Luwian religion to the Israelites.[86] In instances of deportation such as this, the emigres would have comprised all layers of society and not primarily its poorest representatives, so this remains a real possibility. But at no time were conditions more perfect or Palestine, which was perched on the cusp of a new era, more poised to absorb new influences than in the latter half of the thirteenth century.

---

84. Itamar Singer, "A Hittite Signet Ring from Tel Nami," in *Kinattūtu ša dūrâti: Raphael Kutscher Memorial Volume* (ed. Anson F. Rainey; Tel Aviv: Institute of Archaeology, 1993), 189.

85. See, e.g., Haya Ritter Kaplan, "Anatolian Elements in the EB III Culture of Palestine," *ZDPV* 97 (1981): 18–35; William F. Albright, "Dunand's New Byblos Volume: A Lycian at the Byblian Court," *BASOR* 155 (1959): 31–34.

86. As suggested by Hutter, "Widerspiegelungen religiöser Vorstellungen der Luwier," 432; idem, "Aspects of Luwian Religion," 277. However, in my view this is less likely because, as discussed in chapter 2, it is unlikely that there was significant religious continuity between Late Bronze Age Anatolia and eighth-century Syria.

AFTERWORD

WHAT CAN WE CONCLUDE, THEN, ABOUT the Hittites and their world? We have pointed out that theirs is the earliest-attested Indo-European language and that they were the unwitting custodians of the languages and traditions of a variety of peoples, our knowledge of whom depends in large measure, and in some cases entirely, on the Hittite libraries. We have noted their imperialistic ambitions: they dominated the political scene in the Near East in the Late Bronze Age, and the repercussions of their demise were felt politically and economically in the region for centuries afterward. These are reasons enough to justify the Hittites as an object of our study and interest. We may also note as significant, however, that the land of Hatti was a truly multicultural society united by a central authority that provided a focal point for group identity and coherence. In this respect, as well as in the recognition that they were but one among a number of co-equal world powers, the Hittites differed in their ideology from Mesopotamia and Egypt.[1] In recognizing the legitimacy of other sovereign nations, respecting local religious and social customs, and guaranteeing the legal right of every individual to fair and just treatment, the Hittite monarchy was simply upholding the framework within which it understood the universe to operate.

Because time quickly erased them from historical memory, we must seek the legacy of the Hittites not in any cultural features visible in modern Western society but in the lasting impact that they had on the civilizations that followed them and to whom Western civilization can trace its roots more directly. This, perhaps above all, is why their study must be pursued and why it has begun to burgeon in recent years. Hittite civilization was an essential participant in the ancient Near Eastern community, contributing significantly to the intellectual, religious, and political landscape of the region, and thus deserves to share with Mesopotamia the title "ancestor of the West." In this

---

1. Mario Liverani, *Prestige and Interest: International Relations in the Near East ca. 1600–1100 B.C.* (History of the Ancient Near East/Studies 1; Padova: Sargon, 1990), 66–86.

volume I have attention focused on the Hittites' impact on the biblical world, where we may note at a minimum that the notion of the scapegoat entered the Christian tradition, whether via the Greeks or the Israelites,[2] in the person of Christ, who, according to Pauline doctrine, carried away the sins of humanity. Investigations into Anatolia's influence on Greece constitute a much newer pursuit but are yielding no less fascinating results. Most recently, DNA evidence supporting an Anatolian origin for the Etruscans has put an additional spotlight on Anatolia and will provide impetus for further investigation into connections between the peoples of Anatolia and the pre-Roman inhabitants of the Italian peninsula.

The channels through which the Hittites may have impacted the biblical world, insofar as they can be reconstructed, are manifold. A handful of "culture words" that are common to Hittite and biblical Hebrew, including "wine" (Hittite *wiyanaš*; Hebrew *yayin*), "helmet" (Hittite *kubahiš*; Hebrew *kôbaʿ*), "sesame" (Hittite *šapšama*; Hebrew *šumšôm*), "glaze" (Hittite *zapzigi*; Hebrew *sipsīgīm*), and "earth" (Hittite *tegan*, Hebrew *dagān*), may be evidence of a very ancient relationship between the Semitic and Indo-European speakers in the Near East.[3] In addition, we may assume centuries of trade contacts between Anatolia and Palestine, with short periods of more intense contact, as at the end of the thirteenth century. Thus, certain parallels may be no more than two adjacent cultures responding in similar ways to analogous situations. Certain parallels in the legal and social spheres—levirate marriage, for example—may fall into this category.

Other parallels can be understood as areal phenomena; that is, they were traditions that were common to the eastern Mediterranean region. This may be the case, for example, for Elisha's technique for curing the sick child in 2 Kgs 4:32–35 and for the practice of passing between the severed parts of animals as part of a covenant/purification ceremony. Still others are a function of the Hittites and Israelites belonging to the same stream of tradition, namely, the "cuneiform culture" of Mesopotamia. Folkloristic motifs such as the childless couple (see ch. 2), for example, or the topos found in a Middle

---

2. For a discussion, see Jan Bremmer, "The Scapegoat between Hittites, Greeks, Israelites and Christians," *Kult, Konflikt und Versöhnung: Beiträge zur kultischen Sühne in religiösen, sozialen und politischen Auseinandersetzungen des antiken Mittelmeerraumes* (ed. Rainer Albertz; AOAT 285; Münster: Ugarit-Verlag, 2001), 175–86.

3. See Thomas V. Gamkrelidze and Vjacheslav V. Ivanov, *Indo-European and the Indo-Europeans* (Trends in Linguistics Studies and Monographs 80; Berlin: de Gruyter, 1995), 768–79; Singer, "Semitic *dagān* and Indo-European *$d^heĝ^hom$*," 221–32. For a compilation of shared words, see also Chaim Rabin, "Hittite Words in Hebrew," *Or* 32 (1963): 113–39.

Hittite incantation against the demon Wisuriyanza, in which nature prepares for the advent of the deity ("Before you, O god, let the rivers be bridged! Before you let the valleys be leveled! Let the mountains betake themselves down to the vegetation!"),[4] which is reflected in Isa 40:3–4 ("In the desert prepare the road of Yahweh! In the Arabah make a straight highway for our God! Let every valley be elevated; let every mountain and hill be brought low! Let the crooked become straight and the rough places level!"), underscore the shared literary heritage of the two civilizations. Elements of other stories unique to the Hittites, such as the Zalpa Legend, seem to have been absorbed into Israelite tradition eventually to be reconditioned by the biblical authors to suit a new message and audience. By this means, the Hittites have become a part of our own, Western, literary tradition.

The flexible organizational structure of the Hittite kingdom facilitated the flow of goods and people in the Late Bronze Age.[5] The Syrian vassal states formed an effective bridge spanning the geographical distance between Hittite Anatolia and the Levant. Many religious, artistic, and literary ideas must have passed back and forth, facilitated by the permeable borders and loose networks. Moreoever, the trade in luxury commodities within the palace-based gift-exchange networks of the Late Bronze Age involved a range of trained and educated personnel, including artisans, doctors, soldiers, servants, scribes, musicians, singer-poets, priests, and ritual specialists. The borrowing of Hittite ritual terminology into Ugaritic and Hebrew was probably the result of just such exchanges, in this case, of religious personnel.[6] Artistic influences, on the other hand, could have been the result of a conscious adoption of foreign forms, as with the lions at Hazor, or Hittite art may have served as a source of inspiration only, as with the Taanach cult stands. Whether that inspiration was the result of trade or of an exchange of craft personnel is a more difficult thing to determine.

---

4. *KBo* 15.25 (*CTH* 396) obv. 13–15; see Harry A. Hoffner Jr., "Hittites," in *Peoples of the Old Testament World* (ed. Alfred J. Hoerth, Gerald L. Mattingly, and Edwin M. Yamauchi; Grand Rapids: Baker, 1994), 154, who notes also: "Let the mountains be leveled before you, O gods!" *KUB* 15.34 (*CTH* 483) i 45, cf. iii 52.

5. Aslihan Yener, "A View from the Amuq in South-Central Turkey: Societies in Transformation in the Second Millennium BC," in *The Aegean and the Orient in the Second Millennium* (ed. Eric H. Cline and Diane Harris-Cline; Aegeum 18; Liège, Université de Liège, 1998), 275.

6. Harry A. Hoffner Jr., "An Anatolian Cult Term in Ugaritic," *JNES* 23 (1964): 68; idem, "Hittite Equivalents of Old Assyrian *kumrum* and *epattum*," *WZKM* 86 (1996): 151–56. In the latter, Hoffner suggests that Hittite *kumra* be identified with the Hebrew word for pagan priests (*kōmer*) and Hittite *ipantu-* with the biblical ephod.

In the realm of ritual sacrifice, the Hittites and Israelites owe a great deal to a common source, the Hurrians, who inhabited much of the territory between Palestine and Anatolia. Bird sacrifice, burnt offerings, and blood as an agent of purification entered the sacrificial systems of both cultures along with a rich vocabulary of offering terms.

Small groups of emigres from Anatolia may have settled in Palestine at various times over the centuries, but attention has focused primarily on the possibility of a migration of Anatolians to the Levant following the collapse of the Hittite Empire. Here we must distinguish between the proposed surge of refugees into the Neo-Hittite cities of northern Syria and southeastern Anatolia and the Sea Peoples diaspora that occurred along the Levantine coast. While an influx of Hittite refugees (whether large or small) never penetrated as far south as Palestine, certain ideas may well have been carried directly into the southern Levant by Sea Peoples of western Anatolian origin (Sikila, Sherden, and Philistines) who settled along its coast. The guilt offering related in the episode of the Philistines and the ark with its Hittite parallel (see ch. 4) can probably be assigned to this particular migration.

The Neo-Hittite cities also may have played a part in preserving and forwarding ancient traditions to the Israelites, but the exact nature of their role in transmitting cultural artifacts from the Late Bronze is the murkiest of all. Adjacent to the Israelites in time and space and sharing with them similar political pressures, the Neo-Hittites were in a position potentially to funnel customs to the Israelites and appear to have done so in at least one instance, that is, in the importance given to political borders. In other areas, such as religious practices, however, it is not clear how much the Neo-Hittite cities actually shared with their Late Bronze Age predecessors in Anatolia; therefore the degree to which they could have served as intermediaries in transmitting Hittite practices to the southern Levant is open to speculation.

Finally, direct Hittite influence is unmistakable, in my view, in the two most celebrated parallels. The story of David's rise to power was modeled on Hattusili's Apology, a document that likely circulated in Israel/Palestine in the thirteenth century, while the Hittite treaties—the backbone of the entire imperial structure of northern Syria in the Late Bronze Age—served as a model for shaping the covenant between God and the Israelites. The intervening centuries between the floruit of the treaty form and its emergence in the biblical text as covenant form sometime at the end of the eighth (or later) are not an insurmountable chronological barrier, given the likelihood of continuity in the oral and even scribal traditions between the Late Bronze and Iron Ages in Israel.

In an article published in 1958, Cyrus Gordon noted that "the Hittite contribution to Israel will doubtless appear more and more significant during the years ahead. The full meaning of Ezek 16:31 'thy father is the Amorite, and they mother is Hittite' is yet to come."[7] In that article, as it turns out, Gordon was following a false trail, and there have been many more false trails in the search for parallels between the biblical world and that of the Hittites. However, as we have seen, many more profitable leads have panned out beyond all expectations, more than fulfilling Gordon's prediction. In the end, though, what is important is not whether the Israelites borrowed elements of Hittite culture but how a deeper understanding of the world of the Hittites can inform us about the world of the Bible (and vice versa). There can be no doubt that the answer is a great deal indeed.

---

7. Cyrus H. Gordon, "Abraham and the Merchants of Ura," *JNES* 17 (1958): 31 n. 9.

Further Reading

Resources listed here will guide the reader in learning more about the Hittites. Only book-length titles in English are included in this list. Advanced students will find complete bibliographic details for additional primary sources in the notes, along with more on the secondary literature in languages other than English.

General

Beckman, Gary, Richard Beal, and Gregory McMahon. *Hittite Studies in Honor of Harry A. Hoffner Jr. on the Occasion of His 65th Birthday*. Winona Lake, Ind.: Eisenbrauns, 2003.

Burney, Charles. *Historical Dictionary of the Hittites*. Lanham, Md.: Scarecrow, 2004.

Melchert, H. Craig. *The Luwians*. HdO 1/68. Leiden: Brill, 2003.

Yener, K. Aslihan, and Harry A. Hoffner Jr., eds. *Recent Developments in Hittite Archaeology and History*. Winona Lake, Ind.: Eisenbrauns, 2002.

Discovery and Descipherment

Ceram, C. W. *The Secret of the Hittites: The Discovery of an Ancient Empire*. New York: Knopf, 1956. Repr., London: Phoenix, 2001.

History

Bryce, Trevor. *The Kingdom of the Hittites*. 2nd ed. Oxford: Oxford University Press, 2005.

———. *The Trojans and Their Neighbors*. New York: Routledge, 2006.

Kuhrt, Amelie. *The Ancient Near East, c. 3000–330 BC*. 2 vols. London: Routledge, 1994.

Society

Akurgal, Ekrem. *The Art of the Hittites*. New York: Thames & Hudson, 1962.

Bryce, Trevor R. *Life and Society in the Hittite World*. Oxford: Oxford University Press, 2002.

Hoffner, Harry A., Jr., *The Laws of the Hittites: A Critical Edition*. DMOA 23. Leiden: Brill, 1997.

Religion

Beckman, Gary M. *Hittite Birth Rituals*. StBoT 29. Wiesbaden: Harrasowitz, 1983.

Gessel, Ben H. L. van, *Onomasticon of the Hittite Pantheon*. 3 vols. HdO 1/33. Leiden: Brill, 1998–2001.

Hazenbos, Joost. *The Organization of the Anatolian Local Cults during the Thirteenth Century B.C.* CM 21. Brill: Leiden, 2003.

Kassian, Alexei, Andrej Korolëv, and Andrej Sidel'tsev, *Hittite Funerary Ritual: šalliš waštaiš*. AOAT 288. Münster: Ugarit-Verlag, 2002.

Miller, Jared L. *Studies in the Origins, Development and Interpretation of the Kizzuwatna Rituals*. StBoT 46. Wiesbaden: Harrassowitz, 2004.

Taggar-Cohen, Ada. *Hittite Priesthood*. THeth 26; Heidelberg: Universitäts-verlag, 2006.

The Hittites and Biblical Studies

Wright, David P. *The Disposal of Impurity*. SBLDS 101. Atlanta: Scholars Press, 1987.

Reference Works and Primary Sources in Translation

Beckman, Gary. *Hittite Diplomatic Texts*. 2nd ed. SBLWAW 7; Atlanta: Scholars Press, 1999.

Güterbock, Hans G., Harry A. Hoffner Jr., and Theo P. J. van den Hout. *The Hittite Dictionary of the Oriental Institute of the University of Chicago*. Chicago: Oriental Institute of the University of Chicago. 1989–.

Hallo, William H., and K. Lawson Younger Jr., eds. *The Context of Scripture*. 3 vols. Leiden: Brill, 1997–2002.

Hawkins, J. David. *Corpus of Hieroglyphic Luwian Inscriptions*. Vol. 1: *Inscriptions of the Iron Age*. 3 vols. Studies in Indo-European Language and Culture 8. Berlin: de Gruyter, 2000.

Hoffner, Harry A., Jr. *Hittite Myths*. 2nd ed. SBLWAW 2. Atlanta: Scholars Press, 1998.

Hoffner, Harry A., Jr., and H. Craig Melchert. *A Grammar of the Hittite Language*. Part 1: *Reference Grammar*; Part 2: *Tutorial*. Winona Lake, Ind.: Eisenbrauns, forthcoming (2007).

Payne, Annik. *Hieroglyphic Luwian*. ELO 3. Wiesbaden: Harrassowitz, 2004.

Sasson, Jack M., ed. *Civilizations of the Ancient Near East*. 4 vols. New York: Scribner, 1995.

Singer, Itamar. *Hittite Prayers*. SBLWAW 11. Atlanta: Society of Biblical Literature, 2002.

Subject Index

PN = personal name
RN = royal name
RNf = royal name, feminine

DN = divine name
EN = ethnic name
GN = geographical name

A

A.ZU "physician" 180–81
Aaron (PN) 187
Aba (GN) 55
Abdi-Milkutti (RN) 85
Abdu-Hepa (PN) 202
Abecedary 206
Abel, F.-M. 203
Abraham (PN) 198, 208
Acco (GN) 77
Acemhöyük-Purushanda. *See*
    Purushanda (GN)
Achaeans 202
Achilles (PN) 184
Adad-nirari (RN) 57–58, 60–61, 200
Adah (PN) 208
Adana (GN) 13, 76, 86, 201
AGRIG "steward" 113
Ahab (RN) 199
Ahhiyawa (GN) 44, 50, 60, 63–64, 67,
    68–69, 77, 100
Ahhiyawans 53, 76
Ahimelech (PN) 210
Ain Dara (GN) 90
Akhenaton (RN) 54, 142
Akhetaton (GN) 54
Akkad (GN) 142
Akkadian language 4, 11, 29, 32
Akkadian sources 4, 6, 142

Akpınar (GN) 3, 128
Alaca Höyük (GN) 16, 22, 24–25, 80,
    97, 103, 129–30, 192
Alaksandu (PN) 53
Alalakh (GN) 37, 73, 85, 89, 133, 187
Alalu (DN) 151
Alanzu (DN) 140
Alasiya (GN) 44, 69, 73, 77–78. *See*
    also Cyprus
Aleppo (GN) 3, 37, 43, 45–46, 48,
    50–51, 55, 80, 85. *See also* Halpa
Alişar Höyük (Ankuwa) (GN) 12, 16,
    22, 26, 80, 103
Allani (DN) 177
Allatu (DN) 140
Alli (PN) 183
Allumari (PN) 82
Alluwamna (RN) 38
alwanzatar "sorcery" 189
Amazons 1
Ambazzi (PN) 188
Amenhotep III (RN) 4, 32, 45
Amka (GN) 48, 52
Amman airport 215
Ammistamru II (RN) 103
Ammuna (RN) 38, 41
Ammurapi (RN) 73, 75, 77–78
Amorites (EN) 202–3, 209, 212
Amurru (GN) 205

L

INDEX OF ANCIENT TEXTS

BIBLICAL PASSAGES

GENESIS

EXODUS

LEVITICUS

NUMBERS

Maşat Texts

Ras Shamra

Classical Sources

Index of Modern Authors